Media, Communication, Culture

Media, Communication, Culture

A Global Approach

Second edition

James Lull

Columbia University Press
New York

Columbia University Press
PUBLISHERS SINCE 1893
New York   Chichester, West Sussex

Copyright © James Lull, 2000

First edition published 1995

This edition published in 2000 by Polity Press in association with
Blackwell Publishers Ltd in Great Britain

Library of Congress Cataloging-in-Publication Data
Lull, James.
  Media, communication, culture: a global approach / by James Lull. –
2nd ed.
     p. cm.
  Includes bibliographical references and index.
  ISBN 0-231-12073-7 (alk. paper)
  1. Mass media and culture.   I. Title.
  P94.6 L85 2000
  302.23 – dc21   99-054090

Typeset in 10.5 on 12 pt Sabon by Best-set Typesetter Ltd., Hong Kong
Printed in Great Britain by T.J. International Ltd, Padstow, Cornwall
10 9 8 7 6 5 4 3 2 1

Contents

Acknowledgements

My work is made possible by contributions from wonderful people in many parts of the world. It seems impossible to acknowledge everyone who has influenced the work because this book reflects an accumulation of professional and personal experiences that date back to long before I began to write the first edition.

Among those who certainly should be mentioned are Agnes da Silva, Janet Breit, Joe Verballis, Eduardo Neiva, Heloisa Aguiar, Pertti Tiihonen, Mirja Liikkanen, Katarina Eskola, Terhi Rantanen, Juha Kytömäki, Dalmer Pacheco, Tomas Pereira, Guillermo Orozco Gómez, Klaus Bruhn Jensen, Toshie Takahashi Sato, Debbie Johnson, Michael Marx, Steve Hinerman, Maria Immacolata Vassalo Lopes, Dave Morley, Leoncio Barrios, Bo Reimer, Karl Erik Rosengren, Renata Veloso, Stephanie Coopman, Ted Coopman, Dave Elliott, Dennis Jaehne, Tim Hegstrom, Serena Stanford, Mike Real, Paul Messaris, Ien Ang, Thomas Tufte, Federico Varona, Laura Nguyen, Walter Neira, Zhang Li-fen, Lucia Castellon Aguayo, Marcia Terlaje-Salas, Stefanie Izumi, Miguel de Aguilera, Romaldo Lopez, Sam Koplowicz, Marsha Siefert, Brian Sparks, Brett Garland, Patricia Martinez Iguínez, Héctor Gómez, Ricardo "Oso" Morales, Andrew Goodwin, Teresa Velázquez, Juan José Perona Páez, Amparo Huertas Bailén, Juan Luis Manfredi, Nilza Waldeck, Marisa Leal, Rita Monteiro, Robert Avery, Brian Moeran, Claudio Avendaño, and Eleonora Pires.

Very insightful comments on an earlier draft of the manuscript were made by John Tomlinson and Charlotta Kratz.

The staff at Polity Press has been extremely helpful, as always. Once again I wish to thank John B. Thompson for his constant intellectual stimulation, professional advice, and personal friendship. Julia Harsant, Lynn Dunlop, Fiona Sewell, and Sandra Byatt were very encouraging and helpful editors, and Sue Leigh carefully supervised production. Thanks as well to the North American co-publisher of this volume, Columbia University Press, especially Ann Miller and Alexander Thorp, for their enthusiastic editorial guidance and support.

The considerable time I have spent in Brazil and Mexico in recent years has taught me much about media, communication, and culture. In particular, I wish to thank Jorge González, Director of the Culture Program at the University of Colima, Mexico, for sharing with me his great fascination with and knowledge of contemporary Mexican and Latin American culture, as well as his limitless energy and personal kindness. The staff of the Culture Program in Colima, especially Irma Alcaraz, Ana Uribe, Ana Isabel Zermeño, Angelica Rocha, and Genaro Zenteno, have all greatly expanded my knowledge and made life ever so much more enjoyable.

James Lull
San José, California

(JamesLull@aol.com; home page: http://members.aol.com/JamesLull)

The cover painting, 'AD 2000: New York City,' is by the Canadian artist René Milot. Commissioned by the National Geographic Society (of the United States), the painting displays a young woman sitting in her New York apartment, windows barred against urban threats. When not out with friends, she is connected to the world via computer, cell phone, television, and radio – living life remotely, in a barrage of information. A caged iguana, dusty telescope, and potted plant hint at the nature world she has little time to enjoy. Cultural trinkets litter her room, disposable as a pizza box. Craving stimulation, she wouldn't live anywhere else. (By permission of the National Geographic Society, Washington, DC.)

Introduction

I grew up here when California was full of, you know, California type
people. Now it's international.

My plumber, San José, California, 1999

The global is the true state of affairs.

Friedman 1994: 3

As the middle-aged, middle-class professors from the Philippines
droned on sadly about how their traditional island musics were being
replaced by Anglo-American sounds and modern popular music from
Manila, my mind drifted back to my childhood. I recalled my days
as a teenager when I so desperately wanted out of the little "island"
where I was born and raised – a small farm town of Nordic immigrants in southern Minnesota. I depended so much then on top forty
radio stations from Minneapolis and Chicago to feel free, sexy, and
connected to other places. I wanted to explore the unknown, break
the chains, feel alive. I loved the cool music, the smooth, fast-talking
deejays, the dances, the clothes, the city girls – especially Marianne
Fitzgerald, who was by far the cutest ninth grader in all of Minnesota,
and one of the regular dancers on Minneapolis's version of *American Bandstand*.

The big sounds of the metropolis connected so powerfully with my
body, my senses, my dreams. Listening and moving to the big city
beat, I imagined just how much more complex, interesting, and exciting life could be. And I was right! I knew then that I wanted to be
more than just another midwestern American kid who never left
home.

Wake up! Back to reality – an academic conference on popular music. Filipinos lamenting their imagined lost utopias at the hands of the corrupting international music industry and the modern sounds from Manila. I understand where they're coming from, but . . .

This book begins where the wistful Filipino professors' argument leaves off, and concludes much more optimistically. We begin this complex journey into twenty-first-century media, communication,

Photo 1.1 Hanno Möttölä – the globalized Finn (photo by University of Utah Athletic Department)

and culture with an example of a truly globalized man – a young pro-fessional basketball player from Finland who lives in America. We will then summarize how the gaps in comparative socioeconomic status, technology use, information, and knowledge between and among peoples of the world have reached very disturbing levels. We then briefly introduce *structuration theory* as it can be applied to media, communication, and culture. Structuration theory is a useful framework for analyzing how people's lives are structured by, but not limited to, the powerful ideological and cultural forces that surround them.

Box 1.1 International Sport and the Globalized Finn

(The following is based on personal communications with National Basketball Association player, Hanno Möttölä. . . .)

Got his first pair of Air Jordans when he was ten years old. Grew up watching the National Basketball Association (NBA) on TV. Loved the Lakers, hated the Celtics. Really liked Michael Jordan and Hakeem Olajuwon, but Magic Johnson was by far his favorite player. Played hoops with his older brother and friends at the local YMCA. Into U2, Springsteen, and the Rolling Stones.

Some kid from Kansas City?

Try Helsinki.

Head down, fists clenched, arms pulling front to back, a look of great determination on his face, Hanno Möttölä runs down the court to assume a defensive position. He has just scored another two points inside with a fluid duck-under move, a lethal comple-ment to his excellent outside shooting. The big blond is the first man ever from remote, sparsely populated Finland to play in the NBA.

Basketball has become a truly international sport, rivaled only by soccer and hockey. The NBA features famous players from Nigeria, Venezuela, Australia, Germany, France, Serbia, Croatia, Mexico, New Zealand, Canada, Lithuania, Holland, Russia, and several Caribbean islands, among many other global locales.

The rich diversity of players in the NBA today is one spectacu-lar indication of how international sport in particular, and popular culture in general, have been globalized at the outset of the twenty-first century. Hanno Möttölä's story reveals just how connected we have become across the boundaries of time and space.

Not only did Hanno lace up his Air Jordans, watch the NBA on TV, and crank up Bono and U2 on his stereo in Helsinki as a kid, he learned to speak English and Swedish, traveled the world playing for the Finnish national basketball team, and spent a year in San Antonio, Texas, as a foreign exchange student. His father serves as an advisor for Finland's foreign ministry in international relations, and his mother edits the culture section of Helsinki's major daily newspaper.

The globalized Finn maintains constant contact with friends and family via email and telephone, and checks the hockey and soccer scores on-line every day. His family watches him play basketball on America's NBC satellite Superchannel in Finland, and on the Internet.

And what about the game of basketball itself? To watch Hanno play in the NBA is to observe a striking contrast in style. Basketball is the "black man's game" in America, with more than 80 percent of the professional players claiming African-American heritage. For Hanno, "that makes the game much more interesting . . . faster, tougher, more athletic." Still Hanno values and exhibits tremendous discipline, toughness, maturity, and team play – qualities brought from Finland that were refined under coach Rick Majerus where Hanno played college ball – the University of Utah.

In sharp contrast to subdued and modest Finnish culture, the Big American Pop Culture Show has caught up a reluctant Hanno in its midst – lots of money, screaming fans, cheerleaders, pressure to win at all costs. And nationalism: "In the United States you hear the national anthem at every sports game and you see lots of American flags everywhere. Back home these things are not so obvious . . . they're sacred."

Can glitz, glamour, and big money seduce the soul forever? Certainly. But Finland's first NBA player so far resists the temptation. He says he'll go back to Helsinki when his basketball career is over. He loves the history and tradition there. The beautiful old buildings. The people. The culture. The silences. A true cosmopolitan child of globalization who has benefited tremendously from all the advantages the ultra-modern world can bring, Hanno Möttölä still believes one thing: "You'll always be the person from the place you come from . . ."

That place is the most wired nation in the world. Finland has the highest percentage of its population connected to the Internet – way over half. Finns are also among the world's most active users of cellular phones, and the country is home to Nokia, the famous mobile phone maker.[1] Finland's appetite for the latest personal communications devices is more than remarkable given that its people are famous for their quiet, some would say "uncommunicative," social style. Finland is also among the world's leaders in quality education, and despite some rough times in recent years, the country has developed a very high standard of living for the vast majority of its people.

The global gaps

Globalization divides as much as it unites; it divides as it unites.
Bauman 1998: 2

Finland is one of the world's "have" nations. Finns have money and high technology. They have a high literacy rate and an excellent educational system. They have professional opportunities and social guarantees. Finland has the world's most equal social distribution of wealth.[2]

But when we survey all the world's nations and peoples, we find that Finland is truly exceptional in all these respects and is, after all, a small nation with fewer than six million inhabitants. A very troubling trend confronts us as global citizens as we proceed through these early years of the twenty-first century.[3] To put it simply, the world's rich are getting richer, and the poor are getting poorer. Real differences between social and cultural groups in the world are increasing by the minute, and the differences become more striking with every technological advance.

Europe and North America accounted for more than half the world's wealth at the turn of the century, while the developing countries of Africa, Asia, and Latin America (with exceptions like Brazil, Chile, China, and Taiwan) account for a only small percentage. But this is changing. The gaps between and among many of the world's nations are actually getting smaller rather than larger. As a proportion of the world's wealth, European and North American economies are losing ground.

Social class

I am against the kind of globalization that allows one US gentleman to have $90 billion, while another sleeps under a bridge.
Fidel Castro, accepting a medal as an honorary citizen of
Rio de Janeiro, Brazil, 1999

The real gap in socioeconomic status around the world exists *between members of the middle class and the truly poor populations in all countries.* The size of the international middle class is increasing, but the world's underclass population is expanding simultaneously at an even greater rate, and the poor keep getting relatively poorer.

Socioeconomic disparities inside Third World (or "newly industrializing countries," NICs) are particularly extreme. In Asia and Latin America, for example, a tiny number of super-rich people benefit tremendously from international trade and modern information technology while the poor – who procreate at rates much higher than the rich, and therefore increase their numbers faster in absolute and relative terms – fall farther and farther behind.

China, India, Indonesia, Brazil, and Russia have been identified by the World Bank as the largest newly emerging world economies. Their likely future success as nations, however, does not mean that most people or families living in these countries will benefit. National economic development in countries where the differences in socioeconomic standing are great creates explosive social conditions. The World Bank predicts that while China, India, Indonesia, Brazil, and Russia will double their economic output from about 8 to 16 percent of the world's total by the year 2020, serious "social turbulence" will accompany the growth. Indeed, clear symptoms of widespread unrest are manifest in all those countries already. So, while economic development in the coming years will gradually reduce the gap between many nations of the world and expand the size of the middle class in all the emerging world economies, poverty will also grow at a frightening rate. This is not a determined consequence, of course, because nations could direct revenues and resources in ways that would reduce the suffering. But of the five large economies mentioned above, China's socialist system may be the only one able to provide an effective social safety net for its poorest people.

Americans, Brits, Japanese, and Australians are by no means exempt from these global trends. The same internal gaps are developing. Of all the world's large, industrialized countries, the United States has become the most divided by income and wealth. The "gentleman" that Fidel Castro referred to in Brazil is Bill Gates, the world's wealthiest man. The disparity between rich and poor in the United States is systemic. Statistics indicate that roughly the richest 20 percent of the American public now controls more than 80 percent of the nation's wealth, a trend that keeps growing.

The technology gap

Technology never functions in an undifferentiated field of social relations. In our own individual countries, and in the global context too, some people have much greater access to communications technology than others. Socioeconomic class is the most obvious predictor of this difference.

While cellular phones, fax machines, digital video disc players, and all other modern communications technologies are concentrated disproportionately in the hands of the relatively well-to-do, the personal computer really separates rich from poor. While more than 50 percent of North American families had a computer in the home at the turn of the century, information technology remains largely a white-collar phenomenon. Well-paid, highly-educated, young male professionals are most likely to own and use a computer, especially for Internet access.

A US Department of Commerce report explains how the differences between rich and poor in the United States are related to race and technology. Poor people of all races in the United States have few computers in their homes. Blacks and Hispanics make up a disproportionately higher percentage of the American poor, so they are far less likely than whites or Asians to have computers. That clearly limits their opportunities.

This trend is not just related to social class, however. The rate of computer ownership among blacks and Hispanics of all social classes is comparatively low in the United States. More than a third of North Americans who did not own a personal computer in 1998 said they have absolutely no interest in ever having one. Exclusion from and resistance to high technology (and to higher education) thus is related to disadvantages imposed by low social class, but also by cultural values and ways of life.

Higher education, computers, and all forms of high technology are keys to economic success for individuals, families, and nations. Those who do not use computers in today's globalized environment are left behind in many ways. This is what is meant by terms such as the technology gap, the information gap, and the knowledge gap. This worldwide social crisis could not be solved easily even if technological resources were abundant and accessible to everyone, which they most assuredly are not. Technological development cannot simply be mandated in situations where people's basic needs are unfulfilled, where their opportunities are greatly limited, or where their cultural values do not match up well with the razor-sharp rationality of high technology and the competitive demands of global capitalism.

And in global terms, how can we talk about the empowering potential of computers, the Internet, and information technology for India, China, and most countries in Africa and Southeast Asia when the vast majority of families there don't yet have a telephone? With the exception of the relatively small middle-class populations of nations like South Africa and Zimbabwe, sub-Saharan African peoples don't have access to computers at all. The unwired countries of Africa and elsewhere simply function outside the Global Information Infrastructure. In Africa, the technology gap interacts with political turmoil, corruption, the AIDS crisis, and poverty to greatly limit opportunities for economic growth – a goal which requires access to the information superhighway to be realized.

At the same time, the upper classes in developing countries are very sophisticated users of high technology. Many of them have satellite receivers, computers with Internet access, cell phones, DVD machines, fax machines, and every other communications gadget in their homes and offices. They operate in Bombay, Lagos, Sao Paulo, Mexico City, and Kuala Lumpur at a First World standard, safely tucked away in guarded fortresses which isolate them from the threatening, anonymous poor who occupy the streets nearby. The few computers and other information technologies which do exist in developing countries are used mainly to make money rather than improve health, education, family planning, and economic opportunities for the general population.

We have cast our discussion of the global gaps so far mainly in terms of economics and technology. This is a necessary critical orientation, and the world scene in these respects obviously is troubling. But life is not limited to money and computers, and gaps between social groups should not be addressed solely in these terms. Love, beauty, passion, pleasure, and romance, for example, are not taken into account when we focus on the differences between people strictly in terms of economics, technology, and information. By expanding the analysis into *culture*, which includes the emotional dimensions of life as well as the rational sides, we open up lots of interesting possibilities. These will be explored in the chapters which follow.

Structure and agency

We will wrestle mightily with one central theoretical problem throughout this book. The critical issue is by no means unique to the analysis presented here. In one way or another, theorists and writers from all the social sciences have long tried to understand the dynamic relationship between two basic, powerful, and seemingly opposing forces. These forces reflect tensions that have already been raised in this brief introduction.

On one side of the issue, we have *structure*. There are many kinds of structure, but generally we can say that *structure is any force that systemically limits or contains people*. Structures can be quite abstract, and are in some ways even invisible because they can be huge and are therefore taken for granted. The fields of politics, economics, ideology, and culture, for example, all structure social interaction in ways that favor the interests of some people over others. The comments of Zygmunt Bauman and Fidel Castro quoted earlier, for instance, call attention to what these men consider to be structural inequalities in globalization and socioeconomic relations.

On the other side of the issue is human *agency*. This positive force refers to the energy, creativity, purposefulness, and transcendent abilities that individual persons and subgroups set in motion, even unconsciously, to make their lives meaningful and enjoyable. *Agency is the force of liberation and growth*. Agency is exercised at personal and collective social levels.

Apparently we've got a classic "bad guy, good guy" pairing of opposing forces here. In simplified terms, human beings can overcome the confining structures that surround and limit them by exercising their human potential – their agency. This contrasting, dynamic tension provides a productive platform from which we can now begin our explorations and commentaries about global media, communication, and culture.

Structuration theory

The most far-reaching and comprehensive approach for analyzing the controversies of social power that takes structure and agency as its point of departure is the famed British sociologist Anthony Giddens's theory of *structuration* (see especially Giddens 1984; Lull 1992b). A detailed explanation of this very complex social theory goes beyond our purposes here and will not be attempted. But the spirit of the theory can help us find our way round the mosaic that makes up this text. Essentially, Giddens's theory integrates "macrosocial" conditions (reflecting the constraints of structure) with "microsocial" processes (where agency takes form). *Structuration theory is particularly valuable because it explains how structure and agency need not be thought of as entirely opposing forces.* This is a crucial advance in thinking because while structuration theory recognizes the constraints structure clearly imposes on individuals and societies, it does not programmatically blame external forces for everything wrong in the world, an overly simplified conclusion that crops up all too often in "critical" academic theorizing.

We must strike a balance in our thinking about structure and agency in order to fairly evaluate what's really going on in media, communication, and culture at the global level. We want to keep the issue of social power in the forefront of the analysis, of course, but we do not want to simply assume an *a priori* point of view that is overloaded on one side of the social power equation or the other. Too much emphasis on structure exaggerates constraint, making it appear that established social institutions and rules somehow *determine* our realities in an airtight fashion. But by the same token giving too much attention to agency naively grants unwarranted power to individuals and underestimates how dominant forces and guidelines do in fact influence individuals and societies, often even against their best interests.

Communication and connectivity

Communication is necessary for cultural innovation, and cultural innovation is necessary for human survival. This was true more than 40,000 years ago when the first cave art and other symbolic artifacts appeared in Europe and Africa, and it was also true some 400,000 years ago when *Homo sapiens* first developed the physical ability to utter sounds and interact through speech (Kay, Cartmill, and Barlow 1998).

Through communication we create culture, and when we communicate, we communicate culturally: "Culture can be understood as the order of life in which human beings construct meaning through practices of symbolic representation . . . [that is] by communicating with each other" (Tomlinson 1999: 18). In today's complex world communication is the social nexus where interpersonal relations and technological innovations, political-economic incentives and socio-cultural ambitions, light entertainment and serious information, local environments and global influences, form and content, substance and style all intersect, interact, and influence each other.

Human communication is just as necessary today as it was hundreds of centuries ago, but social exchange and the cultural domains that human interactions help create assume radically different forms

Photo 1.2 Do you speak MTV? Globalized media and popular culture like MTV Asia challenge traditional values in every corner of the world, including China (printed with permission of MTV)

and formats in the era of globalization. As British sociologist David Chaney points out, "traditionally, social institutions such as family and religion have been seen as the primary media of [cultural] continuity. More recently . . . the role of ensuring continuity has increasingly been taken over by . . . forms of communication and entertainment" (Chaney 1994: 58).

We live today in an ever-increasingly hyper-interconnected world, a "global ecumene" of communicative interactions and exchanges that stimulates profound cultural transformations and realignments (Hannerz 1996: 7). Any study of culture in the globalized, mass-mediated, Internet-influenced world we live in, therefore, must seriously take into account the most sweeping dimension of communication – *connectivity*. With the Internet and information technology come incredible social opportunities. This is because communication is ultimately an open, undetermined space where the unlimited creativity of people can take form.

Even the most basic, non-mediated, minimally connected communication codes and processes assure tremendous latitude in symbolic exchange. The Canadian anthropologist Grant McCracken offers the analogy of linguistic structure and the way people use language to demonstrate the limits of structure and the vitality of agency in routine social interaction:

> Each speaker of a language is both constrained and empowered by the code that informs his language use. He or she has no choice but to accept the way in which distinctive features have been defined and combined to form phonemes. He or she has no choice but to accept the way in which the phonemes have been defined and combined to form morphemes. The creation of sentences out of morphemes is also constrained, but here the speaker enjoys a limited discretionary power and combinatorial freedom. This discretionary power increases when the speaker combines sentences into utterances. By this stage the action of compulsory rules of combination has ceased altogether. (1990: 63)

About this book

Moving forward then with an overarching philosophy that life's vital trajectories are not predestined, we shall now explore the dynamic interaction of three themes that will make up the core of this book: mass media and information technology, patterns and processes of human communication, and the social construction of diverse cultures.

The book is international, multicultural, and multidisciplinary. Many of the examples refer to cultures outside North America, the United Kingdom, and continental Europe. We study capitalist and communist systems, the First World and the Third, the rich and the poor, the mainstream and the margins. We evaluate media, communication, and culture stretching from California to China, by way of England, Brazil, Mexico, New Zealand, and scores of other places. Theorists from outside the northern loop are prominent contributors to the points of view that evolve in the following pages. We will travel theoretical terrain that encompasses key concepts and issues from communication studies, sociology, cultural studies, political economy, psychology, and anthropology. We visit the premodern, modern, high modern, and postmodern eras.

No facile, easy answers to complex, tough questions will be found in these pages as we strive to explain the forces of structure and agency in contemporary media, communication, and culture. Given the choice of privileging structure over agency, or agency over structure, however, I choose the latter. I prefer to stand in the sunshine, not in the shadows, and I hope that by the end of our journey together readers of this volume will be inspired to do the same.

2

Ideology and Consciousness

We move forward with this critical analysis of media, communication, and culture now by exploring concepts that should be part of any college student's working vocabulary. Ideology and consciousness are the subjects of this chapter, and a related idea, hegemony, will be the focus of the next. We will refer to ideology, consciousness, and hegemony throughout this book. The concepts are complex and overlapping, though each has a unique emphasis and role in social theory. To introduce the first two, we can say that *ideology* is a system of ideas expressed in communication and *consciousness* is the essence or totality of attitudes, opinions, and sensitivities held by individuals or groups.

Ideology

In the most general sense, ideology is organized thought – sets of values, orientations, and predispositions that are expressed through technologically mediated and interpersonal communication. Ideologies are internally coherent *ways of thinking*. They are *points of view* that may or may not be "true;" that is, ideologies are not necessarily grounded in historically or empirically verifiable fact. Ideologies may be tightly or loosely organized. Some are complex and well integrated; others are fragmented. Some ideological lessons are temporary; others endure. Some meet strong resistance; others have immediate and phenomenal impact. But the varying character of ideology should not obscure its importance. Organized thought is never innocent; it always serves a purpose. Ideologies are implicated by their origins, their institutional associations, and the purposes to which they are put, though these histories and relationships may never be entirely clear. In fact society's power holders often prefer that people don't understand or question where ideas come from, or whose interests are served by ideologies, and whose are not.

Ideology is a term we can use to describe the values and public agenda of nations, religious groups, political parties, candidates and movements, business organizations, schools, labor unions, even professional sporting teams, urban gangs, rock bands, and rap groups. But most often the term refers to the relationship between organized thought and social power in large-scale, political-economic contexts. Ideology, therefore, is fundamentally a large-scale, "macro"-level concept. *Selected ways of thinking are advocated through a variety of channels by those in society who have widespread political and economic power.* The ongoing manipulation of public information and imagery by society's power holders constructs a particular kind of ideology – a *dominant ideology* which helps sustain the material and cultural interests of its creators.

Ideology as a system of ideas has persuasive force only when such ideas can be represented and communicated. Naturally, then, the mass media and all other large-scale social institutions play a vital role in the dissemination of ideologies. Fabricators of dominant ideologies become an "information elite." Their power, or dominance, stems directly from their ability to publicly articulate their preferred systems of ideas. Ironically, in today's world many of society's "elites" must depend on non-elite cultural forms – the mass media and popular culture – to circulate their ideologies in order to maintain their elevated social status.

The origins of ideology as a critical concept in social theory can be traced to late eighteenth-century France (Thompson 1990). Since then, by one definition or another, ideology has been a central concern of historians, literary critics, sociologists, philosophers, semioticians, political scientists, rhetoricians – theorists representing virtually every niche in the humanities and social sciences. European intellectuals in particular have given ideology a sharp critical edge. British social theorists, for example – living in a blatantly class-divided society famous for its kings and queens, princes and princesses, lords and ladies – often define ideology in terms of how information is used by one socioeconomic group (the elite or "ruling class") to dominate the rest – especially the poor and the working class. Raymond Williams, one of the most respected communication theorists of years past, called ideology "the set of ideas which arises from a given set of *material* interests or, more broadly, from a definite class or group" (1976: 156; italics mine). He was saying that ideology is closely connected to economic interests. Persons and institutions with political or economic power will try to use ideology to maintain their privileged position at all costs. To give a particularly consequential example, during the Vietnam War of the 1960s and early 1970s the corporate manu-facturers of military weapons, equipment, and supplies vigorously supported the ideological assertion, "My Country Right or Wrong!" in order to keep the profitable war going as long as possible.

Because "systems of ideas" are used in ways that favor the inter-ests of some people over others, we must never trivialize the meaning of ideology. For this reason, the British sociologist John B. Thomp-son insists that ideology is best understood in the aforementioned, more narrow sense of "dominant ideology," wherein "symbolic forms" including language, media content, political platforms, insti-tutional messages from governments, schools, organized religion, and so on are used by those with power to "establish and sustain rela-tions of domination" (1990: 58). However, Thompson argues, "spe-cific symbolic forms are not ideological as such: they are ideological only in so far as they serve, in particular circumstances, to establish and sustain systematically asymmetrical relations of power" (Thomp-son 1995: 213). The socioeconomic elites can saturate society with their preferred ideological agenda partly because they have great influence, often ownership, over the institutions that author and dispense symbolic forms of communication, including the culture industries and the mass media.

Ideology, then, is a very good place to begin a critique of media, communication, and culture. Our reflection begins with the term itself. Simply to refer to any system of ideas as "ideology" calls at-tention to the nature of that system of ideas, and opens the door for meaningful analysis. The expressions "capitalist ideology" and "socialist ideology," for example, call attention to the fundamental principles that make up the two contrasting, often competing, political-economic-cultural systems. Using the term "ideology" directs attention to the values and practices of capitalism and socialism as political-economic-cultural schemas that are constructed and repre-sented rather than natural and self-evident. It problematizes capital-ism and socialism as sets of values, perspectives, and conforming social practices. A seemingly minor shift of language – from "capital-ism" to "capitalist ideology," for example – thus facilitates analysis and debate. That is a main reason why ideology is a favorite term of critical observers and theorists. However, the term can also be used in a way that discourages critical reflection. Some American politicians, citizens, and media complain of the "communist ideology" of "Castro's Cuba" or of "red China," for example. When used in this pejorative manner, the term "ideology" nearly becomes a synonym for "communism." It is the communists who suffer from ideology, according to this interpretation, as if Americans and others in the "free world" don't have to worry about any such political manipulations.

Ideology and the mass media

Some ideologies are elevated and amplified by the mass media, given great legitimacy by them, and distributed persuasively, often glamorously, to large audiences. In the process, ideas assume ever-increasing importance, reinforcing their original meanings and extending their social impact. Television has the unparalleled ability to expose, dramatize, and popularize cultural bits and fragments of information. It does so in the routine transmission of entertainment programs, news, and commercials. The bits and fragments then become ideological currency in social exchange. People talk a lot about what they read, see, and hear on the mass media and the Internet. Media fragments don't stand alone – not in the media, and not in our conversations. Various bits of information often congeal to form ideological sets that overrepresent the interests of the powerful and underrepresent the interests of the less rich or simply less visible people. Although television may be the most obvious conveyer of such dominant ideologies, all mass media, including seldom recognized forms such as postage stamps, store windows, breakfast cereal boxes, automobile bumper stickers, tee-shirts, grocery receipts, golf tees, matchbook covers, restaurant menus, even the bottom of urinals carry messages that serve the interests of some groups and not others. Consider, for instance, the (dominant) ideological lessons given in these familiar American bumper stickers:

- He Who Dies with the Most Toys Wins.
- I Owe, I Owe, So Off to Work I Go.
- My Other Car is a Porsche.
- My Boss Was a Jewish Carpenter.

Image systems

Image . . . is everything.

Tennis professional Andre Agassi in a TV commercial for a Japanese camera manufacturer

Image . . . is nothing.

Professional basketball star Grant Hill in a TV commercial for an American soft drink company

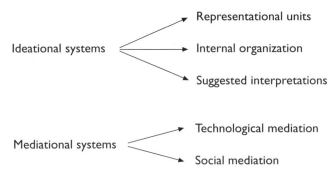

Figure 2.1 Image systems

The Sprite commercial, of course, is meant to be heavily ironic. The soft drink company *depends* on Grant Hill's image to claim that "image is nothing!" Appearances are extremely important in a mass-mediated world. The effective spread of dominant ideologies – those mainstream sets of ideas that reinforce the status quo – depends on the strategic use of *image systems*, of which there are two basic types: *ideational* and *mediational* (figure 2.1). *Ideational image systems refer to how ideas take form. Mediational image systems refer to how ideas circulate in society.* The key word in both cases is "system." Ideologies make sense because their internal elements hang together in systematic patterns. Those patterns then become familiar and accepted because they are delivered to us systematically via the mass media, and are further circulated in the personal conversations we have with our families, friends, co-workers, teachers, fellow students, neighbors, email correspondents, chat-room partners, and others. Image systems, therefore, refer to the articulation of layers of ideological representation and the tactical use of modern communications technology to distribute the representations, which, when successful, encourage audience acceptance and reproduction of the dominant themes, thus reinforcing relationships of power that are already in place. We use the term "image systems" to emphasize that *ideology depends on the patterned construction, representation, and transmission of ways of thinking in order to be influential.*

Ideational image systems

Let's concentrate first on ideas. As we are learning, ideas are never neutral and they rarely stand alone. They are grouped together for strategic purposes, refer to each other, and reinforce each other. A comparison with language may help clarify how systems of ideas work. When people speak a language, they utter sounds that are organized into words, phrases, sentences, and so forth. Language as a system encourages certain responses and understandings, and not others. It is not a closed system – there is room for misunderstanding, disagreement, and invention – but it is a system that is structured sufficiently well so that people who share the code can communicate and coordinate their actions according to mutually intelligible assumptions and rules. The same basic process characterizes how systems of ideas take shape and move about.

Let's consider an extended example of an ideational image system – commercial advertising – a $200-billion industry in the USA alone. What commercial advertisers sell are not just products, services, or isolated ideas. Advertisers sell multilayered, integrated ideational systems that embrace, interpret, and project interdependent images of products, cheerful consumers benefiting from the products, corporations that profit from sale of the products, and, most important, the overarching political-economic-cultural structure – and the values and social activity it embraces – that presumably makes all the consumer activity possible. Advertisers want people not only to like the brands and product groups they put up for sale, but to believe in the economic system that underlies the very idea that "to consume is good." Some ideas thus are acceptable to the economic elite who sponsor the advertising, while other idea are not. One idea that does *not* fit well with the ideational image system of advertising, for example, is the well-documented scientific claim that current patterns of natural resource consumption on a global scale – especially at rates evident in the more developed countries of the northern hemisphere – are destroying the earth's ecological balance and threatening the planet's very survival.

Without much regard for environmental or social consequences, advertisers try to turn media audience members into consumers. Through advertising people are encouraged to become personally involved with commercial products by imagining contexts – the physical scenes, emotional circumstances, and actual social situations in which they would be able to use various products. These projected *imagined situations* are grounded in an overarching *value structure* with which the consumer is already familiar. Advertising's success thus depends largely on the interpretative chemistry of plausible imagined consumptive situations interacting with familiar and accepted value structures. So, for example, a Nissan automobile commercial encourages viewers to buy one of their sleek-looking but competitively priced cars "Because rich guys shouldn't have all the fun!" These eight words sell much more than Nissans. They are used to construct an imagined situation framed by a value structure that embraces unabashed materialist competition, a commodified definition of pleasure, reinforcement of the "naturalness" of a socially stratified society, an assumption that social aggressiveness is the territory of men, and permission to use the product in order to deceive others into thinking you've got a car that reflects high socioeconomic status. This example demonstrates how the various internal elements of a television commercial – the audiovisual cues, cultural values, and assumptions – all work together to create an ideational image system.

Repetition is extremely important. Repeated presentation of dominant ideological messages continues to define or "indicate" culture, particularly for people who are heavily exposed to media. For example, the "heavy viewer" of television (30 hours or more per week) tends to perceive the world in a way that is much more consistent with the images presented on the tube than those who watch less than ten hours weekly (Gerbner 1973; Gerbner and Gross 1976). Mass media greatly influence how people make sense of even the most basic features of their societies. The media give strong, repeated impressions about society's racial and gender composition and roles, for example, as well as its vocational alternatives, political options, and levels of violence. In the United States we see lots of white and black people on TV, but few Latinos, Asians, or Middle Easterners. Most jobs apparently are quite glamorous, men are single and women married, very few children or elderly people exist, there are only two political parties, almost everybody is heterosexual, and the chances are excellent you will be shot the minute you walk out your front door. Television's common themes regularly stereotype people and things, reinforce the status quo, and support the dominant ideology that is behind these ideas. As Gerbner and Gross say, "TV is an agency of the established order and as such serves primarily to extend and maintain rather than alter, threaten, or weaken conventional conceptions, beliefs, and behaviors . . . its chief cultural function is to spread and stabilize social patterns" (1976: 175). Consistent with the perspective we are developing in this chapter, Gerbner and Gross consider the content of television to be an ideologically loaded "message system."

The flood of commercials capitalizing on the national mood in the United States following the Gulf War in the early 1990s illustrates well how culturally based value structures can be used to sell products. In these commercials, sponsors positioned their products inside the emotional context of nationalism, patriotism, and militarism that swept America after Iraq surrendered – to "go with the glow," in advertising terms. Post-war accolades in political rhetoric and corporate advertising incessantly celebrated what was called America's freedom-loving spirit, its selfless determination, and its technological superiority. As we've seen, a fundamental objective of corporate advertising is to gain and maintain credibility by embedding specific messages in more abstract and encompassing ideologies in order to create ideational image systems. In the case of the post-Gulf War rhetoric, commercial messages were reinforced almost daily by former president George Bush's pronouncements of America's prominent role in what he called the "New World Order." The "New World Order" is actually an ideological term created to promote US political and economic interests on a global scale.

Photo 2.1 Freedom to consume . . . if you've got the money. American advertising links ideology and nationalism with a marketing strategy, even in Moscow (photo by James Lull)

Nationalist rhetoric and flag waving in television commercials long predate the self-congratulatory indulgences that saturated the air-waves following the Gulf War or the more current exercises in Japan and China bashing. A common technique has been to ridicule other nations and peoples. Films, television programs, and commercials chastised Germans and Japanese for years after World War II ended. The Cold War ideological standoff in effect after World War II until the collapse of the Berlin Wall and the ultimate disintegration of the Soviet Union provided a political context in which American nationalism and capitalism were exalted by blatant negative stereotyping of communist nations and peoples. The typical strategy has been to create or promote good feelings about American culture (of which the product is a part) by encouraging the audience to laugh at the dramatized cultural (and racial) incompetencies of foreigners. Russians were frequent targets in the 1980s (Real 1989). Since China's military crackdown at Tiananmen Square in Beijing in 1989, the Chinese often have been posed as the feared and hated "other," a perspective that emanates from, and fuels, political purposes on the right and the left in the USA. The action movie *Red Corner*, for example, is a particularly horrible and misleading representation of Chinese culture.

The red, white, and blue flag-shaped logo of the Tommy Hilfiger line of sports apparel is a noteworthy recent example of how familiar, patriotic symbolism continues to be used as a marketing strategy. But in the multicultural realities of today, the "market for loyalties" (Price 1994) is complex. One of the Spanish-language radio stations in San José, California, for instance, uses the red, white, and green colors of the Mexican flag in all its public promotions to compete with other stations. Inside Mexico, red, white, and green banners are used by the powerful political party *Partido Revolucionario Institucional (PRI)*, a tactic some observers believe tricks semi-literate voters into thinking that when they vote for a PRI candidate, they are voting for Mexico.

Commercial advertising not only asserts, references, and reinforces preferred ideologies, it often suggests that products and services exist to help create a better world, despite strong evidence to the contrary in many cases. Specific campaigns are designed to sell images of companies as socially responsible as much as to sell their products. This indirect technique is called institutional advertising. Warm, fuzzy, incomplete, often misleading claims – all designed to make us feel good about the sponsor and about ourselves – are regularly made on TV to accomplish this goal. International Business Machines (IBM), for example, claims to be "helping to put information to work for people," without spelling out which people benefit, in what ways, and at whose expense. A West Coast telephone company claims that "technology will give people more time to be more human" and that we should turn responsibility for managing the technology over to them. Dow Chemical, the company that scorched Vietnam with napalm and Agent Orange, now presents dreamy *National Geographic*-style visuals on its TV ads while claiming to be the company that "protects wildlife." Xerox unblinkingly says it is "documenting the world." Citicorp Bank opines that its services are necessary "because Americans want to succeed, not just survive." Federal Express is "the way the world works." A TV "public service announcement" produced by the Ad Council, a federation of American advertising agencies, tells citizens that "people cause pollution, people can stop it," ignoring the fact that the most damaging environmental polluters are industrial corporations who refuse to accept the responsibility.

Advertising reinforces the class-based structure of society by symbolically rewarding workers' contributions to the system, thereby further legitimating the system itself. The working class is commonly saluted on American television. The humor and lifestyles of the working class are imitated in television programming, especially situation comedies, reinforcing many central beliefs and values held by American workers and their families, thereby helping to keep them amused with representations of themselves while they are encouraged to keep working and consuming. Working-class spirit – a great Western culture myth – is especially celebrated in American beer commercials. Blue-collar work settings and leisure-time activities are shown while the narrator gives the verbal reward: "For all the men and women who have served this great country, this Bud's for you" or "Buy that man a Miller."

Explicit advertising claims are sometimes repeated so frequently over time that they become part of audience members' assumptive worlds. Perhaps the best example is Bayer aspirin. The assertion for years that Bayer is the "best" aspirin has contributed, along with other marketing strategies, to a widespread perception of this brand as superior to its competitors, even though Bayer, like all other brands, contains only five-grain aspirin. Similarly, General Motors' fictitious, friendly, fair, and ever-so-competent "Mr Goodwrench" became America's generic mechanic thanks to an advertising campaign that went on for years. Even the body can be normalized ideologically. In an American television commercial for the cosmetic product Porcelaire (a cream that covers liver spots), a woman calls the spots on the back of her hands "beauty spots." The spokeswoman for the product quickly interjects, "Some people call those *age* spots!," correcting a healthy perception of the woman's skin to conform to the sponsor's objectives. And when things go wrong in marketing and advertising, sheer repetition of a positive message in the face of criticism – commercial stonewalling – is a way to overcome a damaging perception. A major lumber company indicted for irresponsibly slashing and cutting the emerald hills of America's Great Northwest, for example, referred to itself for years in TV commercials as "the tree growing company." In the unctuous wake of the Alaska oil spill some years ago, Exxon still vigorously promotes an "environmentally conscious" image.

Dominant ideologies reflect the values of society's politically or economically powerful institutions and persons, regardless of the type of system in place. In capitalist countries, corporate executives greatly influence media content by sponsoring programs and advertising products. Because media content in those nations is not financed directly by government or associated in the minds of most people with administrative authority, its ideological tones and trajectories are not easily detected, a fact that helps magnify the ideological impact. Dictators in authoritarian regimes, on the other hand, restrict access to information and to communications technology in order to maintain control. Socialist nations use mass media to promote political, economic, and cultural programs that are decided upon democratically in some cases, imposed in others. In the few remaining communist nations, party officials develop explicit ideological objectives and lessons which are then sent to the people through media programming. In China, for example, television and other media remain full of glaringly biased news reports, programs that salute "model workers" and "model citizens," politically correct dramas, documentaries that praise socialism and the Communist Party, and bluntly didactic editorials. Communist ideology is straightforwardly prescriptive, no apologies made. The Communist Party, after all, supposedly acts in the best interests of the people who are said to need and want ideological supervision.

Sources of ideology and the image systems they help create often go unrecognized. To refer to a profitable use of computer software as a "killer app" (application), or to say that a marketing scheme remains "on target," locates such businessworld activity within a familiar lexicon that subtly reinforces aggression and militarism. City skylines, the height and shape of skyscrapers, bridges, theme parks, and tourist sites are all developed to create certain impressions and feelings inspired by global competition for business and tourist dollars. At county fairs in Mexico, the tallest, most exciting, and most expensive ride children and adults can experience is "Kamikaze" (sometimes known in the USA as "The Hammer"). This huge pendulum features two opposing silver-colored, cylindrical cabins which hold people as they swing violently, right-side up, upside down, round and round for a few terrifying minutes. As the cabins slice through the air, huge national flags attached to the pods stream along gloriously to increase the visual impact for viewers on the ground and attract riders. Which national flags are chosen for this awesome power display? The United States, Germany, and Japan.

Mediational image systems

Ideology in any political-economic-cultural context is represented partly *in* language and interpreted *through* language and other highly elaborated codes and modes – including visual forms and music – which are then further interpreted and used by people in routine social interaction. These communication processes all contribute to the ideological effect. They comprise mediational image systems, which can be further divided into technological mediation and social mediation.

Technological mediation refers to the intervention of communications technology in social interaction. Let me again use the case of commercial advertising to illustrate the point. Billions of dollars are spent each year to find just the right mediational systems for the purposes of profit-obsessed commercial advertisers. Advertisers' strategies take advantage of the full range of mass media's persuasive potential. Selection of corporate spokespersons, visual logos, audio jingles, catchy slogans, the style and pace of commercials, special technical effects, editing conventions, product packaging, and the melding of print, electronic media, and interactive media campaigns, to name several central factors, all combine to generate the desired result, selling big and bright products and the political-economic-cultural infrastructure that goes along with them.

Even mass media's presentational formats cue certain expectations and responses. When commercial advertising first appeared on television in the United States, for example, sponsors concentrated strictly on the attributes of their own products. No mention was made of competitors' products, except for occasional comparisons with "Brand X." This advertising practice changed in the 1970s so that names of marketplace rivals were mentioned in commercials. When this happened, the public cried "foul!" Many people complained that it is unethical to identify the loser in a product comparison, even though this practice was never legally prohibited. The public reaction to the change reveals a crucial dimension of mass media's role as a transmitter and shaper of ideology – its power to establish and uphold widespread patterns of thought not only by repeatedly calling positive attention to particular objects of content, but by framing content in such a way that standardized presentational formats themselves connote particular ways to think. Such conventions influence not only audiences, but the creators of popular culture too. Most pop musicians, for instance, have adopted a song-writing style where the predictable formula – verse/chorus/verse/chorus/bridge/chorus – has become the norm. Global advertising, news programs, talk shows, and music television formats are likewise structured, imitative, and predictable.

Modern communication technologies deliver values, perspectives, and ideas to people of various cultures, social classes, and ages all over the world. Young children, of course, are particularly enthusiastic media users. Consequently, pervasive popular culture figures (human and otherwise, it doesn't matter much) such as Ronald McDonald, Will Smith, Madonna, Tony the Tiger, Michael Jordan, the Spice Girls, the Teenage Mutant Ninja Turtles, and Xuxa become celebrated acquaintances and purveyors of ideology – and not just in media-saturated North America or Europe. A compilation of Walt Disney cartoons, *Mickey Mouse and Donald Duck*, became the most popular television program in the People's Republic of China by the late 1980s. Its characters challenged the sanctity and popularity of children's Chinese folk heroes such as Chi-kung, the "crazy Buddha." In order for Chi-kung to maintain an elevated position in Chinese culture today, he must appear on television. Donald Duck and his family of Disney pals have also become more familiar to children in some South American countries than the heroes of their own history and folklore (Dorfman and Mattelart 1972). Brazilian villagers could more easily identify Michael Jackson from a photo than they could any of their own presidential candidates in a recent election, although, in general, Brazilian media are far more attentive to their own cultural heroes than they are to foreign personalities (Kottak 1990). A transformation of folkloric characters and stories from print media to television is taking place all over the world.

A mass medium is not just a "vessel" which carries ideas from one place to another, but is itself a subjective, interpretative, ideological form (Martín-Barbero 1993: 102). As the famous media theorist

Marshall McLuhan put it: "the medium is the message." This means that the technical form used to move information from one place to another communicates something itself that is just as important as, if not more important than, the medium's apparent "content." As a simple example from American culture, there is quite a difference between sending mother a card on Mother's Day and calling her by telephone with a greeting. The *way* the message arrives will itself mean something important to dear old mom. *What* it means, however, is not the same for every person. Some mothers prefer cards because they believe cards show planning and thoughtfulness on the part of the sender. Other moms would much rather hear their child's voice, and may consider a card to be a "cold" way to send a personal greeting. Preferences often differ by culture; the more print-oriented northerners of the world frequently prefer cards, while oral traditions of the southern regions may suggest that for others a spoken message is better. The new global personal communications medium – email – combines features of print (written, private) and orality (immediate, informal) to make the choice of which medium to use even more complex.

Just as language and other communication codes are learned and reinforced in everyday social interaction, ideology is likewise made familiar and normal in routine social intercourse. These are the processes of *social mediation*. Mass media's ideological representations are recognized, interpreted, edited, and used in audience members' social construction of daily life. Children, for example, regularly put TV's commonly known imagery to work in their everyday communication. They often refer to TV characters, programs, and themes to explain or clarify real-world situations, enter adult conversations, and play games with their peers. But television and film provide much imagery useful to adults in their routine communications too. People commonly retell each other news stories they see on television, for instance. Men re-create sporting events, and women commiserate over dramas. Even as the first Gulf War was heating up in the early 1990s, Iraq's Saddam Hussein warned the Americans that the war was "not going to be another *Rambo* movie." He promised instead the "mother of all battles." When the mother of all battles failed to materialize, Americans picked up and exploited the phrase, even commercially. For years now we have heard about the "mother of all comebacks" on sporting fields, the "mother of all examinations" in classrooms, and the "mother of all sales" at local retail stores. Pizza Hut was still hyping the "mother of all pizzas" a decade after the war ended.

What may seem to be trivial extracts from TV commercials, news, entertainment programs, and movies assume more ideological impact when they are circulated through social interaction. John B. Thompson (1990) calls this the "discursive elaboration" of ideology. As ideological messages pass from one person to another, or from one medium to another, the ideas they contain are embellished, reinforced, and extended. Consider how the following media messages are given increased impact by their reproduction in communication:

▨ Cable Network News (CNN) shows a United Nations aircraft preparing to bomb Bosnian Serbs in the 1990s. Arnold Schwarzenegger's famous line "Hasta La Vista, Baby" (from the movie *Terminator 2: Judgment Day*) is scrawled on the side of the plane.

▨ Mexican crafts vendors walk the beach in front of Mazatlan's luxury hotels enticing North American tourists with sales pitches that feature English-language media expressions:
"Hey, K-Mart shoppers . . ."
"Please buy something, lady . . . go ahead, make my day!"
"Happy hour now . . . two bracelets for the price of one."

▨ I explain to a checkout clerk at a supermarket near my home that I'm eating a candy bar in the late afternoon because "it's snack time." She notes what I'm eating and asks, "Isn't that supposed to be a Snickers?," referring to the candy company's advertising pitch as the snack that satisfies between meals.

▨ Some brand names become normative language, referring to ideas and actions that transcend the product:
"Let's have a Coke."
"I have to Xerox this report."
"This is a Kodak moment."

▨ The United States Defense Department calls a press conference to urge increased military presence in Somalia in order to "Give Peace a Chance."

▨ An announcer for the Atlanta Braves baseball team says during a broadcast that it's time for one of the team's pitchers to throw a "Visine ball." Visine is an eye-clearing product that claims it "will get the red out." Atlanta was playing the Cincinnati Reds.

▨ Boston Celtics basketball coach Rick Pitino claims that when his team wins games "[we] start doing the Toyota commercial" (where everyone jumps up and down).

- Americans frequently hum the "do-do-do-do, do-do-do-do" music from the TV show *Twilight Zone* when something unexplainable happens.
- San Francisco Bay Area women are told to be wary of "Radar," a serial rapist said to resemble the meek character from the film and TV show *M.A.S.H.*
- After hearing an airline captain make his pre-takeoff remarks, a passenger says, "Wow, he sounds just like the comedian I saw on TV the other night."

These seemingly innocuous examples help illustrate how media-originated ideological fragments are creatively used in routine social interaction – sometimes further mediated by public institutions, including other mass media. Selected values, ideas, slogans, and products become popularized in the process. In cases such as these, the social mediation of ideology contributes to its expansive, integrative, systemic character. All the verbalizations "work" because of the widespread familiarity and stereotypicality of the images to which they refer, a condition that is directly traceable to the distributive capability of mass media technology. When people refer to media images in everyday conversations, privileged ideological themes are once again articulated and validated. Complex ideas are frequently reduced to catchy sound bites and advertising slogans. Furthermore, reality is framed according to prior media representations and their underlying assumptions and analogs so that mediated imagery becomes the referent with which the "real world" is often compared. This inversion occurs routinely for children, for example, whose *primary* store of knowledge often comes from television, video games, popular music, and other mediated sources. Not only the messages have an impact, however. When audience members repeat a phrase from mass media the utility and credibility of the media technology itself are also reinforced once again.

Consciousness

Ideological image systems cannot *impose* or *confer* meaning on people. The consequences of communication do not always match message senders' objectives. Still, to the undeniable benefit of those who have the power to dominate the media's agenda, most people in the world's more developed societies are not only massively exposed to media, they depend on them for many things. In the United States, for instance, the typical family keeps at least one TV set turned on more than seven hours daily. Two-thirds of the American public gets all its news from TV. Consequently, Americans routinely encounter key social themes that are weighted substantially in line with sponsors' values and objectives and are fitted within the ideological contours of mainstream culture and politics. Mass media transmit highly selective images framed with ready-made viewpoints on many issues that lie outside most audience members' personal knowledge and experience. This is particularly true of global political matters. People the world over, for instance, were entirely dependent on media and government (as reported by media) for accounts of American military incursions into Lebanon, Granada, Panama, Iraq, Somalia, Haiti, Bosnia-Herzegovina, and Serbia during the past decade or so alone.

Consciousness is influenced by the transmission of the dominant ideology to the extent that society's powerful institutions can infiltrate thinking and affect human action. The definition we gave at the beginning of this chapter suggests that consciousness is the essence or totality of attitudes, opinions, and sensitivities held by individuals or groups. That sounds rather vague and general, but such is the nature of consciousness. Consciousness is a mindset – a synthesis of *what* a person or group of people knows or thinks about, and *how* they think. Clearly, the mass media play a very influential role in consciousness formation. Even when audience members flatly reject ideas expressed by the media, they do so only after being introduced to and, at some level, recognizing and contemplating the ideological themes contained in the messages. Of course, consciousness is not fixed; it is impermanent and malleable. It is shaped by the media, but by other information sources too. Nonetheless, consciousness reflects the inevitable inculcation of ideological themes delivered by mainstream media in ways that inspire concordant thought and social behavior. Furthermore, consciousness formation is not always self-evident. Like the fish who don't problematize the water in which they swim, people certainly don't always analyze how their everyday environments, including media messages, shape thinking. Consciousness, thus, broadly reflects the dominant subjects and patterns of mass-mediated ideological representation.

What we think about, and how we think, can never be completely determined by any single source of information. Still, sheer repetition of ideological themes sends ideas deep into individual and collective consciousness. Commercial advertisers, for instance, depend on such repetition. One of the primary objectives of the advertising business is to determine the optimum frequency of message repetition so as not to waste money while achieving the maximum persuasive impact. Teachers, parents, and others with motives that are quite different from advertisers' also depend on repetition of key information to achieve their goals. Producers of the famous American children's television show *Sesame Street*, for instance, use constant repetition to teach the alphabet and other basic lessons. The idea is to saturate your human subjects – potential consumers, students, children, whomever – with information you want them to retain.

The "saturation effect" works constantly. Particular expressions, and the values and assumptions they uphold, reside like a recessive inventory of ideas in the memory systems of people. These ideological memory traces are evoked contextually. This dynamic relation between the presence of particular messages and individual consciousness can be illustrated by how people listen and respond to popular music. If you are asked to recite the lyrics of a popular song, for instance, you probably cannot do so. But if a recording of the song is played, you very well may be able to sing along perfectly. Something quite interesting and important happens when the music starts – a sonic context is established, acting like a cueing system that stimulates not only recall of the words, but how they should be sung, the melody, and, frequently, vivid sentimental associations with people and events – interacting layers of ideology and meaning. The same basic process occurs at the collective level in society. Consciousness also reflects the "collective memory" of a people – shared ideological resources that are put to work in complex ways by groups.

Two important factors in consciousness formation, then, are *direction* and *repetition*. By directing people's attention to certain ideas, and repeating the key information, especially if it can be packaged in clever ways, the potential for creating the desired awareness is developed. That's how ideology and consciousness are connected. *Ideology refers mainly to the representation of ideas; consciousness is the impression those ideas leave on individuals and groups.* Because consciousness is not a closed or permanent state of mind, we sometimes hear terms like "consciousness raising" or "changing people's consciousness." Still, consciousness is not easily altered. It's easier for most people to keep believing what they already think is right and true rather than challenge their values and beliefs. That's one reason, for example, why splinter political groups and candidates, environmental organizations, gay and lesbian rights groups, sufferers from uncommon diseases, and others often encounter cold indifference or resistance from mainstream society.

We all remember that one of British Princess Diana's humanistic projects was to express great public concern over the devastation brought about by land mines in places such as Bosnia, Angola, and Cambodia. She used television and other media to call attention to the issue, thereby bringing the problem into mainstream consciousness. The emotional nature of the land mine issue (where innocent children are the main victims) and Diana's positive public image combined to catch people's interest in a favorable way. The princess may have detested the intrusion of media into her private life – and some people even (wrongly) blame the paparazzi for her death – but putting the unglamorous land mine issue on the world's moral agenda could only have been accomplished by linking the appeal of a celebrity person with the technological reach and impact of mass media.

Let's consider an even more far-reaching example of how ideology, media, and consciousness interact. Television didn't become a common household appliance for families in the People's Republic of China until the 1980s when the government's "modernization" plan was put into effect. Although the authorities tried to control television programming in order to promote the values and policies of Chinese communism, people were suddenly exposed to images they had never seen before. For the first time Chinese people could see places like Tokyo, Hong Kong, New York, London, and Paris, for example, by watching television news. They could tune in to professional basketball games from the United States, see international football (soccer) games from the UK and Europe, watch Japanese soap operas, and learn about fashion, cosmetics, rock music, and Western-influenced lifestyles and popular culture in general. The most common response to the new medium by people in China was to consider it a "mind opener." From the beginning, Chinese people used television to stimulate vicarious travel and to compare China with the rest of the world (Lull 1991: 170–7).

Television "turned on" the mainland Chinese by expanding their cultural consciousness, leading to what John B. Thompson calls a "symbolic distancing from the spatial-temporal contexts of everyday life" (Thompson 1995: 175). The social construction of just such a critical distance, particularly among urban dwellers, became one of the main inspirations for the student–worker revolt at Tiananmen Square just a few years after television had become a common domestic appliance in China. In fact, the overthrow of communism in all the nations which made up the former Soviet Union – especially East Germany – was inspired largely by media, particularly television, whose sparkling images interacted with the drab realities of everyday life in those places. The ideological challenges to communism are among only the most recent and sensational illustrations of how television expands human consciousness. When television first became part of American culture in the 1950s, for example, especially in the more remote, agricultural parts of the country, people enthused about how the new medium had expanded their worlds. I can tell you from personal experience that growing up in the farmlands of Minnesota, I couldn't wait to get to California after watching *Route 66* on TV and listening to Beach Boys albums on my stereo system.

The subconscious

Consciousness is profoundly mental, but it does not imply complete or current awareness. Many media messages are more implicit than explicit and are not intended to be interpreted with focused, full awareness in the first place. An extreme example of indirect, low-awareness ideological influence is subliminal persuasion – the attempt to manipulate behavior by infiltrating the human *subconscious*. Subliminal persuasion captured the public's interest in recent years and has been the subject of some academic studies in the psychology of perception. Interest in subliminal persuasion was aroused primarily by three provocative but highly speculative books written some time ago (Key 1973; 1976; 1980). Unfortunately, the titles of these short books (*Subliminal Seduction*, *Media Sexploitation*, *The Clam Plate Orgy*) and the author's sensationalized treatment have undermined serious consideration of the topic.

Subliminal messages are embedded in advertising texts and in other media content. They are often designed to enhance the attractiveness of a product by appealing to subconscious, unarticulated desires. Based on motivational principles deriving from Freudian psychoanalytic theory, the persuasiveness of subliminal messages stems from their ability to provoke subconscious release of repressed sexual energy and by appealing to the "death wish." According to this way of thinking, if advertisers can associate their products with our powerful but repressed sexual drives, or with the fascination we have with our own physical demise, then they have tapped into highly emotional but subliminal (below the level of conscious awareness) channels which may help provoke the consumer responses they desire.

Photo 2.2 Let it flow. Subliminal sexual intercourse in magazine advertising (reprinted with permission)

Subliminal messages are buried in media texts in ways that defy conscious perception. For example, visual subliminal messages are embedded in films, TV, and videos and are flashed on the screen for only a fraction of a second so that viewers receive, but don't actually "see," the decontextualized messages. In recorded music, spoken messages are inserted on discs and tapes in a way that cannot be consciously heard, or can be detected only by playing the song backwards. Print media, especially magazine advertising, contain below-the-level-of-consciousness suggestions in their photographs and graphic art. When we scan the image we get an impression, a feeling, but we don't stop to critically review the content for its subtle messages. We are influenced by such messages, the theory goes, without knowing it or being able to defend ourselves in a rational way.

Despite considerable popular attention given to subliminal persuasion and the fact that it has been debated and banned by several government agencies and industry organizations in many countries, we have little scientific knowledge about it. Analyzing the effects of subliminal messages is difficult because audience members do not recognize the images. That's the point. Subliminal persuasion depends on undetected influence. In spite of the mysterious and charlatan nature of subliminal persuasion and the way it has been proselytized for profit, however, the phenomenon is not sheer folly. Subliminal messages are simply among the most subtle forms of mass media persuasion in an informational/media environment that is so competitive all possible channels of influence will be exploited.

Temporal and spatial consciousness

So far we've been discussing consciousness mainly in terms of media forms, message content, national cultures, and political history. But modern mass media, especially electronic media, also influence human consciousness in ways that are even more fundamental to the human being. Consciousness is not only about "sense," or what we commonly know, but about "sense making." Because consciousness reflects both *what* the world appears to be, and *how* we perceive that world, what could be more important than the way(s) we conceive of and use *time and space*, the most basic structural features of our environment?

We are concerned with two basic processes here. First, media industries have the ability to overcome the limitations of unmediated ("real") time and space by applying their technologies in ways that promote their interests. Second, audience members interpret and use mediated time and space in ways that differ from their unmediated, "real-time" experiences that also work to their benefit. Living in an increasingly mediated world, industries and audiences therefore combine to "produce" new meanings of time and space. Still, there are crucial differences between the domains of industry and of audience in this transformation of the assumptions and flow of everyday life.

How media industries use technology to affect human perceptions of and relations to time and space is an important and enduring theoretical question. Harold Innis, a Canadian social theorist whose commentaries appeared just as television began to saturate North America after World War II, was the first writer to systematically address this issue (Innis 1950; 1951; 1952). Rather than celebrate the technological wizardry of modern media, a common view expressed in the popular press at the time, Innis worried about the media's economic, political, and cultural consequences. He was especially concerned with the electronic media's ability to radically alter the meaning of time and space. Innis began by examining what the term *mass communication* implies – that *messages become detached from their senders and from the times and contexts of original production.* Mediated messages are then received by a great number of people at many different times in a wide range of places and circumstances. This observation may seem like old news to us today, accustomed as we are to living in a mass-mediated world where time and space can be routinely shifted about for whim or convenience.

The origins of mass media's pervasive influence on consciousness can be traced to a time that precedes the introduction of electronic communications technology. Invention of the high-speed rotary printing press, the linotype machine, and the start of mass publishing widened the gap between rich and poor because these groups have very different levels of print literacy. Next came railways and roads, followed by the telegraph, the telephone, radio, and television. At the same time banking and financial institutions expanded the industrial and technological base for trade and investment. Moving commodities and messages around competitively has always been a central feature of industrial and post-industrial capitalism; it's happening today on a global scale.

Modern mass media – especially the electronic forms – thus make possible an unprecedented technological *conquering* of time and space. However, this achievement must be qualified. In the process of spanning time and space with tremendous speed and efficiency, media technologies also influence the assumptions and flow of everyday life in ways that provide great advantage to those in positions to profit from such temporal and geographic compressions and reconfigurations. Much like advanced twentieth-century transportation forms which stimulated an economic boom for urban industrialists, communications media also "bind" space, according to Harold Innis, in ways that regulate how business is conducted. Modern forms of transportation and communication give certain individuals an advantage because those few people with money enough to buy the equipment can manage time and space more effectively than everyone else.

A critical observer, Harold Innis worried about a world where time and space could be managed by media industrialists to unfair and unhealthy economic, political, and cultural advantage; specifically, that a measure of control over two of life's most basic resources was being turned over to an elite group of urban businessmen whose only motivation is to make a profit. Under the expansionist tendencies of capitalist ideology and the development of mass media, time and

Fortunately, every day comes with an evening.

Photo 2.3 Media divide and capitalize the natural rhythms of time to meet the ideological preferences and production schedules of the economic elite (reprinted with permission)

space have thus become more and more unevenly distributed in the human population. That owners of modern communications media can dramatically reduce physical distance and compress time in ways that reward them financially is a form of "economic neocolonialism," according to this way of thinking.

An American communication theorist, Joshua Meyrowitz, tried to expand the sociological dimension of McLuhan's perspective. Meyrowitz (1985) attempts to specify what radical changes the mass media stimulate in our sense of time and space by discussing how actual social situations have been altered since the electronic media

Box 2.1 Life in Marshall McLuhan's Global Village

Harold Innis's writing set the stage for many more commentaries on the crucial relationship between technological form, time and space, and community. Most notable is the work of his fellow Canadian, the literature professor and media theorist Marshall McLuhan (1962; 1964; McLuhan and Fiore 1967).

Whereas Innis explicitly warned of the dangers he thought modem communications technology pose to society, McLuhan was far less critical. Nonetheless, McLuhan's theories about mass media have become world famous. His books, articles, videos, and other work are crammed with fascinating, controversial insights. He invented many catchy phrases to describe how he believed communications technology shapes human consciousness. The most important contribution he made was to focus attention not on the *content* of media, but on their *forms*. The form that communications technology takes, McLuhan argued, influences the meanings that people take away from their mediated social interactions as much as or more than the message content does. In today's terms, we might say that McLuhan emphasized the hardware more than software.

Marshall McLuhan wrote essays about the sociohistorical development of communications media. He claimed that each new communications medium manipulates time and space uniquely ("the medium is the message and the massage," "hot and cool media") and, consequently, that each medium in its own way greatly influences, even determines, human perception and social organization (see figure 2.2). Specifically, he argued that print media such as books and newspapers, whose linear forms emphasize rationality and privacy, led world cultures away from their oral, nonlinear, holistic "tribal" roots. McLuhan pointed out how dramatically the world changed when the printing press, print literacy, and acts of writing and reading became part of Western societies. Print media, he said, "detribalized" culture.

Oral	Print	Electronic	Digital
Tribal	Detribalized	Retribalized	Virtual tribes
Nonlinear	Linear	Nonlinear	Mainly linear
Push	Pull	Push	Pull
Spoken	Written	Visual/spoken	Written/all senses
Small audiences	Large audiences	Huge audiences	Global audiences
Local	Gradually global	Global	Global
Communal	Private	Communal	Private/virtual
Storytelling, rhetoric, oratory	Books, newspapers, journals	Radio, TV, cable, satellites	Computers, information technology
Collective memory, traditions, history, cultural rituals	Literature, journalism, archives, libraries, publishing industry	Electronic storytelling, popular culture, media industries, audio/videotape, time shift	Global database, unregulated, potentially democratic, connectivity
No literacy	Print literacy	Visual literacy	Computer literacy
Emotion	Reason	Emotion	Reason
Spontaneous	Edited	Programmed	Spontaneous
Popular	Elite	Popular	Elite
Interactive	One-way	Mainly one-way	Interactive
"Real" time	Delayed	Immediate/delayed	Internet time

Figure 2.2 Stages of communication

But according to McLuhan, when the electronic media appeared at the beginning of the twentieth century, they "retribalized" people into a global society. He claimed that electricity (and electronic media) radically "abolish time and space." What has followed in the wake of such a remarkable technological development is a wired "global village." McLuhan argued that electronic media, especially television, activate the same sensory channels as those that characterize communication in face-to-face "tribal" societies. He was convinced that people worldwide were being connected and united through widely shared visceral, emotional experiences facilitated by breakthroughs in electronic communications technology.

The "global village" described by McLuhan became a feel-good term that makes it sound like everybody everywhere is joined together in some positive way by radio, television, cable, and satellites. The phrase inspires a "We are the World!" image, where people join hands and sing in harmony as they struggle together to end world hunger and create everlasting peace. Many media critics, however, harshly criticize McLuhan's ideas because they believe the electronic media have actually done just the opposite – that electronic media do more to divide the world than to unite it:

> The retribalization of the world creates no tribe. The global village is no village, and the television screen no village square. We are better off understanding the present world of media (or world *with* media, not to take too much for granted about their importance) on its own terms, rather than by way of these metaphors. (Hannerz 1992: 28)

Moreover, while McLuhan suggested that electronic media's refashioning of time and space has shocking implications for society, his theory of mediated communication was never very coherent and certainly not critical. He didn't have much to say about who the chiefs of the global village are, for instance, how much they pay their workers, or where they dump their waste.

Marshall McLuhan died before the Internet explosion of today. Nothwithstanding the criticism his work invites, it would have been fascinating to hear what he would have to say about the "digital revolution." In figure 2.2 I have identified key comparative characteristics of McLuhan's oral, print, and electronic media stages. Following his logic, I have extended the stages of communication into the digital era too.

arrived full force. Meyrowitz is optimistic about what these changes mean for society. Social situations are no longer tied to physical locations, according to Meyrowitz, and as a result our social categories and normative forms and places of interaction are blurred. The electronic media produce a new social order, one in which distinctions between childhood and adulthood are reconstituted, gender and racial statuses and roles merge, and political authority and power relations are recast in a more democratic way. Ultimately, Meyrowitz claims that the "unique power" of television is to "break down the distinctions between here and there, live and mediated, and personal and public" (p. 308). The mediation of human experience can be a good thing overall, Meyrowitz believes, because it tears down traditional social differences and hierarchies.

The shifting significance of physical space in the age of electronic media includes a substantial transformation of public ("on-stage") and private ("back-stage") behavior, according to Meyrowitz. This perspective – based on the work of Erving Goffman (1959; 1963; 1967; 1969) – also informs the theoretical work of Anthony Giddens and John B. Thompson. Giddens's (1984) theory of structuration and Thompson's (1990; 1995) theory of mediazation both try to account for how time and space are experienced in modern societies. But more like Innis than McLuhan or Meyrowitz, the British theorists attend to social structure as a critical factor in how time and space are perceived and used. So while Meyrowitz concludes that our world is now "relatively placeless," Thompson (1990) argues instead for a new understanding of how the mass media "extend the availability of symbolic forms in time and space" (p. 221) in order "to establish and sustain relations of domination" (p. 106).

At the same time, Thompson (1995) and others acknowledge that electronic media also hold society's political-economic-cultural power brokers accountable to their constituents, clients, and publics in a way that cannot be matched by any other system of checks and balances. Television makes powerful people *visible* like never before. It's more difficult now for politicians, billionaire businesspeople, sports heroes, movie stars, pop singers, or members of the royal family for that matter, to keep their "back-stage" behaviors out of public view. Who can argue sensibly that the media *only* glamorize and empower people like Bill Clinton, O. J. Simpson, Hugh Grant, Jim Bakker, Richard Nixon, Prince Charles, Maradona, or Carlos Salinas de Gortari? Even the highest-level officials of the Communist Party in China – who before the advent of TV were able to stay completely out of public view and scrutiny – now must make regular appearances in order to pacify the people.

Domestic time, space, and place

The electronic media not only transmit ideological themes and prompt a rethinking and reorganization of time and space, they also influence our domestic sites – how we perceive, arrange, and use our living areas and how we interact with others who reside there. It is in domestic venues and within the contingencies of everyday routines where new communication technologies alter people's worlds, sometimes radically so. But it is also at home where time and space certainly have not been abolished, where social categories have not always merged, and where traditional lines of authority often persist, sometimes becoming even stronger with the introduction of consumer technologies. Patterns of family television viewing, uses of personal computers and VCR machines, and management of TV, VCR, and compact disc remote control devices, for example, all reflect gender and generational hierarchies.

Introduction of new communications equipment into the home necessarily alters the living space, how it is interpreted, and how it is used. So, for instance, when a family brings home its first TV set, regardless of where in the world it happens, domestic space and its meanings change. When my parents bought their first TV set in the early 1950s in the United States, for example, they placed it at the end of the rectangular living (or "sitting") room in the front part of the house. But from the point of view of my parents, television became an unwanted intrusion on family life within a few years. My mother insisted that we add a small room to the house especially for TV viewing – the "TV room." Placing the TV set out of the way restored the living room to its original purpose – for reading and relaxing without distraction, and a setting to entertain guests.

This example reveals at least five fundamental dimensions of how a family's experience with mass media interacts with domestic space, time, and place: *reception* of television programs is *micro-social activity* that dynamically intermingles with *interpersonal relations* that are embedded within *cultural* contexts that are further affected by *social structure.* So our family's characteristic TV viewing activity, which influenced the interpretations we made of TV programs, took place under circumstances set by a parent who determined what role television should play in family life and was supported by financial conditions sufficient to permit a range of relevant options.

Photos 2.4, 2.5 WebTV. Every technological advance reshapes temporal and spatial consciousness. The integration of television and computers may radically alter how domestic space is perceived and used (reprinted with permission of Microsoft)

Today the personal computer has become a significant domestic issue in the world's more developed countries. Computers became part of the "media ensemble" (Rogge and Jensen 1988) at home. The degree to which the computer has been accommodated into domestic life, however, depends on several factors. First and foremost is economics. Personal computers are simply out of financial reach for the vast majority of the world's families. There are still very few home computers in sub-Saharan Africa, for instance, and fewer than one telephone line (necessary for most computer-based communications functions) for every 200 families there, according to World Bank and International Monetary Fund data. China, India, and the nations of Southeast Asia also have a very low penetration of computers and telephones. At the other extreme is the wealthy, high-tech environment of Silicon Valley in northern California where nearly every family has a telephone and two-thirds of homes have at least one computer. Overall, more than half of American families have a computer at home, a proportion that continues to grow, and many have more than one. In general, the more rich the country, the higher the penetration of computers.

How the computer fits in with television, video, and other electronic equipment as domestic appliances, though, is still being worked out both at home and in the laboratories and marketing departments of computer manufacturers. One industry solution is to combine technologies, and change patterns of domestic activity. Microsoft, for instance, has successfully marketed WebTV – a system that allows users to navigate the World Wide Web and send and receive email using the television screen as a monitor. The Intel Corporation, the world's largest producer of microprocessors, is working on a project to encourage families to gather around the "family computer" much like the family TV set (and earlier the family radio) for "social computing." The family computer, sold as "Family Room PC," features a large screen, smart TV receiver, surround sound, and all the accessories, including digital video discs, a message center for telephone and email, and video conferencing. Intel is attempting to turn the personal computer from an individually used appliance into a multi-person technology. They are not simply selling a new piece of equipment. Intel wants to change how we think about domestic time, space, and place. Moreover, the company is trying to meld two media normally used for very different purposes – the TV and VCR for entertainment and relaxation, the computer for information and work. Such technological fusions, however, can never be forced on society. Only time will tell if people are willing to restructure their domestic routines to coincide with the merchandizing recommendations of the high-tech companies.

The role of culture

Culture is a vital factor to consider in understanding how media technologies become a part of everyday life. There are many ways to live in the global village. The meaning of home, family, time, and leisure differs greatly from culture to culture, as does routine domestic activity, including patterns in the flow of human traffic in and out of the living space, the specific functions of domestic space, gender roles enacted there, and characteristic modes of mass media reception. *Media technologies enter cultural settings in ways that extend the characteristic traditions, values, and styles that are already in place while at the same they also challenge and transform the foundations of culture* (Lull 1988). The free-form quality of the Internet, for example, has sent governments all over the world scrambling to decide what, if anything, can be done to "protect" their cultures from this technological interloper while at the same time upgrading their technological infrastructures to accommodate demands of the new global economy.

A stark cultural contrast to the West is the People's Republic of China, a nation where television entered nearly every urban household during the economic boom of the early 1980s. Despite the political-economic-cultural authority wielded by the Communist Party, China is becoming a "consumer society." At the top of the list of consumer items Chinese families want are electrical appliances, especially media equipment (Yi 1997). Indeed, more and more families have been able to buy color TVs, VCRs, audio and video disc players, and personal computers lately. Unfortunately, however, China's impressive recent economic growth has done little to improve living conditions for many families in terms of domestic space. In Shanghai, for example, many families of four or five members still live in one or two small rooms. Television's impact under these conditions is necessarily immense – different from other cultures – affecting the most basic assumptions and practices of daily life. Requirements such as providing adequate study time and space for children, assuring prime-time entertainment for working adults, respecting the program preferences of elderly family members, and getting enough sleep, to name some key cultural considerations, is complex family work. Domestic TV viewing in China occurs in "public home space" compared to the relatively "private home space" characteristic of larger living areas more available in several other countries.

India signals still other contrasts. In rural India, introduction of TV into the household has restructured family members' perceptions and uses of time during the day and week in ways that have radically challenged some long-standing traditions concerning gender roles and relations, work routines, child raising, and domestic tasks. Natural time – the demarcation of temporal increments by the rising and setting of the sun – has given way to television time. Sunday has become a "TV day" in India; night-time activity now focuses on TV viewing, thereby bringing men and women together for a common form of entertainment; food and the way it is prepared have changed in the interest of preserving time for TV viewing. According to Indian researcher Neena Behl (1988), these changes in rural India's family life have made some aspects of domestic relations more democratic. Behl claims that TV smoothes out sharp status differences between males and females and differences between old and young viewers. At the same time, however, other key features of radically stratified Indian society are reinforced in acts of television viewing. Where people sit when they watch TV, for instance, typically reflects caste differences between viewers of unrelated families and differences between gender-based statuses within families. Those with higher status – males, elders, and members of higher religious castes and socioeconomic classes – are given the best seats for TV viewing. This example from rural India shows how the introduction of new technology both changes and reinforces cultural traditions.

Television's influence on how time, space, and place are perceived can be seen in shifting patterns of touch, talk, sleep, food preparation and consumption, and other routine forms of communication and domestic activity all over the world. Without doubt, social assimilations of communications technology and the modifications of consciousness it stimulates have deep implications for gender relations and family life in general. Exactly *what* those modifications are, however, is a cultural matter. Women in Germany, for instance, often complain that television destroys marital communication, while rural Indian women say that the medium brings them closer to their husbands (Rogge and Jensen 1988; Behl 1988). Contrasts in television's role in the domestic life of these two nations stem in part from differences in national development. TV has simply been a part of life in Germany longer. But the dissimilarities also reflect real differences in cultural values and their corresponding social practices.

Another sharp cultural contrast can be shown by comparing South American with North American and northern European families. For example, in Venezuela women are heads of the household in a majority of homes and routinely control the domestic agenda, including choice of television programs and the establishment of desired viewing environments (Barrios 1988). Many Brazilian women, like their Venezuelan counterparts, spend their evenings watching national soap operas (*telenovelas*) in an atmosphere dictated by them. Family television viewing in North American, northern European, and British families, on the other hand, is far more dominated by men, at least when they are employed outside the home (Morley 1986; 1988; 1992; Lull 1988; 1990). For example, David Morley has shown how men in working-class London families exercise greater power than women over what programs are watched at night and on weekends, that they plan their viewing more, watch with less domestic distractions, dominate the remote control device, and feel less guilty than their wives about watching TV. In Japan another domestic development is taking place. Because of the tremendous amount of time Japanese men spend at work and in traffic every day, women and children have gradually assumed more and more influence over television and video viewing, and other home activities.

The different ways males and females of all ages watch television and video, use the computer and compact disc player, read the newspaper, and participate in every other kind of media activity reflects their social roles in general. Preferences for media content – TV, movies, video games, computer programs, and music especially – differ for males and females in similarly patterned ways all over the world. Boys and girls and men and women respond differently to the media they engage. Boys, for example, act more aggressively than girls when watching violent TV or movies. The media environment and interpersonal realities reinforce each other, and a gender-based cycle of difference stays in motion.

Just as families, houses, homes, everyday activities, and conceptions of time, space, and place vary within and among nations and cultures, so too do the institutional features of television, its content, and its modes of transmission. The number of channels available for viewing, program priorities and types, program scheduling, and the availability of VCRs, for instance, all extend certain cultural values and practices, thereby influencing how people watch television (Lull 1988). Even television audiences' "rhythms of viewing" are conditioned largely by the way program segments are divided up. A commercial format, for instance, creates a sequence of timing expectations. Program segments of ten minutes, for example are followed by commercial clusters of five minutes, then back to the program, then the commercials again, ad infinitum. Years of exposure to these patterns create expectations that are felt close to the bone. When Americans travel to England and watch commercial-free BBC television, for example, the change in viewing rhythm can actually be unsettling ("But when do I make a sandwich or go the bathroom?").

And it works the other way too. Europeans accustomed to non-commercial television adjust uncomfortably to the frequent program interruptions when they visit the USA. Commercials are placed in clusters outside programming in many parts of the world; however, the relatively recent triumph of cable and satellite television on a global scale is breaking down the protected national systems and creating cultural crises in the process (for example, see Gripsrud 1995; 1999).

Although TV clearly impacts on domestic life in different ways all over the world, audiences in those same places have influenced the institution of television too. The electronic medium doesn't just dictate expectations and regulate social activity; it also responds to social and cultural patterns. This has often been said of program ratings, for example, in the sense that statistical approximations of audience acceptance ultimately determine the success of a program. In the end what we have is a "give and take" between industries and audiences, with a fair amount of power to shape consciousness held by parties on both sides of the equation.

No individual person, social group, or institution dispenses ideology as attractively and continuously as the mass media. Despite this awesome power, people are not unthinkingly stimulated by mediated representations of political positions, product advertising, or any other ideological domain. Ideational and mediational image systems ultimately are not perfect unities or closed systems and people are not imitating dupes in any political-economic-cultural environment anyway. Individual and collective consciousness is never simply a product of ideological representation or technological influence. The meanings we give to our symbolic environments take shape in the routine social exchanges of everyday life. Consciousness formation, therefore, is an interpretative process, and "this process of interpretation is interpersonal . . . individual experience is to some extent dependent upon categories made available through others' activity" (Chaney 1994: 66). But interpretation of the worlds we live in never leads to any uniform point of view: "just as there is no individual existence, there can be no singular thought. Our consciousness is but a meeting ground, the crystallization of various currents which . . . intersect, attract, or repel on another" (Maffesoli 1996: 68). One way to understand how the many possible outcomes of this complex interplay of ideology, consciousness, and social interaction develop is the subject of the next chapter – hegemony.

3

Hegemony

Hegemony is the power or dominance that one social group holds over others. This power differential can be found in political-economic-cultural relations between nation-states, and between social classes within any nation or territory. Hegemony is "dominance and subordination in the field of relations structured by power" (Hall 1985). But *hegemony is more than the sum of differences in social power; it is a method for gaining and maintaining power*. If ideology is a system of structured representations, and consciousness is a structure of mind that reflects those representations, then *hegemony is the linking mechanism between dominant ideology and consciousness*. We shall sometimes refer to hegemony therefore as ideological hegemony.

Today, more than a century after Karl Marx and Friedrich Engels wrote their classic treatises about capitalist exploitation of the working class (see especially Marx 1867, 1885, 1894; Marx and Engels 1845; 1848), economic disparities still underlie and help reproduce social inequalities in industrialized societies. In that important, basic sense, Marxism and Marxist critical theory, which have been so badly maligned in the rhetoric surrounding the downfall of many communist nations at the close of the twentieth century, remain accurate in many ways. Technological developments of the past century in the field of communication, however, have made the manner of social domination much more complex than before. Power and class differences in today's world are not determined solely or directly by the economic structures and processes of industrial production and consumption. Although workplace conditions and marketplace realities continue to divide human beings into socioeconomic classes, ideological influence has become crucial in the "communication age" today where mediated social interaction is commonplace.

The early twentieth-century Italian intellectual Antonio Gramsci – to whom the term hegemony is attributed – broadened Marxist theory from economics into the realm of ideology. Persecuted by Italy's fascist government of the 1930s and writing from prison, Gramsci emphasized what he called society's "superstructure," its ideology-producing institutions, in his theories of meaning and power (1971; 1973; 1978; see also Boggs 1976; Sassoon 1980; and Simon 1982). Gramsci was trying to explain how the Italian and German fascists could manipulate people so effectively. By calling attention to how governments and economic institutions produce and circulate ideas, Gramsci helped shift critical theory away from its focus on capitalist society's "base" – its economic foundation. His theory of ideological hegemony stresses how mass media are used by ruling elites to "perpetuate their power, wealth, and status [by popularizing] their own philosophy, culture and morality" (Boggs 1976: 39). Ideology-producing superstructures correlate with, but are not the same as, economic structures and processes of industrial production. They must be analyzed in a different way.

Base	Superstructure
Economic relations	Consciousness
Workplace and market	Ideological institutions and everyday life
Material	Symbolic
Direct influence	Framing
Compliance	Consent
Determined effects	Hegemony

Figure 3.1 Gramsci's theory of social power

Such a theoretical turn seems natural and necessary in an era when communications technology is such a pervasive and potent ideological force. The electronic media had just arrived on the scene when Antonio Gramsci was writing. In Gramsci's time and continuing today, owners and managers of media industries are able to produce and reproduce ideological content, inflections, and tones far more easily than other people in society because the elites manage the key socializing institutions, thereby guaranteeing that their points of view are constantly and attractively cast into the public arena. The fascists of Gramsci's day used propaganda. The capitalists of today use advertising and other informational campaigns to accomplish the same goals.

Hegemony extends the systemic logic of image systems to achieve ideological saturation. The mass-mediated dominant ideology is corroborated and strengthened by an interlocking system of information-distributing agencies and taken-for-granted communication practices that permeate every corner of social and cultural reality. Messages supportive of status quo ideology emanate from schools, businesses, political organizations, trade unions, religious groups, the military, and the mass media. They all dovetail together. *This inter-articulating, mutually reinforcing process of ideological influence is the essence of hegemony.* Society's most entrenched and powerful institutions – which all depend in one way or another on the same sources of economic support – fundamentally agree with each other. Hegemony therefore depends on widespread circulation and social acceptance of the dominant ideology.

Hegemony works on a grand scale, but in a subtle way. It is not a *direct* stimulation of thought or action. According to Stuart Hall, hegemony is a "framing [of] all competing definitions of reality within [the dominant class's] range, bringing all alternatives within their horizons of thought. [The dominant class] sets the limits – mental and structural – within which subordinate classes 'live' and make sense of their subordination in such a way as to sustain the dominance of those ruling over them" (1977: 333). The most potent effect of mass media is how they inconspicuously influence their audiences to perceive social roles and routine personal activities. This "mainstreaming" effect is accomplished largely by the way mass media's symbolic content frames "reality." The economic and information elite in society use the mass media to provide a "rhetoric [through] which [social roles and 'normal' behavior] are labeled, evaluated, and explained" (Elliott 1974: 262). Television commercials, for example, encourage audiences to think of themselves as "markets rather than as a public, as consumers rather than citizens" (Gitlin 1979: 255).

But hegemony does not mature strictly from ideological articulation. Dominant streams of thought must be subsequently reproduced in the activities of our most basic social units – families, workplace networks, and friendship groups in the many sites and undertakings of everyday life. Gramsci's theory of hegemony, therefore, connects ideological representation to culture through everyday social interaction. *Hegemony requires that ideological assertions become self-evident cultural assumptions.* The effectiveness of hegemony depends on subordinated peoples accepting the dominant ideology as "normal reality or common sense . . . in active forms of experience and consciousness" (Williams 1976: 145). Or as communication theorist Eduardo Neiva puts it, "as everything is integrated, nothing is without sense, and the sense of any social fragment is given by its integration in the social framework" (Neiva 2000: in press). Because information and entertainment technology is so thoroughly integrated into the everyday realities of modern societies, mass media's social influence is not always recognized, discussed, or criticized, particularly where the overall standard of living is relatively high. The enormous scale and complexity of society can mask its ideological foundations. Hegemony, therefore, can easily go undetected (Bausinger 1984).

Photo 3.1 The commercial organization of experience. A sign at Disneyland in California suggests places for taking pictures, mainstreaming tourists' experiences and memories (photo by James Lull)

Hegemony implies a tacit willingness by people to be governed by principles, rules, and laws they believe operate in their best interests, even though in actual practice they may not. Social consent is a necessary part of the process. Consent is a far more effective long-term means of social control than is coercion or force. For hegemony to work, people must believe in their system of governance and in their dominant culture. As Raymond Williams explained, "The idea of hegemony, in its wide sense, is . . . especially important in societies [where] electoral politics and public opinion are significant factors, and in which social practice is seen to depend on consent to certain dominant ideas which in fact express the needs of a dominant class" (1976: 145). Thus, in the words of Colombian communication theorist Jesús Martín-Barbero, "one class exercises hegemony to the extent that the dominating class has interests which the subaltern [dominated] classes recognize as being in some degree their interests too" (1993: 74). The idea is to keep people believing in the governments, economic institutions, and cultures they inhabit and help reproduce. One true test of hegemony's power in a society is whether or not young men are willing to march off to war in order to defend the system in which they live.

Today we generally think of hegemony in terms of the economic and political power that elites hold over the rest of us, but religion is also a potent hegemonic force, and certainly not just in Western societies. Discussing his work in India, for instance, the cultural anthropologist and photographer Stephen P. Huyler (1999) told a newspaper reporter:

> Religion permeates every aspect of every person's daily life in India. And they don't even *think* of it in terms of religion, in many cases. It's just the way people acknowledge the spirit in order to maintain the balance of their daily lives. Many [Indians] are surprised when I point out that this ritual or that observance would be viewed by others as an expression of religion. They simply tell me, "This is just our custom. This just what we do in our family." (*San José Mercury News*, September 25, 1999)

Our "customs" and "just what we do in our family," particularly when we don't reflect on what motivates such orientations and behavior or whose interests they ultimately serve, are precisely how hegemony takes form in everyday life.

The role of media and popular culture

People say the home run race is bringing the country together . . . so be it. Let's bring the country together.

> Baseball player Mark McGwire in 1998 as the
> televised competition for "home run king" distracted
> some Americans from the Clinton–Lewinsky scandal
> going on at the same time.

Central to hegemony is a strong connection between the major information-diffusing, socializing institutions of a society and the ideological lessons they create and sustain in that society. Media legitimize certain ideas, making it more likely that those ideas will be accepted by the population. Let's make our discussion of hegemony more concrete by calling out some examples. We can begin with a real ideological behemoth – the American commercial television industry. Commercial television connects financially and symbolically with many other large industries, especially advertising companies, but also with hundreds of national and multinational corporations that produce, distribute, and market a wide range of commodities. The media and the products and services they advertise work together to help create the dominant ideology.

Examples can be found in all types of television programming. For instance, commercial TV networks dedicate tremendous resources to capture the "child audience." But they almost never buy original children's shows. TV program executives want ideas that are already associated with successful retail products marketed to children – toys, mainly – thereby lessening the risk of investment. Children then want toys they have seen on TV. They are far less concerned with the merits of the toys themselves than with the magical image certain toys achieve from TV exposure. The toy industry and the television industry thus meld into one mutually reinforcing and very profitable enterprise that narrows the range of available products while it makes the economic process more efficient for the industries involved. The toy tie-in functions well with movies and fast-food chains too. In America at the end of the last decade, McDonald's was selling Tarzan dolls timed to match Disney's release of the film. Beanie Babies were all the craze months earlier. Godzilla and the Spanish-speaking Chihuahua were hooked into the Mexican fast-food chain, Taco Bell.

Television has the ability to absorb and transform other major social institutions – organized religion and sports, for instance – by turning them into entertainment and popular culture. Religious television, and especially the evangelical programs, have become enormous financial successes, a phenomenon that is now spreading around the globe. These programs often mimic the celebrity talk-show format of a Rosie O'Donnell or Dave Letterman, for instance, complete with studio orchestras and audiences. The religious shows depend greatly on the star appeal of their charismatic servants of God to grab high ratings. The sports industry has become even more intertwined with electronic media, to the point where a "television time-out" (a break in the action created solely to make room for additional commercials) now seems like a normal part of the game. Viewers are further encouraged to check out the TV networks' website (and the commercial messages that appear there) for even more sports images, statistics, analyses, and hype.

The history of American commercial broadcasting clearly shows how capitalist economic forces cooperate with and often override government's supposed role as defender of the people's interests. Legislation was passed by Congress in the 1920s to assure that radio and television would not be given over to commercial interests alone. Broadcasting stations were said to be public resources, not unlike national parks, rivers, and lakes, to be protected. In return, the electronic media were supposed to act in the "public interest" or stations' owners could have their extremely profitable licenses revoked. Slowly but surely, unfortunately, the Federal Communications Commission stepped aside as commercial broadcasters amassed great economic power and political influence. Radio and television stations, of course, decide how much news coverage to give congressmen and congresswomen. Furthermore, government regulators typically are recruited from, and return to, the very communications industries they are supposed to monitor. By the end of the twentieth century, the public service requirement for broadcasters in the United States had been almost completely forgotten. In Europe and other parts of the world fierce competition from commercial television, cable, and satellite broadcasting has challenged the sanctity of "responsible" state media like the BBC too.

Hegemony is a process of convergence, consent, and subordination. Ideas, social institutions, industries, and ways of living are synthesized into a mosaic which serves to preserve the economic, political, and cultural advantages of the already powerful.

The mass media play an extraordinary role in the process. Within the media industries themselves we find dramatically increasing patterns of convergence. Perhaps the most troubling phenomenon is the fact that more and more media outlets are owned by fewer and fewer individuals and companies (Bagdikian 1997). This concentration of ownership is developing not only within single media forms such as television stations, or among related technologies like radio and television, but across many types of communications media and across many different entertainment and information industries. For example, in just the past few years Time Warner merged with Turner Broadcasting Service and then with America Online, Disney with Capital Cities Broadcasting/ABC, and Westinghouse Broadcasting and Viacom with the CBS network. British Telecommunications PLC merged international operations with America's AT&T to do business in more than 280 countries producing revenues of about $10 billion in 2000. AT&T then merged with TCI Cablevision in the US to create AT&T Cable Services. General Electric owns NBC. Electric companies now offer telephone service. Telephone companies sell cable TV subscriptions. Long-distance telephone companies break into local markets. Cable companies buy up satellite TV systems. Merger mania is reaching new heights with the explosion of the Internet's global popularity. America Online's acquisition of Netscape gave AOL an extraordinary market share of residential Internet users. Disney's purchase of Infoseek, WorldCom's merger with MCI, who later merged with Sprint, and General Electric's purchase of Cnet were other significant early deals on this new economic and cultural frontier.

Media ownership spills over into many related industries, including those industries that provide content for the media themselves. For example, multi-billionaire media mogul Rupert Murdoch, who owns Newscorp, the Fox Group in the United States, a host of British and Australian media, and satellite systems around the world, including Star TV over China, recently paid more than $300 million to buy the Los Angeles Dodgers baseball team (whose games appear on his TV stations). The California Angels baseball team is owned by Disney/ABC, the Atlanta Braves by Time-Warner, the Chicago Cubs by the Tribune company. The Ackerly media group (radio and outdoor billboards) bought the Seattle Supersonics basketball team. Mergers such as these are consummated primarily to guarantee that the extremely profitable games played by the teams involved will be carried on radio and television stations owned by the same companies. The arenas in which the teams play are often named after their corporate owners too. Or they are put up for sale to the highest bidder: Pacific Bell Park (telephone company) in San Francisco; Great Western (bank) Forum in Los Angeles, Arco (gasoline) Arena in Sacramento, United (airlines) Center in Chicago (where United Airlines tickets are dispensed by machine in the lobby), are just a few examples.

And the big home run hitter quoted at the beginning of this section, Cardinal's star Mark McGwire, hits many of his four-baggers into "Big Mac Land," a section of Busch (beer) Stadium in St Louis, a commercial tie-in to the McDonald's hamburger chain.

We may not have seen the limits of this hegemonic commercial logic. Imagine that sports teams stop being identified with the geographic locations they have traditionally represented, and take on corporate identities instead: the Seattle Mariners could become the Microsoft Mariners. The Chicago Bulls become the United Airlines Bulls. The Indianapolis Colts take the field as the RCA Colts, and so on. Better yet, why not give individual players the right to sell *themselves* to corporate sponsors? Imagine a radio play-by-play announcer excitedly describing a baseball game where "3M hits a hot grounder to Texaco . . . he scoops it up and flips it underhand to General Motors who relays the throw to American Online! Double Play! Texaco robbed 3M of a hit, and GM made a perfect relay to first!"

The corporate influence over popular culture should not be underestimated. When American rock singer Sheryl Crow released the hit song "Love is a Good Thing" in 1996 it was immediately pulled out of the huge Wal-Mart department store chain, limiting overall sales. Why? The song contains the line, "Watch our children as they kill each other with guns they bought at the Wal-Mart discount stores." Freedom of speech often ends where corporate discomfort begins.

Media technologies and genres frequently converge to reinforce each other hegemonically. Popular radio and video songs, for example, can also be commercials. Genesis's "Tonight, Tonight, Tonight" and Steve Winwood's "Do You Know What the Night Can Do?" have the same melodies as, and similar lyrics to, the Michelob beer commercials these artists also sing. America's first prime-time, network TV, Spanish-language commercial featured Puerto Rican pop singer Chayanne reworking the lyrics of his hit song on the Latin charts, "Éste Ritmo se Baila Así," into a Pepsi-Cola endorsement. A paid-for Pepsi logo pops up in a Nintendo video game. Video games, computer games, toys, and board games pick up media/military sloganeering such as "A Line in the Sand" and "Gulf Strike." The highly rated video game Street Fighter II inspires production of a movie by the same name. Nike animated TV commercials featuring Michael Jordan inspired the movie *Space Jam*. The original *Star Wars* trilogy becomes an exhibit at the Smithsonian National Air and Space Museum. Props from movies like the park bench from *Forest Gump* and John Travolta's disco outfit from *Saturday Night Fever* are sold in public auctions. Sylvester Stallone's and Wesley Snipes's *Demolition Man* becomes a movie-length commercial for Taco Bell. Bill Cosby parlays his widespread recognition as a TV character into best-selling pop books on fatherhood and sales pitches for "fat-free Jell-O puddings." Commercial logos become products themselves and are reproduced on tee-shirts, posters, beach towels, and other informal media. The rhetoric of TV commercials and programs is recycled in the lyrics of rap music and in the routines of stand-up comedians performing live and on television. A romantic encounter depicted in a TV commercial for coffee (Taster's Choice in the USA; Nescafé Gold Blend in the UK) is turned into a commercial video and novel. Postcards, tourist magazines, and travel posters reproduce the skylines, skyscrapers, monuments, and museums of cities and nations, glorifying and extending the original structures which are themselves loaded with values representing the dominant ideology and culture.

Cable television ushers in an era of program-length infomercials. There are films made for television, magazines published about television, and television news magazines. The best-known national newspaper in the United States, *USA Today*, is sold nationwide in vending boxes that resemble TV sets. Television commercials appear on Channel One, an educational news channel shown to students in American elementary-school classrooms. Logos that advertise only national gasoline, food, and motel chains appear on government highway signs, advising travelers of their availability at upcoming freeway exits. Expensive public relations campaigns of major corporations distribute "informational" supplementary textbooks to elementary and secondary-school systems. Major business organizations send digests of their annual reports and other promotional materials to college instructors, hoping this biased information will be incorporated into teaching and research. Similar materials are sent to political and religious leaders so they will pass the information along to their constituencies and congregations. School uniforms are required of students to assure their compliance, their "uniformity," with the authorities' values.

In the United States, non-mainstream political ideologies, parties, and candidates, as well as suggestions of consumer alternatives to the commercial frenzy stimulated and reinforced by advertising and other marketing techniques, are rarely seen on the popular media. Truly radical ideas typically appear only on underfinanced, non-commercial radio and TV stations and in low-budget print media. These media have tiny public followings compared to commercial television and video outlets, metropolitan daily newspapers, and national magazines. When genuinely divergent views appear on mainstream media, the information is frequently shown in an unfavorable light or is modified and co-opted to surrender to the embrace of mainstream thought. Thus former presidential candidate Jesse Jackson modified his political platform to fit into the unthreatening ideology of the Democratic Party; the long-haired look of "anti-establishment" young men in the 1960s became a popular hairstyle of middle-aged businessmen two decades later; roughly textured punk rock turned quickly into "new wave" dance music and was used to market radical chic department-store fashion a decade later; the anti-fashion grunge look of the 1990s is packaged for sale by fashion designer Perry Ellis; urban black culture becomes commodified as "hip-hop" fashion and is put up for sale in suburban malls; the Smothers Brothers comedy team, who championed the cause of socialist folk singer Pete Seeger in the 1960s, do TV commercials for the Kentucky Fried Chicken franchise; the Jefferson Starship rock band (formerly the Jefferson Airplane, known for "We Gotta Have a Revolution") sells the rights to a hit song ("We Built This City") to International Telephone and Telegraph (ITT) where the song becomes an anthem for a TV commercial campaign titled "We Built This Business," and so on. The mass media help create an impression that even society's roughest edges ultimately must conform to the conventional contours of dominant ideologies. This normalizing activity is key to ideological hegemony.

Do people who work for the mass media and popular culture industries knowingly or purposefully create hegemonic conditions? In some cases, yes. Mexico, for example, has a long history of government officials openly paying off journalists to assure favorable coverage (a practice that has been declining lately). But as British cultural studies researcher Shaun Moores observes about broadcast news: "the operations of ideology have much more to do with a taken-for-granted reproduction of dominant definitions and an adherence to accepted professional conventions than they have with the deliberate biases of broadcasters or the institutions in which they operate" (Moores 1993: 28).

Global capitalist hegemony

This is My Planet.
Reebok International advertising campaign

Solutions for a Small Planet.
IBM international advertising campaign

Business schools on college and university campuses throughout the United States and in other relatively developed countries now routinely offer courses with titles such as "Global Management." Think of how pretentious and taken-for-granted such an idea is – that some class or category of persons and institutions would take it upon themselves to "manage" the globe. Still, everybody's "going global" in the business world. The world is the market. This tendency is not new. It follows directly from the logic and practices of centuries of economic and cultural colonialism that can be traced back at least to the Roman Empire, right through the expeditions of the Scandinavian

Vikings, the Portuguese, English, Spanish, French, and Dutch, to the more contemporary exploits of the Germans, Americans, and Japanese. Today the dynamic combination of jet air travel and fast, efficient communications technology has produced a "global information infrastructure" that gives the players in this game real opportunities to "manage the globe" in a way that has never been possible before. The unfairness and dangers of this global economic and ideological hegemony have been signaled by several academic observers. Perhaps most notable among them is Immanuel Wallerstein, who emphasizes the same term we stressed last chapter in our critique of ideology – system. Wallerstein calls the global economy "a modern world-system" (Wallerstein 1974, 1980; 1990). According to this view, ideology and communication are used to gain and maintain economic power and exercise social influence at the global level in a tight system of winners and losers. The flow of ideas, data, and points of view serves the global elite to the detriment of everyone else. Multinational corporations have actually assumed greater control over the destiny of the world's population than governments in the global scenario, making politics nearly irrelevant in some cases.

Box 3.1 Microsoft: Hegemony for the Digital Age?

The only thing I'd rather own than Windows is English, or Chinese, or Spanish, so I could charge you $249 US for a license to speak.

> Scott McNealy, Chief Executive Officer of Sun Microsystems, commenting on the dominance of Microsoft Windows operating system in 1998 US Senate hearings on the alleged monopolistic marketing practices of Microsoft

The most stunning thing about the software business continues to be how USA-centric it is. There has never been an industry that was so dominated by one country.

> Bill Gates, Chairman of Microsoft

As the twentieth century drew to a close, one major US corporation, Microsoft, became a symbol of just how dominant a single business organization, and one country, can be in the economics of global communication. Microsoft was rivaled only by IBM as the most admired company in the United States at the end of last century. Bill Gates had become the wealthiest "working man" in the world, according to *Forbes* magazine, with an estimated net worth

Photo 3.2 Microsoft meets NBC to create satellite and cable TV Channel MSNBC (printed with permission of Microsoft)

of $93 billion in 1999. At the same time America had recovered its rating as the world's "most competitive nation" in conditions that create wealth for a country, the Japanese economy having taken a downward slide in the Asian economic crisis.

But while Microsoft was exerting world leadership in software development, it was also bundling its operating systems (Windows 95 and 98) with its Internet browser in a way that many people believe forcibly monopolized the market. A massive anti-trust investigation was conducted by the US government. The government's top economic expert witness testified at the trial that Microsoft is a monopoly because (1) it has a stable market share of more than 90 percent with no change in sight, (2) it would be almost impossible for another company to successfully introduce another competitive operating system, (3) Microsoft's profit margins and equity are very high, and (4) the company threatened to revoke Windows licenses from computer manufacturers if they hide Microsoft's web-browser icon on desktop systems (*San José Mercury News*, November 19, 1998).

Moreover, any software operating system like Windows is much more than a technological development and a business venture. The digitized integrating function of Windows never just moves information around the world without bias. Windows is ideological and cultural too. The domination of the English language, together with all the Anglo-American pop culture that is celebrated on the Internet, contributes to the hegemonic effect. Microsoft's actions affect everyone, not just the company's business competitors.

Just as significant ideologically as the link between Microsoft's operating systems and its Internet browser is the connection the software company made with one of the major American commercial television networks, NBC, in the late 1990s. The most visible product of the joint venture was formation of a cable news channel, MSNBC, which combines the tradition and lofty status of NBC News with the look and feel of computer software. An example of the channel's programming is "News Chat," where the host and his attractive "techie" assistant interact simultaneously with news personalities, analysts, telephone callers, and email correspondents, all the while directing viewers' attention not only to themselves, but to a variety of MSNBC websites and on-line chat rooms. The NBC news network also provides information for the Microsoft Network, a commercial on-line service for consumers who buy Windows operating systems. The Channel bar on Windows 98 steers users directly to websites usually owned by Microsoft, or its partners – MSNBC for news, for example.

For years Microsoft vigorously defended its aggressive business practices and offered no compromise. Gates and his lieutenants claimed that Microsoft is not a self-interested monopoly, but an "innovator" whose creativity, productivity, and market strategies are necessary for the company to succeed, and for the global information revolution to continue on schedule.

The company was dealt a serious blow in late 1999, however, when a US federal judge ruled that indeed Microsoft was a monopoly. The judge concluded that "Through its actions ... Microsoft has demonstrated that it will use its prodigious market power and immense profits to harm any firm that insists on pursuing initiatives that could intensify competition against one of Microsoft's core products" (*San José Mercury News*, November 6, 1999). Ironically, the judge found that instead of promoting innovation in the high-tech field, Microsoft was suppressing it unfairly.

Why should we worry about this? Bill Gates says he doesn't think it's a problem! But others fear that journalistic integrity is seriously compromised by a conflict of interest in agreements like the one between Microsoft and NBC. Presumably NBC would not be eager to investigate Microsoft very carefully in its routine coverage of the news, for example, a fear that was in fact confirmed by MSNBC's sketchy coverage of the software company's anti-trust hearings. An earlier interview of Bill Gates by NBC anchorman Tom Brokaw didn't contain any tough questions either. Microsoft is only the largest and best-known of high-technology companies which are developing working agreements and financial ties with content providers, Internet services, and news organizations. America Online, for instance, has been hooking up with metropolitan daily newspapers and commercial advertisers as main sources of revenue for what was originally an Internet access service. Search engines are programmed to navigate selectively to sites that represent commercial interests, and to default to sponsored home pages.

And while Microsoft may produce software, the company has always had much interest in the development of personal computer hardware, such as the computer–television interface discussed in chapter 2.

Communist hegemony

Although most critical theorists think of hegemony in terms of ideological control in capitalist countries, hegemony has been central to the management of ideology in communist nations too, though it develops differently. The ideological planning of communist governments and their creation of propaganda to inform and advise "the people," represent the same basic intention capitalists have – to protect the political and economic interests of the ruling elites. Competition for the hearts and minds of the people is supposed to be eliminated in communist systems. Other systems of ideas – religions, for example – had been declared illegal in places such as China and Cuba, though such restrictions have proven very difficult to enforce. Sloganeering is a common strategy. In China, for example, "Respect the Four Cardinal Principles of Socialism" and "Unite Behind the Material and Spiritual Modernization" are all too familiar to the people. Educational institutions in China are required not only to teach Communist Party ideology, but to discourage any questioning of the official agenda. Journalists are supposed to find facts to support official positions rather than try to more objectively report news events. Newspapers, television, radio, and billboards praise "model workers" – men and women who have made some long-term, selfless contribution to the system – which really means that they have gone along with communist dominant ideology in some extremely dedicated and visible way.

The collapse of political authority in Eastern and Central Europe and the former Soviet Union was a breakdown in communist ideological hegemony. Conflict between culture producers and young audiences in East Germany and Hungary is typical of what happened in the Soviet bloc (Wicke 1992; Szemere 1985). Young rock musicians and their enthusiastic audiences led a cultural and political struggle against the repressive institutions and the ideology behind them. Trying to contain and control rebellious youth, the former communist governments attempted in sinister ways to defuse the politically charged musical and cultural activity by incorporating and sponsoring it – a purely hegemonic maneuver. Young people and other dissenters saw through the strategy, however, challenged the hegemony, and stimulated policy changes that later contributed to the dramatic downfall of the European communist governments. In China, the extraordinary student and worker uprising in 1989 was but the most visible sign of widespread resistance among that country's disaffected urban population. Television and other mass media – widely believed to be under the control of Chinese government authorities – actually facilitated popular protest (Lull 1991). Indeed, "modern broadcasting devices, once the perfect instruments for capturing loyalties and maintaining the state, [have become] consummate devices for undermining the established order" (Price 1994: 704). Recent popular revolutions in communist countries developed from widespread discontent with an interacting spectrum of economic, political, and cultural conditions that were made visible in large measure through the mass media. Ironically, then, the workers' uprising that Marx and Engels theorized would take place in repressive, class-based capitalist economies like England and the United States developed instead in communist nations which had proven in many respects to be even more repressive. The communications systems that were put in place to maintain ideological hegemony actually ended up challenging the authority and power of communist governments.

Counter-hegemony:
Do we really do what we're told?

Three leading critical theorists with whom we are already familiar, Raymond Williams, Stuart Hall, and Jesús Martín-Barbero, remind us that hegemony in any political context is indeed fragile. Hegemony requires renewal and modification to stay effective. Hall suggests that "it is crucial to the concept that hegemony is not a 'given' and permanent state of affairs, but it has to be actively won and secured; it can also be lost" (1977: 333). Ideological work is the winning and securing of hegemony over time. Williams (1975) called attention to the idea of "determination." Essentially, he argued that society's socioeconomic elites *will* dominate the rest of us. For him, the huge disparity between rich and poor is inevitable under capitalism; the disparity is *determined*. However, according to Williams, this determination "never [acts] as a wholly controlling, wholly predicting set of causes . . . we have to think of determination not as a single force . . . but as a process in which real determining factors – the distribution of power or of capital, social and physical inheritance, relations of scale and size between groups – set limits and exert pressures, but neither wholly control nor wholly predict the outcome of complex activity" (p. 130). Ideology is composed of "texts that are not closed" according to Hall, who also notes that ideological "counter-tendencies" regularly appear in the seams and cracks of dominant forms (Hall 1985). Furthermore, as Martín-Barbero explains, "Not every assumption of hegemonic power by the underclass is a sign of submission and not every rejection is resistance. Not everything that comes 'from above' represents the values of the dominant class. Some aspects of popular culture respond to logics other than the logic of domination" (Martín-Barbero 1993: 76).

We must therefore stress the *lack* of any fully predictable, determined consequences of the dominant ideology. Mediated communications ranging from popular TV shows and movies to rap and rock music, even graffiti scrawled over surfaces of public spaces, all carry messages that challenge the dominant ideology and mainstream culture. Counter-hegemonic tendencies permeate mediated texts. The interpretations and uses that people make of media content often go against the flow of the dominant ideology and culture too. A key concept here is appropriation. *People creatively modify ("appropriate") the messages they are given from media and elsewhere to fit their own ways of thinking and living.* As with the American soldiers' use of military gas masks as inhaling devices to heighten the effect of marijuana smoke, or the homeless's transformation of supermarket shopping carts into personal storage vehicles, *such ideological resistance and appropriation frequently involve reinventing institutional messages for purposes that differ greatly from their creators' intentions.*

Photo 3.3 Appropriation. A homeless man in Maceió, Brazil, turns an old re-frigerator into a hand-pushed cart for selling fruit and vegetables (photo by James Lull)

When an ideological structure is especially powerful, resistance will likewise be strong. Consider the plight of the Vatican. A Gallup poll in the United States reports that the vast majority of American Catholics believe married couples should be able to choose whatever form of birth control they want, including abortion if necessary. Most Catholics in the United States also favor the idea of women priests and the right of priests to marry. These profound disagreements with papal positions and rules reflect the limited choices people have at the official level. Popular opinion among American Catholics represents resistance to a global religious hegemony imposed by the church. But Catholics everywhere make their own Catholicism. To the horror of the pope, for example, Latin American Catholics have invented various local religions composed of Vatican dogma and liturgy, but also of local customs, beliefs, superstitions, and rituals, including African voodoo rights. Many Latin American Catholics believe in the church at an abstract, spiritual level, but adapt and transform Catholic ideology, authority, rules, and rituals to fit their own personal, group, and cultural feelings in remarkable processes of "collective appropriation" (Giddens 1991: 175; see photo 3.4).

Photo 3.4 Local Catholicism. Venezuelan villagers in the Andes Mountains replace Jesus Christ on the cross with a heroic doctor who saved many lives in the early twentieth century (photo by James Lull)

Like all symbolic forms, language is widely and creatively appropriated for alternative purposes. Dominant ideological themes represented in written language are sometimes reformulated to assert completely resistant or contradictory messages. The more repression, the more expression. Consider these examples:

■ Printed above the inside door of every subway car in London is the following instruction:

> Do not obstruct the door. It causes delay and can be dangerous.

The institutional instructions are recast when London punks blot out some of the words:

> obstruct the door. cause delay be dangerous.

■ The politically correct attitude about animal rights and vegetarianism is abused by the bumper sticker: "I (heart) animals: they're delicious!"

■ The materialist message of bumper stickers that read "My Other Car is a Porsche" becomes "My Other Car is Also a Piece of Crap!"

■ The snow ski lodge "Ski Bear" becomes "Ski Bare."

■ The American "Just Say No To Drugs" campaign resurfaces as "Just Say No To Drug Tests."

■ The environmentalist group Greenpeace uses a website in Holland to broadcast audio recordings of activists battling the crews of boats owned by Shell Oil (a Dutch company) in the North Sea.

■ The website *McSpotlight* calls attention to the nutritional, environmental, and economic destruction its creators believe are caused by the *McDonald's* hamburger franchise.

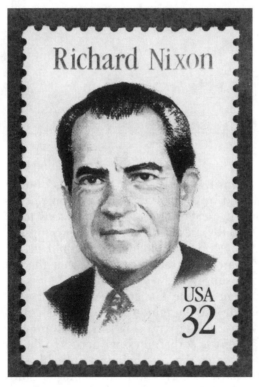

Photo 3.5 (3.6, 3.7 overleaf) The Nixon envelope. Former American President Richard Nixon escaped jail for his crimes when he was alive, but his symbolic institutional image has been creatively incarcerated (printed with permission of the *Santa Cruz Comic News*)

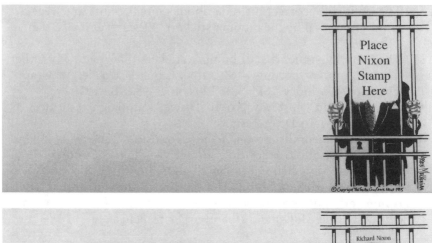

Photos 3.6–3.7

▪ The overly sensitive "I Brake for Animals" bumper sticker has been countered by "I Swerve and Hit People at Random!"

▪ The famous, cynical TV show *The Simpsons* features a cartoon character of Bill Gates addressing Homer Simpson, who miraculously had developed a product that could destroy Microsoft's hegemony. Gates's character says: "Rather than risk competing with you, I'd simply like to buy you out."

▪ Chinese students in the Tiananmen Square protest movement of 1989 ironically use the famous verses of the communist nation's founder, Mao Zedong, and sing official Communist Party revolutionary songs to get their message across to the government and the people, even as they are being assaulted by the army.

▪ Barney, the harmless, ever-so-lovable purple dinosaur who was star of the highest-rated public TV show for children in the United States, *Barney and Friends*, becomes a fierce object of hate. A Barney lookalike was viciously attacked in a Texas shop-

Photo 3.8 But did he inhale? An American organization dedicated to the legalization of marijuana adds some dialogue to the institutional image of George Washington, the first United States president, who is said to have grown hemp, the plant from which the herb is cultivated

ping mall, and an I Hate Barney Secret Society has formed, turning Barney's "I Love You, You Love Me" theme song into "I Hate You, You Hate Me, Let's Go Out and Kill Barney!"

The organization Mothers Against Drunk Driving (MADD) finds opposition from Drunks Against Mad Mothers (DAMM). Witty newspaper columnist Joe Bob Briggs further advises

Photo 3.9 *"Super Barrio."* A Mexican man fighting for the housing rights of poor people appropriates the Superman image to attract attention from the media for his humanitarian cause

WAR against Yugoslavia

CET 23:01 TANJUG javlja: NATO avion i dva helikoptera sa oko 50 pripadnika specijalnih jedinica, koji su dosli iz pravca Bosne, sruseni u oblasti planine Tare, 200 kilometara juzno od Beograda!!! TANJUG reports: NATO airplane and two helicopters with approx. 50 special forces soldiers, coming from Bosnia, are downed near Tara, 200 km southern from Belgrade !!!

22:19 Vazdusni napad na Novi Sad u je toku javio AP. Ali, u Novom Sadu je mirno. Air strikes on Novi Sad reported AP. But, all is quiet in Novis Sad.

22:00 Potparol Pentagona, Kenet Bejkon, izjavio je da su snage vazduhoplovstva SAD, ispalile 50 projektila tipa tomahavk iz strateskih bombardera B 52S sto cini jednu trecinu svih projektila tog tipa u celom svetu, a s kojima raspolaze americka vojske. Pentagon spokesman, Keneth Bacon, said that US AirForces aircrafts B52S launched 50 tomahawk missiles, what makes one third of all of that kind of missiles owned by US Army.

Beograd 01.04.1999. Predsednik Slobodan Milosevic je primio u Beogradu Ibrahima Rugovu, lidera kosovskih albanaca. Oni su razgovarali o problemima na Kosovu i nijhovom politickom resenju. **Belgrade 01.04.1999.** President of FRY, Slobodan Milosevic, met Ibrahim Rugova, leader of ethnic albanians in Kosovo. They were talking about Kosovo problems and political solvation.

21:15 Trojici americkih vojnika koji su uhvaceni od strane VJ, za petak je zakazano sudjenje pred Vojnim sudom u Beogradu, javio je TANJUG. Three american soldiers captured by the Yugoslav Army will be trialed at Friday in front of the Military Court in Belgrade, TANJUG reported.

21:05 Vazdusna opasnost u Beogradu !!! Air raid in Belgrade!!

Danas su u Novom Sadu odrzane demonstracije zbog rusenja starog mosta kojim se Novi Sad spaja sa Petrovaradinom. Demonstrations were held today in Novi Sad bacause of destruction of old bridge which connects Novi Sad and Petrovaradin.

20:50 Vise stotina ljudi krenulo je u litiju preko Pancevackog mosta u Beogradu da sprece NATO bombardovanje beogradskih mostova <real video>. Hundreds of people walking in procession across Pancevo bridge this night to prevent NATO destructing bridges of Belgrade <real video>.

19:30 Ruska flota pronasla je americku podmornicu u podrucju u kom vrsi vojne manevre. Russian fleet found american atomic submarine near the area where Russia is helding manoevres.

17:30 Odrzane demonstracije u Novom Sadu zbog rusenja mosta na Dunavu. Demonstrations were held in Novi Sad because of bridge destruction.

17:05 Jos jedan F117 pogodjen je nocas i spustio se tesko ostecen na zagrebacki aerodrom Pleso, javlja TV Srbije. One more F117 was hit by Yugoslav air defense, and, heavily damaged, landed on Zagred airport Pleso this morning, say TV Serbia.

16:10 Vasington post javlja da su albanski teroristi na Kosmetu potpuno razbijeni, bez oruzja i da upucuju apel NATO da im nekako pomogne jer vise nemaju ni cime da se bore niti ih ima dovoljno. Najavljen je potpuni nestanak terorista. Washington Post, Albanian terorists on Kosovo are very close to desapear. Their forces are destroyed, they have no weapons and also, they ask continuously NATO to help them with weapon and men. There is some prediction that soon there will not be any terorist on Kosovo.

16:10 Milosevic razgovarao sa Ibrahimom Rugovom. Saopsten zajednicki stav da se problem moze resiti samo politickim pregovorima. Milosevic and Rugova met today and made talks. The result of talks was message that all problems have to be politically solved, not by aggression. Milosevic im Gespraech mit Rugova.

16:00 Prestanak vazdusne opasnosti. Cekamo rezultate napada. End of air raid danger. Still waiting for attack results.

Gracanica 31.03.
3 rakete pale u podrucju manastira Gracanica. Manastir je vec pogodjen u napadu pre 2 dana.
Gracanica 31.03.
3 missiles hit Gracanica monastery area. Monastery was hit 2 days ago.
Read <The Art of Gracanica

Photo 3.10 Internet democracy. As bombs dropped on Belgrade in 1999, Yugoslavians mounted a global counter-offensive ("War Against Yugoslavia") with daily updates from the war zone on the Internet

readers: "Mad Mothers got liquor banned on college campuses this year, even though thousands of innocent drunks continue to be killed each year by sober mothers turnin' right out of the left hand lane!"

These examples show that ideological conversions of hegemonic messages can be quite light-hearted and humorous, or they can be deadly serious. The examples reveal an independence of thought, creativity, determination, and resistance that the forces of hegemony cannot contain or destroy. That is why the effects of hegemony are never fully determined. People can and do resist the idea of being channeled in one direction or another.

In general, *hegemony fails when dominant ideology is weaker than social resistance.* Gay subcultures, feminist organizations, environmental groups, radical political parties, and youth – especially music-based youth formations such as punks, B-boys, Rastafarians, and metal heads – all use media and their social networks to endorse counter-hegemonic values and lifestyles.

Furthermore, ways of thinking are always reflexive and embedded in a complex, sometimes contradictory, ideological regress. The widespread, multi-institutional "Just Say No To Drugs" campaign, for instance, is cast within a long-standing, media-perpetuated endorsement of (prescriptive) drugs as solutions to an entire range of problems. Illegal drugs have also been celebrated for years in all forms of art, especially music. A national "safe sex" campaign has not been able to stem the tide of risky sexual behavior. Part of the reason is that the mass media, even with Magic Johnson's still-smiling face on camera, have never stopped gushing positive images of devil-may-care sex. The federal government finally admitted that sexual activity among teenage girls in America has increased sharply recently, despite all the anti-AIDS hype.

Well-coordinated, massively sponsored commercial campaigns can never guarantee success. American business has its tragic commercial defeats, perhaps still best exemplified by the miserable failure of the infamous Ford Edsel, a grandly promoted car in the 1950s, to entice consumers. More recently, Microsoft couldn't sell the supposed innovative, user-friendly interactive software, "Bob." We could list out a million examples of audience-consumers' rejections of what the dominant ideology and culture have to offer them.

But we create a false opposition when we place media and the culture industries in some kind of "us v. them" standoff with audiences. *Resistance to the dominant ideology (to the degree that we can say such a thing exists) comes from inside the culture industries too.*

Horace Newcomb and Paul Hirsch point out that contrary to any theory of capitalist ideological hegemony, television actually emphasizes "contradiction and conflict rather than coherence" in its programs (1987: 62), as we saw in the *Simpsons* example above. In today's global, Internet-connected environment, avenues for communicating counter-hegemonic messages are available like never before, as is evident in the Greenpeace/Shell and McDonald's websites.

A famous recent case of how ideological conflict can develop between hegemonic institutions was the well-publicized standoff between Oprah Winfrey, hostess of America's most popular TV talk show (*Oprah!*), and the American beef industry. After listening to experts explain on her show about how red meat is grown and processed, Oprah took a step back, looked directly into the camera, and said, "I'm never going to eat a hamburger again!" The beef industry of Texas later sued her for that remark, claiming to have suffered a loss of some $34 million traceable to a huge drop in beef consumption for two years after her nationally televised display of disgust. The courts sided with Oprah Winfrey. This conflict demonstrates how powerful, interrelated industries (hamburger chains are among the biggest spenders on TV advertising), which should in theory work together to construct ideational image systems that would stimulate the greatest possible profits for both, *don't* always agree. The beef industry was humiliated by the ordeal, not least because Winfrey moved the production of her show from New York to Texas during the trial in order to fight the cattle ranchers on their own turf, and to benefit visually from the support of her throngs of adoring fans there.

The electronic amplification of contradiction exists in all ideological and cultural contexts. The Chinese government, for instance, has been unable to fully control the ideological agenda of its own mass media, despite surface appearances of effective censorship, which contributed to the student–worker uprising in 1989 (Lull 1991). Lately in China many journalists have their own email addresses and are using the Internet to bypass official propaganda and access international news reporting (Latham 2000). In South Africa during apartheid racial conflict was not discussed in government TV shows, but regularly appeared as the theme of foreign programs, especially American films, scheduled for television airplay by progressive thinkers in the nation's television system.

Priorities cultivated within the economic system can abuse its own ideology too. The late Philippines dictator Ferdinand Marcos, for instance, was cut off mid-sentence in his blatant advocacy of unbridled capitalism on a *Night Line* interview with Ted Koppel when the network satellite contract expired and the picture from Manila went black. As NATO bombs rained heavily on Yugoslavia in 1999, the European Satellite Consortium (Eutelsat, based in Paris) kept transmission of Serbian TV going for months, providing a vital information link inside and outside Yugoslavia for Slobodan Milosovic's forces working against NATO's interests.

Counter-hegemonic messages created by media industries can be even louder and more to the point. Several Hollywood films, for example, have directly called into question the power of the media themselves. Most recent of these are *The Truman Show*, *Tomorrow Never Dies*, and *Mad City*. Other famous cinematic critiques of media power are *Being There*, *Broadcast News*, and *Network*.

Conclusion

We must be very careful not to overromanticize social resistance to hegemony. Ideological hegemony in any society depends in part on the belief that room for the expression of differing opinions is available. Capitalist and communist systems both have their own mechanisms for creating this belief. Hegemony, therefore, is always being constructed; it is never finally and totally achieved. Hegemony is a process of perpetual social domination by the relatively powerful over the relatively powerless. The victims of hegemony don't realize they are being repressed through ideology. Therefore, capitalist democracies can be among the most insidious of hegemonic states because most citizens believe that "unlike the Communists, we have the right to choose our political leaders and the things we want to buy." Indeed, the raucous way democracies air and correct their problems can give the appearance of vulnerability, instability, even chaos, while in fact it is that very (apparently open) process that ultimately makes for stability and continued domination.

In societies where people have a political vote, the common wisdom goes, it is *their* fault if social conditions are problematic, and *their* responsibility to correct the problems through legitimate political procedures. Never mind, for example, that the mainstream media only give time and space for political candidates from the major political parties, thereby purposefully directing voters' attention away from more strident solutions offered by the radical left and right. Never mind that few small businesses can afford to widely advertise their goods and services. What is created in many democracies – the United States and England are two particularly striking examples – is an "illusion of choice" for voters and consumers. This illusion,

critical theorists say, is what keeps people believing in and repro-
ducing their systems of governance. This is what is meant by the
"social reproduction of domination."

Nonetheless, it is surely off the mark to regard the effects of
symbolic imagery and communications technology as one-sided and
exploitative. Such a perspective fails to consider the complex and
indeterminate nature of human communication. I certainly agree with
John B. Thompson that dominant ideologies do exist and that they
frame perceptions and inspire interpretations that serve the interests
of dominant social institutions (Thompson 1990: 7; see also chapter
2 of this volume). But as Thompson himself argues, ideology is "a
creative and constitutive feature of social life which is [not only] sus-
tained and reproduced, [but also] contested and transformed through
actions and interactions which include the ongoing exchange of symbolic forms" (Thompson 1990: 10).

Because ideology must be represented to be effective, its consequences cannot be confidently predicted. We should not equate the
power to expose and frame ideas with the power to control the
response. Like all symbolic displays, even the most systematic and
didactic varieties, ideologies are resources whose significance is manifest not only through representation, but through interpretation and
use. *Social change, the defining characteristic of world history, unmis-
takably demonstrates that ideology is negotiated and contested, not
just imposed and assumed.* Individual persons, social groups, nations,
and cultures therefore should not be considered as simple victims of
dominant social forces. Ideology, media, and social activity all
embrace conformity *and* contestation. We will analyze how these
complex and contradictory forces are organized, related to social
power, and integrated into the culturally situated places and times of
our lives throughout the remainder of this book.

4

Social Rules and Power

Just as we have maps in our heads for navigating our way through physical space, so too do we have mental guidelines for negotiating social territories. We undertake these journeys successfully most of the time because the worlds we encounter are relatively coherent and consistent and because we are skilled at recognizing social prescriptions and patterns, responding and adapting, even transforming them frequently without thinking much about what we are doing. How is this immense coordination of social activity made possible and what are its consequences? What roles do mass media play in the process? In this chapter we shall try to answer these questions by exploring the concept of *rule* and its complex relation to issues raised in the previous chapters, especially the exercise of social power. Specifically, I shall describe what rules are and how they link ideology and hegemony with various forms of authority in symbolic representation and social practice.

Rule

Rule is a term familiar to most everyone. Rules often tell us what is required, what is forbidden, or how to do something. Every bureaucrat and government official in the USA has convened under Roberts' Rules of Order. Judges impose rules of the court and teachers have rules for the classroom. Rules regulate sporting games, etiquette, driving, and countless other situations where safety, fairness, correctness, or efficiency are desired. Books have been written to explain the rules for playing golf, for becoming a successful businesswoman, for constructing nuclear power plants, and for maximizing sexual potential. There are rules for rulers and for radicals, for kings and for housewives, for the mind and for chaos. There are rules for breaking the rules and more rules for dealing with rule breakers. And while many rules are codified and articulated through official channels, the vast majority of rules are rarely, if ever, formalized. Informal rules of social conduct make up the cultural base of societies everywhere. It is no wonder, then, that rule has emerged as a central theoretical concept in academic disciplines such as anthropology, linguistics, sociology, political science, and communication. But rules are certainly not just the domain of academic theorists. Popular epistemologies – how people from all walks of life come to know their worlds and engage with the contours and contingencies of everyday routines – are also based in rules. But what exactly are rules?

Following the influential thinking of the eighteenth-century German philosopher Immanuel Kant, rules are, first of all, *constitutive* expressions. This means that rules suggest possible courses of human thought and action by pre-interpreting the world for us – by constituting, and thereby explaining and prescribing, social reality in certain ways. Constitutive rules (often implicitly) tell us what exists, in what measure, and in what relation. The second type of rule is *regulative*. Rules regulate social behavior inside the structured, prescribed (constituted) reality by specifically guiding and sanctioning human activity in particular ways. Regulative rules are often more formal and explicit. Constitutive and regulative rules impose systems of order on all forms of social interaction.

Thus, rules accomplish two basic tasks: they direct social thought and action (1) by asserting in a complex way *what* is normal, acceptable, or preferred (the constitutive rules) and then (2) by specifying *how* social interaction is to be carried out (the regulative rules). In this way, *rules lead to interpersonally coordinated understandings that underlie and promote patterned social activity*. For example, after years of watching prime-time television we may come to believe that men have certain professional roles in society (for example, more "white-collar" opportunities, more likelihood of being bosses, more freedom to change jobs) or have particular social statuses (for instance, less likelihood of being married or having children, more money, more glamorous lifestyles). Simply through long-term exposure to these mediated images, men and women in society learn what kinds of professional opportunities they might expect, and what a "normal" life for males and females might be like. These lessons are learned in part from the structuring power of constitutive rules. Regulative rules, on the other hand, tend to be more explicit and specific. Automobile speed limits, school dress codes, and voting procedures are examples of regulative rules. Regulative rules, therefore, are sometimes encoded as laws, but they don't have to have this kind of official backing. Even patterns of talk between men and women (who initiates conversation, who interrupts whom, different vocal volume for males and females, and so on) are governed by regulative rules.

Rules structure but do not determine the ways we make sense of the symbolic representations and social patterns we routinely encounter. They reflect cultural values and ideologies that have become legitimized, concretized, and extended through time and space by specific histories of social action. Rules are the perceived matrices of social organization – ephemeral referents that are kept in mind by social actors as they imagine the future in part by referring to the past. Just as the retina of the eye produces an image of an object even after it physically disappears from view, thereby giving continuity to sight, rules assert frameworks for ideological continuity that likewise persist in time and space. They structure the cognitive schemata and emotional inclinations people routinely use to organize, create, and find pleasure in even the most subtle circumstances of their everyday lives. It is the very embeddedness of rules in normative social practice – especially the structuring capability of the implicit, taken-for-granted rules pervading the most mundane recesses of everyday life – that gives them such great influence.

The constitutive and regulative qualities of rules generate a "shared understanding of how people ought to behave" in order to produce "consistency, regularity, and continuity" in their social worlds (Edgerton 1985: 24, 8). When rules are widely known, and where compliance is a shared value, rules "specify 'correct' or 'appropriate' [social] procedures and the attendant community evaluates the performance" (Collett 1977: 8). For rules to effectively prescribe social attitudes and activities, they must be "followable" (Shimanoff 1980). Consistent with our discussion of hegemony in the last chapter, the power of rules springs in large measure from the fact that people *choose* courses of action; they are not coerced. Social actors elect to follow, ignore, break, or modify rules. Even international political relations – negotiations that affect the very future of the planet – are played by "rules of the game" (Kratochwil 1989). The Cold War era policy of nuclear deterrence was an especially dramatic example of this.

Rules in society

Rules help construct and perpetuate the fundamental themes, trajectories, and tones of our social worlds. They do so often in very subtle

and complex ways. *We are socialized not simply by ideas, but by the
way ideas are structured, related to authority, and pertinent to our
needs and interests.* By complying with rules, we forge patterns of
"daily life [that are] known in common with others and with others
taken for granted" (Garfinkel 1967: 35). This very taken-for-
grantedness implies a profound, often subconscious, acceptance of
the terms of social rules. All communication experiences develop
against a field of "background expectancies [whereby] persons . . .
hold each other to agreements whose terms they never actually stip-
ulate" (p. 73). These tacit agreements regulate even the most basic,
pragmatic aspects of social interaction. Practical consciousness "consists of knowing the rules and the tactics whereby daily social life is
constituted and reconstituted" (Giddens 1984: 90). The relative predictability of personal habits and routines based in rule-governed
social patterns helps people feel secure emotionally (Giddens 1984;
1990; 1991) while it simultaneously reinforces the contours of the
dominant ideology and culture.

The American sociologist Harold Garfinkel demonstrated how our
assumptions, routines, and the social order are all connected. He
developed a series of "experiments" that his students carried out at
the University of California, Los Angeles (Garfinkel 1967). The idea
was to challenge the normative assumptions of everyday life. By
purposefully destroying "background expectancies" and routines,
Garfinkel's students instigated social chaos. A simple example is this:
when the students were asked by their friends in routine interaction
"How are you doing?," they were instructed by Garfinkel to ignore
the social convention, which would be to say something like "Fine,
thanks, how are you?" regardless of how one feels and not necessarily with any true interest in knowing how the other is doing.
Instead of giving the expected response, the students answered with
a series of clarifying questions, taking the inquiry "How are you
doing?" seriously. One response might be: "What do you mean, 'How
am I doing?' Physically? Mentally? Spiritually?" Disturbed by this
dismantling of a taken-for-granted way of communicating, the person
who asked "How are you doing?" usually became extremely frus-
trated and sometimes quite angry. What this example and similar
exercises reveal is the deep structure of routine social behavior and
the commitment we have to act normatively in carrying out even the
most seemingly unimportant everyday activities.

Garfinkel coined the term *ethnomethodology*. This expression
refers not to a research strategy (for which it is frequently mistaken),
but to the "methods of life" people use to make sense of their worlds
and construct their everyday activities. These methods are central not

only to practical construction of the worlds we live in, as Garfinkel's norm-breaking experiments show, but to how we view and rationalize that world. *Social actors normalize their experiences by interpreting the world in terms of their structured background expectancies.* To illustrate this, let me provide an example from my own teaching experience. I asked my students at the University of Wisconsin years ago to design and carry out a naturalistic norm-breaking experiment *à la* Garfinkel. Responding to the assignment, two heterosexual midwestern males developed a team project. One of them went into a jewelry store and stood at the counter admiring the rings. The other student, a man of about 21 years, then entered the store. The two didn't acknowledge each other's presence. They were, apparently, strangers. The second student then asked the clerk for some help picking out wedding rings. When the clerk showed some matched sets, the young man explained, in a completely unaffected tone of voice, that he wanted matching rings for *men*. The clerk, quite taken aback, shuffled some boxes around and explained that he was sure something could be worked out. The student-shopper then looked at several possible purchases, maintaining a completely straight demeanor, before thanking the employee, saying he wanted to think about it for a while, and walking out. The first student, still in the store, then moved to a spot where he could overhear the clerk re-create the scene that had just taken place. As the clerk told the story to a fellow employee, the clerk adopted a dripping, completely misleading feminine vocal affectation as he played the role of the apparently gay shopper. The assumptive world disrupted by the shopper had been reconstructed by the clerk. His re-creation of the unsettling scene restored order by reasserting what he perceived as typical gay speech. He could then recoup the reasonableness of what had just happened.

Humor is often used by people in attempts to normalize shattered background expectancies. I watched a tourist in Mexico once try to bargain with a street vendor by offering to pay "only" 300,000 pesos for a beach towel. When his wife pointed out to him that this amount of Mexican currency at that time was worth more than a hundred dollars, the embarrassed man retracted his offer and joked, "Boy, we'd have to frame the sucker at that price!" Underlying such attempts at humor are strategies used to make social interaction normal when it goes wrong.

Most of us willingly abide by social rules most of the time, especially the countless unspoken rules. This is how societies function and avoid disorder. Failure to abide by social rules is even sometimes considered pathological, "dysfunctional behavior," on the part of individuals or groups. But we must be very careful here. Evaluations of functionality are necessarily biased. What is considered functional or dysfunctional, normal or deviant, stabilizing or disruptive is always an interpretation made by individuals or groups in accord with their own world views and motivations. As the famed sociologist Robert Merton (1957) pointed out many years ago, conventional social practices frequently function to the benefit more of powerful subgroups than of marginalized groups or even of society as a whole. To understand rules, their creators, articulators, and enforcers, as well as their consequences, we must always ask: for *whom* do rules function?

Implicit rules are especially subject to strategic interpretation and manipulation. Precisely because they are not formally outlined or limited, and therefore offer little room for appeal or grievance when violated, they can be used to oppress and control. I attended a university faculty meeting once where a graduate teaching assistant was actually terminated from his job not for the official reason, budgetary problems, but because he routinely used an informally unapproved form of transportation, a skateboard, to travel across campus on his way to the classes he was teaching. It became clear during the discussion of his work that several faculty members had simply been insulted by his breaking of an unspoken rule of professional conduct. Normative rules are embedded so deeply in routine social interaction that they often are not brought to conscious awareness until the tacit requirements they embrace are disobeyed.

Although rules are pervasive and influential, they are by no means uniform, permanent, or universal. The basic distinction I have made between explicit and implicit rules reveals how widely they can differ. Some rules are clear while others are ambiguous. Some are specific to certain situations while others apply more generally. Rules vary in their degree of articulated importance and interpreted seriousness. They are hierarchical. Some rules can be broken by some people, but not by others. Some rules remain relatively unchallenged while others are regularly contested. Some rules contradict other rules.

Above all else, rules are flexible. They can be manipulated to serve the purposes of issuing authorities, but they can also be creatively used even by those with little official authority. People do not engage rules uniformly. They often interpret, use, and transform rules in ways that benefit them. Rules are resources. Like the symbolic content of TV programs, music, film, literature, and all the rest of popular culture, rules can also be appropriated in the construction of everyday life. As John B. Thompson puts it:

in drawing upon rules and conventions of various kinds, individuals
... extend and adapt these schemata and rules. Every application
involves responding to circumstances which are, in some respects, new.
Hence the application of rules and schemata cannot be understood as
a mechanical operation, as if actions were rigidly determined by them.
Rather, the application of rules and schemata is a creative process
which often involves some degree of selection and judgment, and in
which the rules and schemata may be modified and transformed in the
very process of application. (1990: 148–9)

Exceptions to rules

A key concept related to rule flexibility is *exception*. When can a rule
be ignored, broken, or modified? How is it done? The American
anthropologist Robert Edgerton argues that rules are routinely
broken depending on a variety of contextual factors including temporary conditions (e.g. when a person is ill or intoxicated); the statuses of the people involved (e.g. rich versus poor, men versus women,
adults versus children); special occasions (e.g. parties, holidays,
rituals); and settings (e.g. public versus private space). Rules are also
broken for a wide variety of political, cultural, social, and personal
reasons. By reframing reality in novel ways, artists of all kinds can
provoke feelings and stimulate unique insights. The shock of a creatively broken rule, a radical divergence from what is expected, draws
attention and stimulates curiosity. Paul Bouissac (1976), for example,
argues that rule breaking is at the heart of why people enjoy the
circus. According to Bouissac, the circus is amusing precisely because
expected patterns of everyday life are shattered into bits, then creatively reconstructed to form a new, perverse reality. At the circus a
horse can make a fool of its trainer. A tiger can ride the back of an
elephant. The elephant can use a telephone or sit at a dinner table.

Disruptive rule breaking can even be heroic. Although rule breakers are generally despised and often punished by institutional authorities, they are frequently celebrated culturally. The American
government recently gave its highest citizen honor – the Congres-
sional Gold Medal – to Rosa Park, the black woman who refused to
give up her seat to a white man in an Alabama bus in 1955, spark-
ing a national fight against segregation. Western mass media create
rule-breaking heroes. Many of the best-known movie stars (for
example, James Dean, Marilyn Monroe, Marlon Brando, Jack
Nicholson, Eddie Murphy) and pop music celebrities (the Beatles,

David Bowie, John Coltrane, Jimi Hendrix, [the artist still best known as] Prince, Madonna, and Marilyn Manson, for instance) have won huge audiences in part because they have routinely broken social and artistic rules. Professional athletes such as Dennis Rodman and Charles Barkley have capitalized on the public's fascination with outrageous behavior. Professional wrestling is a study in rule breaking. An American performance artist, Dennis Leary, observes that he now gets paid big money for doing exactly the same things that got him into serious trouble at home and school. Howard Stern has turned rule breaking into a radio art form. Bart Simpson, Beavis and Butthead, and South Park are among the animated versions of this tendency.

Breaking the rules on purpose has its limits, however, even for those who win fame and fortune by being bad boys and girls. Madonna may have thought she was being cool and outrageous when she pulled a Puerto Rican flag between her legs during a concert in San Juan, for instance, but even her fans had trouble forgiving that politically and culturally ignorant gesture (Santiago-Lucerna 1997). Puerto Rico's uncomfortable relation to mainland USA (and widely perceived "second-class status" as an American "territory;" not a state, and not an independent nation) creates a context where such an abuse of the symbol of Puerto Rico can easily be interpreted as a disrespectful and hegemonic act. For many Puerto Ricans, Madonna's behavior represented exploitation of their land and people by American mainlanders more than any form of heroic, rebellious artistic expression.

Box 4.1 The Clinton Sex Scandal:
Breaking the Rules of Morality

Bill Clinton is a strong, vigorous, young man with a tremendous personality. I'm sure the ladies just go wild over him.

*American evangelistic preacher, author,
and presidential advisor Billy Graham*

What a wonderful country the USA must be. Every woman can feel she can overthrow the most powerful man in the world!

Dutch feminist communication scholar Joke Hermes

A scandal begins when social rules are broken and the violations become public knowledge. In today's globalized, technologically mediated symbolic environment, such transgressions sometimes become "media scandals" (Lull and Hinerman 1997). The media scandal is a basic staple of modern journalism and media performance, especially where the press is relatively free from government influence, and where news is marketed aggressively as a commercial product. This tendency toward sensationalism was not born of twentieth-century morality, politics, and media. News of "sin and corruption" was crucial even to the development of the world's very first true mass medium – the "penny press" newspapers of New York in the 1830s. Since then sensational news has fascinated audiences who attend to all types of mass media.

Media scandals develop when social norms reflecting the dominant morality are violated – that is, when the commonly accepted rules of social conduct are broken. The revelations must be widely circulated via communications media, be effectively narrativized into a story, and then inspire great interest and discussion (Lull and Hinerman 1997: 11–13). A media scandal, thus, is created not by the media, but by a volatile interaction of facts, allegations, and images with the public's desire to know more. In the United States, the Watergate break-in and cover-up of the 1970s – a felonious crime and political boondoggle of major proportions – became the archetype of a media scandal. It led to the resignation of former president Richard Nixon, and set the standard for media scandals of a political nature. The O.J. Simpson murder trial of the 1990s was another famous media scandal, though it remained largely an American obsession. But as the last century came to a close, people everywhere learned of a sexual adventure between a former president of the United States and a flirtatious, buxom young intern at the White House that became the most spectacular media scandal so far. Video clips of Monica Lewinsky hugging the president in a public reception line appeared on TV, allegations flew, the former president denied everything (but we could see in his eyes from the beginning that he was not innocent), and audiences were hooked on the story.

The Clinton sex scandal forced Americans to reflect on the breaking of social rules in at least three ways. They first evaluated their popular political leader in terms of his personal morals. The Lewinsky affair was just the most recent event in a parade of accusations involving not only sex, but also that other eternal source of temptation and compromise – money. A shady real estate deal and a stream of campaign finance violations – including one charge that Clinton's fundraisers were cutting deals with the People's Republic of China – dogged the president at the same time the sexual allegations were flying about. So while the president could apparently balance the budget, if not his testosterone, other issues were becoming ethically and politically problematic as his second term wore on.

Second, the sex scandal led people to reflect on their own moral values and histories. Nearly everyone agreed that Clinton had been "cheating" on his wife. Many people said they thought that was wrong. But what about themselves? Social scientists are quick to point out that in a world of throwaway jobs, friends, spouses, and children, marital infidelity is common in the United States and elsewhere. Husbands, wives, and families thus had to deal in some way with their own moral standards, expectations, and behavior as a consequence of media coverage of the White House tryst.

The third level of moral violation has the most profound implications. Discursively at least, Americans hold their elected officials (and sometimes their colleagues and neighbors, if not themselves) to Puritanical moral expectations shaped largely by the country's Judeo-Christian religious heritage. That moral standard is reflected and codified in the national book of rules – the Constitution of the United States, and the system of laws based on it. The president of the United States of America represents a nation that routinely claims moral superiority, especially in foreign policy. A breach in moral conduct by the president puts at risk not only the president, but the credibility of the nation itself. So at the crucial juncture early in the media scandal when former President Clinton looked into the television camera, cocked his head to the side with unimpeachable authority, wagged his finger at the audience defiantly, and said with a straight face: "I did not have sexual relations with that woman . . . Monica Lewinsky," many Americans wanted to believe him – not for his sake necessarily, but for the sake of the nation. Clinton's claim, of course, turned out to be false, unless you, like the former president, don't consider what those lovebirds were doing in the White House to be "sexual relations." And when Bill Clinton's personal credibility was shattered, negative feedback about America's role in global politics followed immediately. President Clinton's moralizing comments about Saddam Hussein and Mu'ssammar Gadhafi made public that same week seemed particularly hollow and arrogant.

When Americans and everyone else learned that President Clinton's denial of a sexual affair with Monica Lewinsky was a lie, much criticism then became focused on what was commonly considered an even more troubling breach of morality – untruths told under legal oath. Americans felt they couldn't look their president in the (mediated) eye any more. More than his personal reputation had been trashed; the nation had been damaged. Despite all this, and even after his moral and legal transgressions had been exposed, the president's last line of defense was itself a moral claim: that the "right thing" to do would be to "stay focused on the work the American people asked me to do" (and in the process avoid answering questions about the scandal). In the end, the Clinton sex scandal became an enthralling, if rather pathetic, narrative through which America judged not only the ethics of the man it elected president, but the viability of the nation's imagined moral character.[1]

The most significant consequences of the scandal thus are more ideological and cultural than personal or political. Media scandals disturb certain privileges of power by turning the "back-stage" (private) dealings of public figures into "front-stage" (public) knowledge (Thompson 1997). Such revelations can be stressful for everybody, as the Clinton sex scandal made very clear. But in the end this mediated visibility holds accountable those who influence us by means of their political, economic, or cultural power, which itself is often won through media exposure. If we allowed politicians, sports heroes, movie stars, billionaire businesspeople, pop musicians, and members of the royal family to completely determine the contexts in which they are viewed and pondered, then we'd miss lots we should know. Perhaps more troubling than the threat to the privacy of powerful persons is the celebrity status conferred upon them in the first place by media institutions and audiences (Gronbeck 1997), although in the case of Princess Diana, the positive intimacy we felt with her was also generated by the constant media attention – wanted and unwanted – that she got.

The public's appetite for this and other scandals should not be understood as some perverse fascination with the unspeakable, but rather as personal and collective introspection. Much of the appeal and impact of the Clinton affair and many such media scandals rests ultimately on the discontinuity between idealized moral expectations – duly documented and understood through explicit and implicit rules, laws, conventions, and norms – and the often less honorable realm of the everyday lives of real people. That uncomfortable space between the ideal and the real, between morality and desire, is precisely where Bill Clinton, Monica Lewinsky, and the American public found themselves in 1999.

Rules and culture

Rules, and the breaking of rules of all types, is necessarily a cultural matter. Traditional cultures are themselves based on systems of rules. One of the most intriguing aspects of the Clinton sex scandal is the way it was perceived by people around the world. The scandal was by no means interpreted uniformly. Ironically, many people throughout the world found the possibility of impeachment a pre-posterous consequence of an adolescent-sounding sexual fling and unwarranted incursion into the private life of the president of the United States. In China, some people said the intrusion of the press into the sexual affairs of the national leader reminded them of that country's infamous Cultural Revolution of the 1970s, when leaders were humiliated and dispatched ruthlessly from their official posi-tions. In Mexico, where government corruption has long been a way of life, people couldn't believe that the president of their powerful northern neighbor could be subject to such public ridicule for what appeared to be such a relatively minor lapse in private conduct. Clinton was lightheartedly named "*Macho* of the Year" by a Brazil-ian organization devoted to counterbalancing the growing influence of feminism there. Many Russian men, too, were said to celebrate the president's sexual conquests as an impressive demonstration of his virility.

Official rules often clash with rules-in-use. For example, traffic lights and vehicle lane markers in Brazil and other Latin American countries do not function as legally enforced requirements for proper driving. They are interpreted more as suggestions. In Rio, motorists routinely drive through red lights without thinking about stopping unless, of course, another car enters the intersection from the left or right. When a major street crosses a lesser street, the driver on the major street assumes the right of way, even when the signal in his or her direction is red. A driver entering from the lesser street must honk the horn or flash the headlights when approaching the crossway to warn oncoming drivers that he or she intends to enter the intersec-tion, thereby invoking the official rule pertaining to "right of way." This example of driving in Brazil shows that rules are almost always negotiated. The negotiations themselves are rule based and culturally differentiated. A student of mine from Venezuela tells another story about cultural differences in driving. The student had recently vaca-tioned in Germany. As her German hosts drove their car on the out-skirts of a small town late one night the driver insisted on waiting for a red light to change at an obscure intersection where no cars could be seen for miles. Coming from a culture where official rules are much more open to creative interpretation, the Venezuelan simply could not comprehend why the driver wouldn't just drive through the red light. Cultures are characterized not only by their official rules and unofficial, informal rules, but also by patterned ways of obeying and breaking rules.

Motivations for breaking rules, and the behavioral patterns that result, are greatly influenced by relationships between prescribing authorities and rule users/breakers. The way people respond to rules says a lot about how they feel about the societies in which they live. Vehicle drivers in Rio de Janeiro run through red lights partly because they don't much respect the government that put the lights there in the first place. Traffic semaphores in Brazil often appear in extremely illogical places, reminding drivers of the institutional incompetence against which they rebel generally in daily life. In Brazil, traffic lights signal institutional incompetence as much as they do traffic flows. The police there are as likely as anyone else to break the official rules. Prevailing rules are sometimes based more on the relationship between enforcers and violators than on that between the civil state and rule breakers. In Florence, Italy, for example, African street vendors must pick up their illegal displays of sunglasses, African hats, and trinkets and move when the police drive by, only to put their wares back on the exact same spot immediately after the authorities leave. The vendors even smile and wave at the police as they feign concern. Thus, the rule against street vending is not enforced, but a rule that demands public displays of respect for the enforcing authorities must be superficially obeyed as part of a game of social power. Such clashes between official rules and rules-in-use can have far-reaching political and cultural implications. In China and the former communist nations of Europe, for example, people have realized that government officials at the highest level don't play by the rules of social equality that they themselves have set. This double standard is commonly interpreted as a profound breach of ethics which implicitly encourages rule breaking and corruption at all social levels and a total mistrust of government, its laws, and decrees.

Rules are interpreted situationally in all cultures. To behave strictly according to literal rules carries the risk of becoming a "judgmental dope" rather than a "competent rule user" (Garfinkel 1967). Every use of a rule is an interpretation of the rule. As Edgerton points out, creative uses of rules are often motivated by self-interest. He calls this motivated involvement with rules "strategic interactionism." People make the best use of rules for their self-interest, or in the interest of their social affiliations, depending on the situation (Edgerton 1985: 13). Obeying official rules or going along with commonly accepted

ways of doing things is but one option. Rules are more than requirements, restraints, and instructions. They are schemata people use to
choose particular courses of action.

One of the world's most famous rule-breaking contexts is Brazil's
annual Carnival celebration (see also chapter 7, "Carnival culture").
For four days immediately preceding the Christian celebration of
Lent, the usual formal and informal rules of social behavior are
broken with abandon. Normal social and sexual limits give way to
an unspoken rule of freedom and egalitarianism which leads to temporary displays of "social inversion" (DaMatta 1991). Brazil's characteristic social positions and roles are reversed, particularly during
the symbolic highlight of Carnival, the parade of the *escolas de samba*
(samba schools): men can become women, the poor don the garb of
the rich, and the rich applaud the poor *favela* (shanty-town) dwellers
as they rise up temporarily to symbolically control Brazilian culture
during this radical, but clearly demarcated, temporal context.[2] Rules,
then, can be creatively interpreted and put to use, sometimes even in
direct opposition to their originators' intentions or their common
meanings.

Photo 4.1 Carnival! The world's biggest and craziest party, where social rules
are broken in ways that make temporary cultural stars of the poor in Brazil
(printed with permission of TV Globo)

The choices that are made, and the forms of social interaction that are created, however, are not random or democratic. While strategic interactionism (or "tactical rules;" see Lull 1990) rightly emphasizes the elasticity of rules and the creative undertakings of individual rule users, normative rules in particular also have an undeniable ability to shape consciousness and influence social activity. Together with the concept of choice – which speaks to the interpretative freedom, imagination, and creativity of rule users – we must, therefore, also take up the concept of *power* located in the statuses and roles of rule makers and articulators. We need to know who prescribes what ideas and actions and how the prescriptive force of rules relates to socioeconomic realities. The structural contours of a society, and the social formations contained within them, necessarily reflect material and ideological relations wherein power is a central feature. Rules representing institutionalized sources of power are one important type of rule, therefore, and power is the topic to which we now turn.

Power

Rules shape and facilitate dominant ideologies (chapter 2) by linking ideological representations with authority. This is the essence of many social rules – the development and coordination of specific thoughts and courses of action that imply particular ideological positions and rely on the credibility of institutional authority for their effectiveness. Rules simultaneously manifest and reinforce authority. But as I hope to have already shown, many rules gain their legitimacy and prescriptive force not only from their embeddedness in structures of authority or from their hegemonic relation with other institutions. To be effective, many rules must also be perceived by social actors as emotionally satisfying, culturally relevant, socially useful, or otherwise appealing.

The power of rules, therefore, cannot easily be categorized or generalized. Their influence does not resemble traditional definitions of power such as "the capability of an individual or group to exert its will over others" (Giddens 1991: 211). The exercise of rule-based power is not unidirectional and its consequences do not necessarily oppress others. People frequently find rule structures comforting. Most children want rules and enforcement so they feel noticed and loved. Employees want to know workplace rules so they can comply to insure their security. The faithful willingly obey religious codes. Consumers look for guidance.

Rules promote explicit and implicit understandings that inspire patterns of social behavior. But we must distinguish between rules and behavioral patterns. Rules are *not* the patterns themselves; *they are cognitive and emotional frames of reference that encourage the construction and maintenance of certain behavioral patterns.* The patterns take shape in routine communication. The resulting patterns are *conventions* which then themselves assume prescriptive force as *social norms* (Shimanoff 1980: 110). Convention refers to conventional behavior. Norm prescribes what should be done. To summarize the process, rules are concretized in routine communicative interaction. The resulting behavioral patterns, stimulated and shaped by both personal and mediated communication, become social conventions that reflect underlying ideational image systems structured and advocated by rules. Conventions are then often prescriptively interpreted as social norms. Thus, rules help stimulate particular patterns of social interaction (conventions), which, in turn, reinforce the rules (as norms), compounding and repeating the cycle of influence.

Drawing from the work of musicologist Charles Hamm (1983), let me show how this works with an example from the spiritual politics of colonial America. Eighteenth-century psalms sung by enthusiastic members of early American religious congregations at first produced a heterophonous clashing of sounds. To impose order on the situation, religious leaders created songbooks. The songbooks instructed everyone to sing the same notes and words simultaneously, thereby establishing social conformity in the form of a particular type of ritualistic communication – a literal chorus of voices organized on terms set by an agent of institutional religious authority. The church service itself was also structured so that singing could take place only at certain times. A member of the church was thus required to conform to a set of imposed rules comprising the singing of psalms and the conduct of a religious service. These coordinated performances combined to form a sanctioned, structured social convention that systematically introduced institutionally based, rule-governed norms to new members. By defining what is normal in the form and content of the church service, religious leaders were able to institutionalize ideology while asserting their authority by imposing and maintaining rules.

Key to the influence of rules, then, is how they work so closely with ideological predispositions and sources of authority. Furthermore, rules supply references for the ongoing construction of meaning and development of social relations based on configurations and syntheses that have already been made. So, as we have just seen, to join in ritualistic religious activity, or to participate in any other even mildly organized social behavior for that matter, presumes at least tacit reproduction of the ideological assumptions that make up the activity.

The very status of "rule" can be authoritative. We have all heard the simple retort "because it's the rule!" or "because that's the way things are done around here" (from a convention to a norm; from a description "of" behavior to a prescription "for" behavior; see Kratochwil 1989) to justify a policy or action. Rules are often used to rationalize activity or invoke authority, as in the case of a father who instructs his child to do something, "because I say so, that's why!" We often quickly discover who has the power to set and enforce rules locally. More distant rulers are often less identifiable.

Lines of authority

I'm sure the parents of these children think it's cute, but I can assure you that most people don't appreciate being instructed by a four year-old!
From a letter appearing in Ann Landers's syndicated newspaper advice column about the practice of using children's voices on recorded telephone answering machine messages

Tracing lines of authority in rule formation, articulation, and enforcement reveals much about social hierarchies and their forms of power. These hierarchies can be headed by an individual strong man or woman, social coalitions of various types, or larger, more abstract and encompassing sources. In its most basic form, rule-governing authority is biologically conditioned. The world heavyweight boxing champion, for instance, can mightily influence his social world by using brute force to impose his will (at least until another more powerful institution, constitutional law, intervenes and puts him in jail for doing just that, as was Mike Tyson's fate more than once). Male heads of the household, elders, older siblings, and strong persons of many other types impose and maintain order in their zones of influence. Patriarchy in societies all over the world evolved from roles developed in premodern cultures where men's greater physical size and musculature, together with women's biological role as childbearer, led to a gendered division of labor that is still with us. Males became procurers and protectors required to engage the world outside the family. Such profound responsibilities also gave them relatively greater autonomy and opportunity. This division of labor led to development of restricted social roles for both sexes and the creation of differences in power that are more favorable to men in some important ways.

Hierarchies of authority originating in biological difference extend deeply into the public sphere. Men dominate economic, political, and religious institutions everywhere today, often bringing competition and conflict with them. Unfortunately, as Anthony Giddens bluntly points out, it seems that "men's attitude toward the world is essentially an instrumental one, based on domination and manipulation" (1991: 229). The power of rules, then, is closely related to social roles. Presidents of large, technologically advanced nations can impose military force on lesser powers, or on their own people when an uprising occurs, thereby exercising a form of institutionalized patriarchy. Religious leaders are almost always men who, in their own spheres and with a somewhat more gentle touch, command their congregations. Chief executive officers of corporations are respected mainly because of their organizational status and power. Fathers impose their will at home. All these individuals operate within and are legitimated by ideological institutions – politics, religion, business, family. The rules they articulate influence their environments in part simply because the institutions and agencies they represent remain in place and continue to operate.

In today's industrialized and post-industrial societies, many of the most powerful social organizations – transnational corporations, for instance – are utterly faceless except, perhaps, for their corporate media spokesmen and women – actors, actresses, sports personalities, etc., whose authority springs from the world of popular, not corporate, culture. Some of these agencies – IBM is a prime example – have even required dress codes to guarantee an anonymous appearance – the infamous "corporate look." You can often recognize corporate executives by the ties, shoes, and overcoats they wear. The military, of course, takes this thinking to the extreme. Although all social institutions have their temporarily visible personalities, we have been taught to respect "the company," "the church," "the school," "the union," "the army," "the political party," and "the law," for example, as legitimate originators, articulators, and enforcers of rules. In many realms of the modern world, our trust no longer resides so much in personal acquaintances as it does in social institutions and images. It is trust "in a general system of expectations" (Kratochwil 1989: 114) and in the abstract capacities of expert knowledge emanating from a host of distant authorities. This kind of trust is clearly evident every time we step into an airplane, for example (Giddens 1990: 26).

The special authority of electronic media

Radio and television studios and transmitters are among the most valued and protected technical facilities anywhere in the world. Most commercial broadcast stations are enormously profitable; being granted permission to transmit is like having a license to print money. In nations suffering political unrest, government leaders often try to control broadcast facilities militarily. They fear that a takeover of telecommunications installations by revolutionary groups would signal a most serious challenge to political authority. One action taken by the communist government in the People's Republic of China during the 1989 student–worker uprising, for instance, was to impose martial law and seize control of all mass media facilities. In extreme cases such as this, forces that control the electronic media control the country.

The idea of *mass communication* is indeed a weighty sociological concept. Ownership and control of the mass media, especially the electronic media, are unparalleled forms of social power even in the most stable societies. Electronic media are among the modern world's most celebrated and effective conveyers of ideology and articulators of social rules. Media stimulate short-term patterns and long-term conventions that can affect an entire society. Growth in profits attributable to commercial advertising, children reciting themes from television programs, increases in the attendance of live performances given by popular music artists following the airing of a hit record on radio and MTV, even the very attendance by a national audience to a television program are all examples of real media influence.

People in more developed countries tend to be especially critical, even quite cynical, about the mass media, particularly television programs, commercials, and the practice of journalism. Despite the concerns many people have about them, the mass media are among the most potent of modern-day authorities. The vast majority of people in the more developed countries all over the world say they trust television more than any other source of information. Television wins the credibility contest because it is visual, immediate, and convenient (so that it is used habitually, fostering a special kind of trust). Furthermore, television's credibility as a medium interacts with the interpersonal believability of its personalities. Technological capability and personal ethos coalesce to create unequaled institutional legitimacy. The most famous example of this combined authority may be the influence American newscaster Walter Cronkite enjoyed on CBS television for many years. His unsurpassed personal credibility and the widespread public acceptance of television as the most believable news medium worked together to inspire the confidence of millions of viewers. When he signed off every evening with "And that's the way it was this day," Cronkite had effectively circumscribed the world's events into a half-hour capsule gently given to an adoring audience who deeply trusted his fatherly image.

Cronkite's legendary popularity also can help us understand other ways the mass media have become patriarchal authorities. In a sense, the electronic media are extensions of male culture. They were invented by men. The first voices to be heard on radio were those of engineers transmitting signals by tinkering with the tubes and wires. It didn't take long for another male-dominated institution, commerce, to recognize and capitalize on the profit potential of radio once it became technically feasible. Television, following the successful precedent of radio, was born a commercial medium. As a consequence of this marriage between engineering and commerce, males became the first owners, managers, programmers, technicians, regulators, and personalities on radio and television. The electronic media today continue to extend and amplify male authority in even the most subtle ways. To cite but one telling example, more than 90 percent of television "voice overs" (when a disembodied voice is heard over the visuals of a commercial) are done by men, asserting masculine authority in a way that is unlikely to be consciously perceived or criticized by viewers. Institutional voices, especially those of the mass media, are indeed loud and clear. The special authority of electronic media, asserting and reinforcing endless streams of ideologically charged information, is, without question, an impressive social force.

Public images and private practices: media, rules, and the macro/micro question

Electronic media play an especially influential role in contemporary rule-governed interaction. Media help shape and maintain rules and the ideological predispositions underlying them because their unique and powerful technical capabilities and appealing content are the most effective means of information diffusion ever invented. Mass media traverse not only geographic frontiers, but also boundaries of class, race, culture, politics, education, and gender to distribute entertainment and information that instill and refresh particular points of view and ways of making sense as a routine product of transmission. By articulating ideological syntheses that promote certain perspectives and exclude others, and by relating ideological inflections to sources of authority, the mass media help constitute and regulate social reality by structuring some of their audiences' most common and important experiences.

Rules commute from sweeping macrosocial environments, through various mid-range configurations, to the very smallest, most idiosyncratic contexts and activities. Rules link public agendas with private worlds. Some rules promote patterns of thought and social activity in ways that define large populations. But familiar surroundings such as living spaces, workplaces, and social gathering spots of all kinds are likewise structured and governed by rules, some deriving from distant authority, others more local. Of interest is the fluidity of rules across sociocultural contexts, from macro to micro and the reverse, and the ways rules are interpreted and used as they move from place to place. This crossing and intermeshing of social arenas and circumstances help us understand how rules are put to work by their originators, articulators, enforcers, and interpreter-users.

Mass media help break down distance between the macrosocial and the microsocial, between the global and the local. They bring public themes into private environments where they enter into and are influenced by local conditions, orientations, authorities, and practices. The public sphere has been mediated and reconstituted in the electronic age (Thompson 1995), both technologically and socially. News is a clear example. As Anthony Giddens points out, "distant events may become as familiar, or more so, than proximate influences, and integrated into frameworks of personal experience" (1984: 189). The same can be said of virtually all electronic media content. Employing media imagery in the routine construction of interpersonal discourses of all kinds is a common social use of television. But what appears on the mass media is useful not only because it is so available and appealing. Media consumers' own interests, exercised within the circumstances and venues of reception (the endless microsocial contexts), greatly influence how media imagery is interpreted and used too.

Rules in perspective

Pervasive and powerful as they are, rules certainly don't cause or explain everything. Basic reflexes, survival instincts, spontaneous emotional outbursts, and unthinking conditioned behavior, for example, need not be required or suggested by rules. To follow, disobey, ignore, reformulate, or appropriate a rule and its underlying structures of thought and authority is not a cause-and-effect process, but a choice made by individuals and groups in particular contexts, sometimes for reasons we may never fully understand. To conceptualize social interaction in terms of rules is certainly one very productive way to theorize the intricate relation between ideology, authority, and power.

5

Media Audiences

One of the senior scholars of media studies, Denis McQuail, describes the history of the concept of *media audience* this way:

> In the early days of mass communication research, the audience concept stood for the body of actual or intended receivers of messages at the end of a linear process of information transmission. This version has been gradually replaced by a view of the media receiver as more or less active, resistant to influence, and guided by his or her own concerns, depending on the particular social and cultural context. (McQuail 1997: 142)

In this chapter we will explore media audiences by discussing the social processes of mediated communication. Media audiences have been studied systematically by academic and market researchers since the 1930s when radio first became a mass medium. In many key respects, the ways audience members use the mass media have not changed much since then; it's just taken the researchers this long to be able to better describe the complex relationships between sources of electronic communication and their interpreter/users. Technology and society are changing constantly too, of course, throwing additional challenges toward anyone who tries to describe and explain audiences.

The very first media researchers were sociologists, psychologists, political scientists, and marketers interested in media's broad social effects: mass persuasion, information diffusion, political and consumer behavior, and socialization. These researchers focused mainly on categories of media content and aggregated, statistical groups of audience members – how much of this or that was being consumed by whom?

A main concern from the beginning was the media's ability to persuade people. The underlying premise of the early research was that mass media's symbolic imagery almost automatically provokes conforming responses from audiences. This belief was understandable given the historical context. Imagine what it must have been like for society to move into the electronic media world. By the 1930s families throughout the United States and many other Western countries could buy a handsome new device, a radio, that magically brought fresh and impressive voices, ideas, culture, entertainment, and music into the home. Radios were admired and used so much they often were made the centerpiece of the living space in much the same way that the first black-and-white TVs, then color TVs, and now home entertainment centers, including the latest WebTV configurations, occupy the focal point of many domiciles around the world today. Who wouldn't have thought that radio would inspire audiences to pay attention to and follow suggestions emanating from the little box? When television came along a few years later, the social concerns were magnified. While radio could attract and amuse listeners for hours, television seemed able to nearly hypnotize them for even longer periods of time.

Direct effects

The first stage of media audience research reflects these strong impressions of the electronic media as powerful, persuasive forces in society. The early studies of radio and television understandably is often called "direct effects" research. There was little question early last century that the electronic media affect people. The job of researchers at the time was simply to document the chain of influence as it moves from "sender" to "receiver" in order to measure the effects. Two main factors in the process of communication were considered: the *content* of media, and the *behavior* of audiences. Certain types of content were believed to cause predictable social responses.

One extremely important line of media direct effects research has endured for decades now, and still serves as the best way to illustrate this way of thinking about the relationship between media content and audiences. I refer here to the large number of empirical studies undertaken originally by American social scientists concerning the influence of violent TV programs on children. Analyzing these social influences has been the most significant achievement of audience research that relies on a straightforward cause-and-effect theoretical model and statistical data as evidence. This is because the cause or "stimulus" (violent TV shows) and the effect or "response" (aggressive behavior) on or of child audiences can be relatively easily isolated and measured through content analysis and in the laboratories of social psychologists and communication researchers.

By studying the short-term and long-term consequences of violent TV, social scientists documented just what parents feared all along. Only the truly cynical, massively uninformed, or profoundly compromised person could deny that this body of research cumulatively reveals that violent programming helps stir up aggressive behavior (National Television Violence Study 1997; Murray, Rubinstein, and Comstock 1994; National Institute of Mental Health 1982; Gerbner and Gross 1976). This does not mean that violent television or any other form of popular culture *by itself* causes children or adults to commit antisocial acts. Media and popular culture are part of a set of factors that contribute to social violence including especially unhappy or violent family life, bad neighborhood conditions, and the ready availability of dangerous weapons.

Television systems in nations all over the world have been developed with strict limits on the amount and type of violence they can show. American media institutions have lacked such supervision. Concern in the United States about violent television (and video games, violent film, computer games, rap, and heavy metal music) has grown to epic proportions since the Littleton, Colorado, massacre in 1999. More vigilant industry monitoring has begun, but the culture industries are extremely reluctant to suspend or cut back on their financially successful violent productions. Academic research over the years reveals that levels of violent TV and other media programming remain very high despite all the warning signs. It will stay high unless some extraordinary government intervention takes place, which is unlikely. The treasured right of "free speech" is routinely invoked by industry in order to protect their profits.

Apart from the violence studies, however, the "direct effects" model of media influence has certainly not been able to explain the many complex processes of technologically mediated human communication. It's no easy matter to measure human thought and activity or to know precisely how the media influence their audiences.

How can we determine the particular impact of mass media compared to other environmental influences when analyzing human consciousness and behavior? Claims made by researchers about "media effects," therefore, are usually stated in highly equivocal terms. In his classic analysis of media's impact on audiences, for example, Joseph Klapper (1960) concluded that the mass media generally do more to reinforce pre-existing human behavior than to change it. Wilbur Schramm's often-quoted conclusion from the early days of mass communication research – that the media influence some people, some of the time, about some things – perhaps still best exemplifies the complexities and uncertainties of media direct effects theory (Schramm, Lyle, and Parker 1961).

Limited effects

Eventually, hopes and fears that media technology and messages simply overwhelm audiences were substantially qualified. Media influence has been shown over the years to depend on many intervening contextual factors. Most important of these is that communications media themselves are "mediated by a variety of social relationships that serve to guide, filter, and interpret media experience" (McQuail 1997: 8). That is, *people* mediate the influence of the media. As a simple example, imagine that a small group of people is watching television. A commercial advertisement hyping a new product appears on the screen. One of the viewers who has tried the product, but with disappointing results, yells back at the TV, "You're a bunch of liars!" This person has effectively "mediated" the TV message for the other viewers, and probably limited the ad's potential to recruit clients from this group. Social mediations have proven effective in many other situations too. A parent can significantly reduce the impact of TV violence, for instance, by questioning and criticizing violent imagery when it appears while viewing with children. Parents can also talk to children about "prosocial" themes on TV such as helping and sharing in order to reinforce positive messages. Teachers have been able to use video and television in the classroom to teach vocabulary and thinking skills. Such mediating social influences vary across cultural contexts as well, adding additional layers of uncertainty to processes of media influence.[1]

History's second wave of media research reflects this active role of audiences. It is less pessimistic than the direct effects perspective because it gives people credit for confronting the mass media in significant ways on their own terms. No one claims that the media don't affect people. But the media's effects are not determined or absolute, as was first thought. Given this more complex understanding, audiences could no longer be reasonably theorized only as "victims" of media influence. The more sophisticated theoretical view is known as the *limited effects* perspective. Whatever effects the media have on audiences are mediated, and therefore limited, by other factors.

The limited effects view took hold when researchers began to realize how common it is for people to willingly engage media to advance their personal and social interests. For example, radio listeners in the 1940s used quiz programs and soap operas to get advice for solving personal problems and for learning social roles generally (Herzog 1944). Radio listeners quickly employed the medium to establish moods, bracket the day, find companionship, put themselves at ease socially, and be entertained and informed (Suchman 1942; Mendelsohn 1964). Reading the daily newspaper is a way for adults to participate meaningfully in public life (Berelson 1949). Families used television programs emanating from the very first black-and-white sets to entertain visitors and provide group entertainment (McDonagh 1950), and as a conversational resource, fantasy stimulant, and coin of exchange in peer group interaction (Riley and Riley 1951). An ethnographic study of Boston's East End Italian population of the 1950s documented how family discussions about TV programs help people define and reinforce gender roles, solve everyday problems, and chastise social institutions (Gans 1962).

Uses and Gratifications

Another important strain of media audience theory that departs sharply from the direct effects research tradition and its usual focus on the negative impact of media emerged during the 1970s. It is known as the audience *uses and gratifications* perspective. Proponents of this theory straightforwardly claim that people actively *use* the mass media to *gratify* specifiable human *needs*. According to these theorists, it isn't enough just to recognize the limits of media's effects; to be more true to reality, a positive spin must be put on audience behavior. Instead of asking what the media do to people, uses and gratifications researched turn the question around: *"what do people do with the media?"* (Katz 1977). Lots of studies and theorizing in many countries have been undertaken from this theoretical vantage point (see Blumler and Katz 1974 and Rosengren, Wenner, and Palmgreen 1985 for summaries of this work).

A uses and gratifications approach

I will now present a uses and gratification model which outlines one way to think about *how* and *why* individual audience members use the media. The approach we consider is based on a psychological approach to the study of audiences. We shall focus on human *needs* and the media-based *methods* that people construct to gratify those needs. Throughout the discussion we shall reflect critically on the significance of each stage in the process, and on the very concepts and labels we employ to describe the way people use the media to gratify their needs.

Needs

Virtually all uses and gratifications theorists recommend using a central psychological concept – need – as the starting point in their analyses. Inevitably, they defer to conceptions of need that are grounded in time-tested psychological theories of motivation such as the self-actualization approach of Abraham Maslow (1954; 1962) or the psychosexual/psychosocial synthesis of Erik Erikson (1982). Because needs are not directly observable, we can only speculate about their origins and forms. It has been useful, therefore, to turn to psychologists for definitions and typologies. And for good reason. Within psychology the concept "need" is the foundation of much important theoretical work including cognitive dissonance theory, social exchange theory, attribution theory, and some strains of psychoanalytic theory.

The American psychologist Frederick Samuels (1984) has reviewed the history of need as a psychological concept. He points out that survival (physiological) needs – such as the requirement for food, water, and sleep – are undeniable, essential human needs. The needs for personal safety, social belongingness, and self-esteem may even "lie within the pre-self core of every human being at birth," according to Samuels (p. 203). Other more abstract conceptions of need such as self-actualization, cognitive needs (such as curiosity), aesthetic needs, and expressive needs are less clearly delivered with us at birth, but are nonetheless central to human experience. Furthermore, needs are not independent from one another. Some needs are contained within or overlap other needs.

The very term "need" implies a state of deprivation such as hunger or thirst, or a requirement for essentials such as shelter, personal safety, and cognitive and social stability. No doubt these needs are fundamental to the individual's well-being. But gratifying a need means much more than responding to biological or psychological deficiencies. Most psychologists believe that human beings are also driven to discover, grow, transcend, and share. These advanced needs are discussed, for example, in Maslow's famous hierarchy of needs. The higher-level needs become salient when biological and safety needs are met.

No matter how essential needs are to people everywhere, they are not universal in form. As the British psychologist Rom Harré and his colleagues argue, "It may even be the case that different cultures, by emphasizing one sort of emotion rather than another, may produce people whose physiological systems differ from one another" (Harré, Clarke, and De Carlo 1985: 7). Furthermore, they point out "biological imperatives demand that we eat; but cultural imperatives determine the cuisine, our table manners, and the ritual significance with which many meals are taken" (p. 31). Needs are influenced by culture not only in the ways they are formed, but in how they are gratified. Our need to "belong," for instance, is gratified in terms of experiences and sentiments that surround family, race, ethnicity, gender, religion, social class, and nation (Samuels 1984: 205). Thus, culturally situated social experience reinforces basic biological and psychological needs while simultaneously giving direction to their sources of gratification. This is a crucial point because it means that we must carefully consider the actual contexts of need gratification. It is here that the mass media enter the picture, and understandings about exactly what needs are, where they originate, and how they are gratified become quite perplexing. Need is a concept that can even be manipulated for profit.

Beyond basic survival requirements, what does the human being truly need? From whose point of view, and with what costs and benefits for whom? If some needs are socially constructed, isn't it then the case that people may be told they need things they can do very well without? Questions such as these constitute the classic anti-capitalist critique of needs made by Herbert Marcuse in his book *One Dimensional Man* (1964). Marcuse argued that market forces try to persuade us to believe in "false needs" which differ from "true needs." False needs are:

> superimposed upon the individual by particular social interests in [the social actor's] repression . . . No matter how much such needs may have become the individual's own, reproduced and fortified by the conditions of his existence; no matter how much he identifies himself with

them and finds himself in their satisfaction, they continue to be what they were from the beginning – products of a society whose dominant interest demands repression. (Marcuse 1964: 5)[2]

It is precisely the confusion about what needs really are that commercial advertisers try to exploit. Even without considering the political polemics that Marcuse's argument inspires, we see again that the concept is not something easily agreed upon. Critical theorists insist that if many needs are learned (or "cultivated;" Giddens 1991: 170–1), then isn't it essential to identify, focus on, and analyze the social forces that shape needs? In an incisive critique of uses and gratifications theory, the British sociologist Phillip Elliott argued that the *active* audience member is still primarily a *social* actor subject to ideological and cultural influence: "To reject the idea of an active, purposive audience out of hand would be to adopt a completely determinist view . . . [but] it is necessary to suggest that he orients his behavior toward the external world rather than internal mental states" (Elliott 1974: 255). People thus intentionally engage the "external" social world in order to gratify their needs. When people attempt to gratify their need for love, social acceptance, or belonging, for instance, they are being constantly exposed to suggestions about how to gratify those inner necessities. There is a dynamic relation, therefore, between inner agitations of the self and the organization of the external world: "What people orient to in everyday life, what they feel is worth discussing, and trying to manage, are their hopes and fears, their dreams, anxieties, guilts, worries, and so on, and the structural properties of the social relations and institutions in which they find themselves enmeshed" (Harré, Clarke, and De Carlo 1985: 29–30). It is exactly this contested emotional space that some information agents – advertisers, for example – try to influence by cultivating "unhappiness . . . fears, anxieties and the sufferings of personal inadequacy" (Bauman 1989: 189). Commercial solutions are then proposed. Need-based human activity proceeds toward gratification and other consequences. The direction this process takes for any individual is influenced by contact with a culture's characteristic themes which are mobilized by its primary vehicles of socialization and cultivation – the mass media.

Methods

I no longer feel impelled to go out in the hot sun to play softball with the young bloods at the department picnic. The perceived need to uphold the "macho" image has diminished. Now it should be noted that maintaining a "macho" image is – strictly speaking – not an actual need; it is thus a misperceived need. However, it may be legitimately considered as one possible way, as a *means*, to satisfy an actual basic need – self-esteem. In my older age I find other ways than knocking around a horsehide sphere to obtain self-esteem.

Samuels 1984: 18

In this little story, Frederick Samuels makes the crucial distinction between need and *means*, or what I call *method*. The concept of method is extremely important. Recalling our discussion of ethnomethodology from the last chapter, method refers to the fundamental, purposeful, and methodical ways people go about constructing their routine activities. We all have methods for accomplishing our personal and social goals. I prefer to use "method" instead of "means" therefore in order to emphasize the strategic and systematic aspects of this goal-directed social activity.

In the uses and gratifications approach to media audiences, *a method is a means for gratifying a need*. In the account given above the method is composed of a cognitive plan (maintaining a "macho" image) and an activity (playing softball) both of which are designed to gratify a need (for self-esteem). Methods such as this one may or may not be consciously planned or recognized. They may or may not be successful. They are constantly revised. Furthermore, much human behavior – including contact with the mass media – is *not* motivated by a desire to gratify a need. In the next few pages I will untangle and expand upon these distinctions and give several examples to show how social actors construct methods and use the media for various purposes. I will hold onto the basic assumptions of the psychology-based uses and gratifications perspective in my theoretical elaboration, though this manner of theorizing by no means represents my overall point of view. I will not limit the analysis of cognitive operations as if these mental processes occur unaffected by ideology and culture. As I argue throughout this book, analyzing the ways microsocial communication processes interact with social structure should be at the heart of theory. By focusing on method, we can keep the delicate synthesis of social structure and social action at the forefront of analysis where it belongs.

In their attempts to sell commercial products, sponsors of mass-mediated imagery often try to confuse need with method. *Advertisers attempt to create a perception of need in the minds of audience members by suggesting potentially successful methods.* Let me illustrate how this works with a straightforward example from tele-vision. For years the primary advertising campaign undertaken by a major Japanese automobile manufacturer featured the slogan "You Need This Car!" This example typifies commercial short-circuiting of the reasoning process. The often-repeated suggestion that the con-sumer "needs" a product is designed to provoke a genuine feeling that the commodity itself is the need. But in the example given above, for instance, the product (the car) is actually a method, not a need. The Japanese automaker Suzuki went even more directly to the point in the late 1990s when it called one of its line of cars the "Suzuki Esteem." There are many ways to achieve self-esteem and certainly not all of them are accomplished through material displays. One could feel quite gratified by volunteering for the Red Cross, for example, or by organizing or participating in an AIDS walk, or helping out at the local elementary school, among limitless other possibilities.

The print advertisement shown as figure 5.1 is another clear example of how advertisers try to substitute their products or ser-vices for needs. The California telephone company Pacific Bell iden-tifies the "basic human needs" as food, water, and "phone." The true psychological need that is being referred to and exploited is for "social belonging," which human communication can help create. The "need" certainly is not for a telephone. Using the telephone (with profits headed straight to Pacific Bell) is but one method that can be used to maintain interpersonal contact.

Figure 5.1 Basic human "needs"

The attempt to assert material goods as needs is part of an overall strategy used by advertisers to deliberately confuse and "displace" meaning. The Canadian anthropologist Grant McCracken (1990) offers an interesting perspective on how this works. He says that advertisers market their products in ways that are designed to capture (or recapture) emotional conditions, social circumstances, and life-styles that have been purposefully displaced and made distant in the ad itself. Commodities are then made available to help the consumer gain (or regain) that which is made to appear out of reach – the golden past, the bright future, or the alternative present. Consumer goods are promoted as the "objective correlatives" of displaced meaning – "purchases [that can] give the consumer access to displaced ideals" (McCracken 1990: 116). The frenzy to chase displaced ideals engenders a never-ending search for self-satisfaction. As Anthony Giddens relates, "the project of the self becomes translated into one of the possession of desired goods and the pursuit of artificially framed styles of life . . . the consumption of ever-novel goods becomes in some part a substitute for the genuine development of the self" (1991: 198). The effect is exponential. As McCracken points out, "from the moment of introduction, the new good begins to demand new companion goods. The individual who assents to the first demand finds that it is followed by a hundred others . . . higher and higher levels of consumption are seen as the loci of pleasure where in fact they are only dulling, boring comfort" (1990: 125, 128). Or as Zygmunt Bauman argues, the main message advertisers send is "Above all, do not delay gratification if you can help it. Whatever you are after, try to get it now, you cannot know whether the gratification you seek today will still be gratifying tomorrow" (Bauman 1996: 25).

For purposes of our discussion here, the point is this: mass media endlessly suggest methods for gratifying human needs. These methods are sometimes substituted rhetorically for needs, and meaning is displaced away from the real to the ideal as part of a design to constantly promote consumer anxiety and provide a multitude of profitable short-term material solutions. The sponsored images may even accumulate to represent particular cultural norms. They are further differentiated by gender. Women are told they need certain things and men other things. But as we know, such cultural representations are not uncritically consumed by audiences. In the end this tension between the ability of mass media to influence thought and activity, and the strong tendency of individuals to use media and symbolic resources for their own purposes, must be accommodated by our theory of media, communication, and culture.

Methods and need gratification

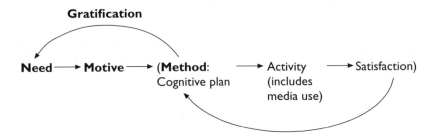

Figure 5.2 Method-satisfaction/need-gratification model

Let's look closely at the concept of "method." Methods are cognitive plans and activities designed and undertaken by social actors (sometimes outside their conscious awareness) to accomplish particular goals that can gratify needs (figure 5.2). People routinely turn to the media for all kinds of social reasons. Such mediated experiences apparently are considered quite satisfying. Empirical research shows that across a wide range of everyday activities, human beings physiologically, cognitively, and emotionally experience interaction with television, computers, and new media as if they are just as "real" as unmediated social exchanges (Reeves and Nass 1996). Just such tendencies were theorized many years ago as "parasocial interaction" – mediated human interaction that feels like unmediated interaction (Horton and Wohl 1956). So, for example, if a person feels lonely and wants to socialize, but is shy or inhibited in typical social situations, he or she might turn to the media for vicarious interaction and need fulfillment. Television is an obvious candidate. Soap-opera stars, newscasters, and talk-show hosts receive literally tons of mail from lonely viewers who use certain television shows to interact with other human beings. The person thus might try parasocial interaction (a method) in order to gratify a desire for social belonging (the need). When a mass medium is employed for such purposes, this is a "use" of the medium. The use is part of the method.[3]

But the methods don't always work. It is often the case, for instance, that the principal outcome of media activity (for example, degree of perceived social interaction obtained through TV viewing) may not be deemed sufficient by the viewer. This failure may encourage the person to try something else in order to realize the same objective. In uses and gratifications parlance, the person turns to a "functional alternative." This could involve engaging another mass medium or taking part in unmediated social activity. The mass media, people, the Internet, parties, the telephone, drugs, even sleep are all sources of potential need gratification. So, to watch TV, write an email letter, listen to music, attend a party, check out some websites, or call someone on the phone could all potentially gratify one or more needs. The person may try several alternatives before succeeding. So, need gratification occurs in two stages. First, the activity must satisfy the intrinsic requirements of the method. Second, the method (now realized in terms of the activity undertaken) must be able to gratify the need.

To further illustrate the process of need gratification, let me provide some additional examples. A responsible father or mother may determine that one method that could gratify the need to belong is to be perceived by other family members as a good parent. The parent may then construct a variety of everyday activities that could produce this recognition and appreciation. This is a purposeful plan of practical action – a method. Television can be put to use to satisfy the method and gratify the need because children's TV viewing is activity over which parents can have considerable influence. Such a role performance can make it clear to everyone that the parent is a valued member of the family group.

Here is another example. A person is motivated to gratify the need for self-esteem. The cognitive plan fashioned by the person for this purpose is to become an expert on a topic of cultural interest (world affairs, computer technology, popular music, fashion, etc.). Developing such expertise potentially qualifies the individual as possessor of important, useful, or otherwise desirable information. Media activities that could be undertaken to achieve this objective include, for instance, subscribing to specialty magazines, reading the newspaper carefully every day, viewing appropriate TV programs, and so on. To the degree that these media activities successfully facilitate the requirements of the method, we can say that the first level of satisfaction has been reached. The person has become an expert. The adequacy of the method is then cognitively tested against the need for self-esteem. The person determines, often unconsciously, if the method has "worked." Two types of success or failure can thus occur. First, the particular activity may or may not develop into a successful enactment of a method. Second, the method itself may or may not then gratify a need.

How people use media to gratify their needs is limited only by the imagination. They can use television, for example, to illustrate their experiences and feelings, establish common ground with others, enter conversations, reduce interpersonal anxieties, set the agenda for talk, clarify, promote, and transmit values, establish physical and verbal contact and neglect, develop family solidarity and relaxation, reduce conflicts, maintain relationships, learn social behavior, make decisions, model behavior, solve problems, support opinions, disseminate information, enact and reinforce roles, exercise authority, filter experience, and facilitate arguments (Lull 1980; 1990). Such uses matter because television and other media are vital components of the communication systems of families and other viewing groups. Power among family members, for example, is frequently exercised and fought over through everyday domestic use of television and other media. Who controls the remote control device, who knows how to work the VCR or DVD player, and who plans viewing schedules, for example, are negotiations that are typically waged in terms of gender and generational differences (Morley 1986; Lull 1990; Press 1991), but also differ culturally (Lull 1988; 1990). In a highly social culture like Brazil, for example, television is regularly used for conversation, group viewing, and social navigation: "In a culture where people like to be alone, TV may contribute to greater isolation. However, in one where people like to be with others, it may lead to greater social interaction" (Kottak 1990: 148).

Wants

Human involvement with mass media is not always motivated by the desire to gratify a need or needs. We also use media to *satisfy wants*. Compared to needs, wants are far more of the moment and less central to the well-being of the person. Still, they call out for particular courses of action that often demand immediate satisfaction. For example, a person may flick on the TV for momentary distraction while he or she waits for a friend to call at home. Someone else may pick up a newspaper to glance at the sports results at breakfast. Another person turns on the radio for company while doing housework. In cases such as these, audience members' uses of media cannot really be considered responses to biological or psychological needs. That would be a gross overstatement. These kinds of involvements are motivated by wants. *A want is something desired but not needed*. The normative environment – both its cultural characteristics and its microsocial expectations – helps shape wants too. The person develops cognitive predispositions that are influenced in large measure by what society expects and what local environments permit.

Although wants and needs have been discussed separately here, I do not mean to imply that they are mutually exclusive. Nor am I suggesting that they are the only foundations of human activity. Wants and needs should be regarded as points along a continuum of the motivational basis of human activity. Furthermore, although I have specifically discussed television as a resource for need gratification, other media and symbolic forms – music and computers especially – are also used to gratify needs, although their contexts and specific applications differ from those of the visual medium. Because of their pervasive presence and appeal, television and video remain frequently used social resources for constructing need-gratifying methods.

The functionalist tradition

Over the years researchers have documented an impressive variety of audience members' personal and social uses of the mass media. This has been an enormous improvement over the too-simple and too-pessimistic "direct effects" perspective. Uses and gratifications style media research is still being conducted today, and maintains a very respectable place in the history of communication research. Despite the substantial empirical evidence these studies have generated, and the historical credibility of the perspective, uses and gratifications theory has been strongly criticized. Why?

Because the uses and gratifications perspective assumes that people *willingly engage* the mass media and *benefit* from the experience, it is often associated with the highly criticized notion that mass media *function* positively for society. Functionalist mass communication theory can be traced to a four-part inventory about the mass media developed by the American political scientist Harold Laswell in the 1940s. Laswell (1948) claimed that the media perform four basic functions for society: they survey the environment (the news and information function); they correlate a response to this information (the editorial function); they entertain (the diversion function); and they transmit the culture to future generations (the socialization function).

The functionalist perspective – in a way similar to uses and gratifications theory – implies that media are resources put to use by individuals in society. Critics have claimed that this way of thinking about the relationship between people and mass media is naive and misleading because it explains audience members' contact with media in individualistic, mentalistic terms that are claimed, in the aggregate, to advance the social good (Elliott 1974). A more insightful analysis of mass communication might begin by examining media institutions, sponsors, and messages. When the objectives and practices of media owners and their financial backers are taken into account, it becomes clear that the mass media present an agenda of direct suggestions (for example, commercials) and indirect suggestions (such as themes in TV programs) that reinforce the dominant ideology and a system of unequal social relations. Uses and gratifications theory, according to the critics, only documents and concretizes this domination by claiming that people are routinely gratified by their experiences with media. So, in sociological terms, critics say that while audience members may exercise considerable influence over their media experiences at the personal and interpersonal (the "micro") levels, they are subject to profound constraints, are even dominated, at the societal (or "macro") level.

In a classic text, *Mass Communication: A Sociological Perspective*, the American sociologist Charles R. Wright made Harold Laswell's theory of "media functions" more comprehensive and critical by questioning the taken-for-grantedness of a function (Wright 1975). Wright asked: "What are the manifest [apparent] and latent [not so apparent] functions *and dysfunctions* of mass communicated surveillance, correlation, entertainment, and cultural transmission for the society, the individual, subgroups, and cultural systems?" (1975: 11; italics mine). Wright formulated an elaborate scheme to assess these complex, interrelated issues. He pointed out, for example, that when media provide necessary information about a natural catastrophe (an earthquake, for instance) society as a whole can respond effectively and positively. In this sense media function for society. But, he said, the very same newscasts and emergency alerts can simultaneously induce panic or "anti-social attempts at survival" among individuals and subgroups (such as looting in the wake of the disaster). This development is a media dysfunction. Mass media are functional or dysfunctional to the degree and in the ways that audience members use them.

The mass audience

Despite the ebb and flow of theoretical fashions in the academy, in practice, the idea of a mass audience has dominated how we think of audiences and will probably do so in the years to come.

Webster and Phalen 1997: 115

So far we have focused primarily on media audiences as *individuals*. We first asked whether or not individual persons are directly persuaded or harmed by media programming. Then we showed how audience members take considerable control over their media experiences as "active audiences," limiting the effects. We presented a uses and gratifications model that emphasizes the ability of individuals to develop methods for using media to advance their interests.

But there is another level of "audience" that we must also consider. This is the idea of audience not as individuals, but as *groups* of people who have something in common, usually some media-related behavior or habit. We routinely use the expression "audience" to describe these groups, for example, when we refer to "the TV audience," or "readers of *Cosmopolitan*," or the "target audience" of advertisers. The ease with which the word "audience" passes over our lips, however, worries some observers. For some critics, the idea of a big, anonymous audience implies incorrectly that people who attend to media are nothing but a faceless, passive lump of humanity. People who differ greatly from one another are dumped into a common pool of undifferentiated souls, becoming an aggregated presence, a mass, loaded up with negative characteristics and connotations. The "couch potato" viewer, the soap-opera addict, the TV talk-show regular, and the beer-drinking, TV-watching football fan are some classic stereotypes of this way of thinking about human beings as media audiences.

When the term "mass" is applied to the media – as in "mass media" – relatively little harm seems to be done because the expression refers to the capability of communications hardware to traverse great distances and reach lots of people. The emphasis is on technical potential. Even the term "mass communication" describes a rather abstract social process. But when we describe real people by using "mass" as an adjective – as in "mass audience" – the significance changes considerably. In Western societies in particular, with their emphasis on individual rights and freedoms, few people cherish the idea of being thought of as part of the "masses." Social class differences are implied by "mass" in a judgmental way too; using the term divides the world into elites and the rest of us – the great, unwashed masses.

Mass audiences become statistics which are bought and sold. When a commercial television network wants to convince a potential client to advertise, for instance, it tries to sell the audience it has for any particular program. This seemingly dehumanizing transformation of people from flesh-and-blood, living-and-breathing individual human beings into faceless statistics became the focus of a book about media audiences by Australian cultural studies scholar Ien Ang (1991). Writing in her previous home in Holland with its strong public service television system, and at a time when American commercial television was spreading rapidly throughout Europe, Ang sharply criticized the way commercial media industries construct and use the concept "audience." She was especially concerned about the ways audience ratings data are used to manufacture "fictional" audiences who are then marketed without conscience by the brokers of media advertising.

The mass society

Even more condemning, media audiences have been associated with what social theorists call the "mass society." As Western societies became industrialized and modernized over the past two centuries, observers realized that the pace and scale of all social life were expanding rapidly. In the process, modern societies were creating not only mass media and mass communication, but also mass industrial production, mass education, mass health care, mass marketing, mass taste, mass everything. And who lives in the midst of such massification? The masses, of course. Where do they live? In a mass society.

The idea of a mass society is based on an early twentieth-century model of the social organization of industrializing Western capitalist societies (O'Sullivan et al. 1994: 173), especially in northern Europe and North America. The industrializing nations were composed of a vast workforce of men and women, the theory goes, who lived isolated and unfulfilling lives. They were like slaves to their jobs and to their bosses, were forced to live away from the security of their extended families, and often migrated from the peaceful countryside to the dangerous cities to find work. They were like atoms caught in the confines of some huge, oppressive, material structure over which they had no control. Defined by dull, repetitive, low-paying, unsatisfying labor, and disconnected from many of their previous meaningful social relations, these were the "alienated masses" that the famous critical theorist Karl Marx (1975; 1977; Marx and Engels 1970) thought would eventually stage a worldwide socialist workers' revolution. That revolution has not materialized, but the general critique of labor and life under capitalism that mass society theory describes still rings true in many respects today.

Members of the first mass societies were also said to be disconnected from true knowledge and emotion. They were psychologically
adrift in an impersonal and threatening environment that offered
little joy or comfort. Because of their miserable living conditions and
limited range and quality of human contact, men and women of the
mass society were forced to depend on indirect forms of human communication for information, entertainment, and companionship – the
mass media.

Exploited at work and isolated socially, people living in the mass
societies of the last century were considered easy targets of media
influence. As we saw in our discussion of "direct effects" theory
earlier in this chapter, the mass media initially were believed to have
an enormous impact on their audiences. Under certain conditions,
mass audiences were thought to be "at the mercy of totalitarian ideologies and propaganda" (O'Sullivan et al. 1994: 173). This scenario
is said to have applied to audiences in all Western industrial societies
of the time, but one particularly troubling historical example stands
out. Caught in a global economic depression, fearing the future, con-
fident of their "ethnic superiority," and stirred to collective action by
powerful leaders and a punishing system of sanctions, the populations of Germany and Italy became pawns in the rise of fascism and
Nazism in industrialized Europe during the 1930s. The media played
a crucial role.

It's understandable that fierce social criticism would emerge in the
wake of the Nazi terror in Europe. Critical theorists were trying to
explain what could have possibly provoked human beings to act in
such a horrific way. The most important school of critical theory
which dealt with this grave problem emanated from the very heart
of former Nazi territory – Frankfurt, Germany. "Frankfurt School"
theorists took the mass media and the culture industries as primary
subjects of intense critical scrutiny. Two scholars in particular –
Theodor Adorno and Max Horkheimer – blamed the media for the
rise of fascism (Adorno and Horkheimer 1972; Horkheimer 1972;
Adorno 1989; 1991). They argued that the new propagandistic
power of fascist media had overwhelmed rationality and civility,
setting off barbaric, insane collective behavior. The concept of "the
masses" made sense in this historical context.

The case of Nazi Germany is but the most extreme illustration of
the devastation that the mass media can help bring about. Audiences
as masses were becoming firmly established in social theory. When
Adorno and Horkheimer first came to the United States after World
War II they feared that the newly formed and flourishing industries
of American popular culture had the same dangerous potential to

undermine human rationality and the standards of civil behavior that had broken down in Europe. Adorno and Horkheimer were "highly cultured European men and yet they found themselves in a world they utterly failed to understand; the world of Hollywood and Mickey Mouse" (Tester 1994: 35). Cultural products like Hollywood movies, commercial TV, and popular music, in their view, could only seduce, pacify, and distract the masses. These theorists argued that the media only reinforce and reproduce the masses' limited consciousness, while degrading true art and culture in the process. Now, many years after the harsh critiques of Adorno, Horkheimer, and other Frankfurt School theorists were originally published, their ideas are generally regarded as reactionary and elitist. Their writing has nonetheless served an important purpose in the evolution of critical social theory. Adorno's and Horkheimer's work reflects the grim reality of Europe before and during World War II, and the destructive role of media under fascism, which forever alerted societies everywhere to the destructive potential of media as instruments of manipulation and social control.

Many basic assumptions of mass society theory also underlay the first theories of mass communication in the United States before and after World War II. Audiences were thought to be easy targets of commercial advertisers and political campaigners. Violent media content could stimulate audiences, especially children, to be more aggressive. Media were also said to act like a narcotic drug (the "narcotizing dysfunction"), substituting vicarious action for real-world behavior. People end up depending on the media for nearly everything, according to the mass society perspective, and the media also desensitize us from the environments where we live, and from our inner selves. Heavy exposure to television is claimed to almost automatically cultivate beliefs among TV viewers (Gerbner et al. 1986). Aggression, narcotization, dependency, desensitization, and cultivation are all types of "direct effects" suffered by the mass audience in the mass society (O'Sullivan et al. 1994: 174).

Rethinking the mass audience

Not all media scholars today, however, think that collective audience behavior is necessarily a bad thing. They insist that the "mass audience" should not be confused with the "mass society." Furthermore, "many theorists have wrongly equated a *mass* audience with a *passive* audience" (Webster and Phalen 1997: 116; italics mine). In their book, *The Mass Audience: Rediscovering the Dominant Model*, American communication scholars James Webster and Patricia Phalen (1997) argue that mass audiences are not pushed around, but powerful. Webster and Phalen defend the industrial and academic practice of aggregating human beings into media audiences. They believe that "far from taming viewers, aggregating individuals empowers them. It amplifies their voices and recasts them in a form to which institutions must respond." By categorizing people as audiences, "something new and formidable" is created (p. 21). That something new and formidable is *collective opinion* that is stronger than opinions which can be expressed by any *individual* member of the group.

Webster and Phalen make two arguments about why audiences as aggregates of people have real populist-style power. The first concerns the media themselves. Media industries, after all, have to *please* their audiences. If commercial media cannot attract a large number of willing consumers, they will not be able to sell advertising. In this sense, audiences have real power in their sheer numbers, which are reflected in program ratings data. Audiences collectively pick and choose content that appeals to them. Programs must attract a "critical mass," or they will disappear. Of course this is the same argument that executives in the media industries use to defend themselves when their programs are criticized. The critics then usually respond to the executives by saying that audience members can only choose to read, listen, or watch from a menu that is offered to them by industry in the first place. But this argument has become much less convincing lately because the amount and variety of media content offered to media consumers worldwide have expanded dramatically, offering many more choices than before.

A second formidable defense is that the mass audience as a collectivity can inspire political action against powerful advocates of the dominant ideology. Such a view of course runs completely contrary to the Frankfurt School theory of media manipulation discussed in the previous paragraphs. Webster and Phalen offer the case of the 1968 Democratic National Convention in Chicago as historical evidence to support this defense. The famous Chicago convention took place at a time when many Americans were strenuously objecting to the Vietnam War. Protesters on the streets of Chicago clashed violently with police outside the convention hall. The major television networks captured the bloody confrontations on video, and beamed shocking images of riot police savagely beating unarmed protesters. As the brutality continued under the vigilant gaze of news cameras, the protesters shouted a slogan that is now etched in social history: "The Whole World is Watching! The Whole World is Watching!" The "whole world," of course, is the "mass audience." The anti-war protesters in Chicago counted on a worldwide mass audience to be outraged by what they saw on TV and demand that the government intervene to stop the brutality in Chicago and the war in Southeast Asia. In fact, one of the great lessons of the 1968 Chicago riots was that revolutionary groups must learn how to manipulate the media to their advantage. This strategy presumes that the "mass audience" is not only out there, but is paying attention and ready to act.

Let's see how this principle took form twenty years later in a very different political and cultural context – the People's Republic of China.

Box 5.1 The Chinese Audience: A Collective Response to Communism

(This case study is based on Lull 1991.)

When television was made available to Chinese people nationally in the 1980s, many people had already begun to distrust the Communist Party and its propaganda. The infamous 1989 student–worker uprising in Tiananmen Square was motivated in part by just such resistance to official ideology and culture. The mass media, especially television, played a pivotal role in the uprising. How could this have happened in a communist country?

Chinese communist ideology since 1980 has promoted two principal ideas: "modernization" and "reform," which refer to China's attempt to extensively upgrade its agriculture, industry, national defense, science, and technology. By the 1980s, however, many Chinese people simply didn't trust the government's sincerity or its ability to follow through on these objectives. They cynically regarded government propaganda about reform as nothing but a smokescreen that would lead nowhere while it would continue to protect the despised privileges of the elite communist leaders. The "people" themselves would not benefit.

People began to more openly resist the teacherly, misleading, overblown propaganda about modernization and reform that appeared on television and in China's other mass media. They ridiculed the Communist Party's simple-minded self-promotion, its blatantly biased news reports, the laughable TV "model worker" programs, the exaggerated advertising claims made about domestic products, and the unavailability of advertised foreign goods. Viewers watched TV with hypercritical sensitivity. Families ignored the official narrations which accompany TV newscasts, focusing their attention on the less-manipulated visuals instead. What really struck many Chinese about a televised visit the late national leader Deng Xiaoping made to Tokyo, for example, was not the trade agreement he consummated, or the pomp and circumstance surrounding his foreign travel, but Japan's modern skyscrapers, cars, fashions, and busy lifestyles that were plainly shown by the television cameras. A television drama imported by China from Japan, *Oshin*, was interpreted by Chinese viewers mainly in terms of the free-market economic opportunities enjoyed by the lead character. And viewers questioned how communism could be better than capitalism when imported American TV programs playing on the Chinese system taught them that "in the West, even terrible people can own cars!"

Two Chinese television programs appearing on the national TV system in the late 1980s contributed greatly to the resistance movement of 1989. The first of these, *New Star (Xin Xing)*, was a 12-part docudrama serial that portrayed a power struggle between two men who represent strikingly differing styles of leadership within the Communist Party. One character, Li, exhibited a humanistic, fair, and modern approach to leadership. The other character, Gu, carried on in the repressive old style, arranging privileges for himself and his family through blatant graft and corruption, and punishing idealistic young people for their innovative ideas. Recognizing that the dismal situation portrayed by old Gu was closer to their reality than the hope generated by young Li, the Chinese "mass audience" reacted strongly and loudly to the series. They demanded that the Party act on its promise of reform. A second documentary-style series, *River Elegy (He Shang)*, was likewise interpreted by the enormous Chinese audience as a call for revolutionary change in the communist system. The program focused on China's persistent inward orientation, its fixation on its own land, which has isolated the nation from the rest of the world for many generations. The audience widely believed this program shows that China is still trapped within the confines of its feudalist past. Audience members became intimately involved with *New Star* and *River Elegy* because of the inviting, open-ended structure of the two television series, which

Photo 5.1 *New Star.* Li (left) and his corrupt adversary Gu. Viewers passionately responded to the program because the characters represented two very different futures for the People's Republic of China

contrasted so sharply with the didactic propaganda messages to which they are so accustomed.

The Chinese audience for the first time ever felt empowered by its collective response to mass media. The economic depression, political repression, and cultural suffocation suffered in the 1970s and 1980s set the stage for a mass reaction. Media technology and content became salient resources for resistance. The television audience rejected the blatant propaganda while it was attracted to alternative possible worlds presented on the very same media. The consequences were irreversible. Although the Chinese Communist Party still rules the country today on official levels in the political sphere, the economic and cultural conditions of contemporary China reflect enormous changes in styles and quality of life. Those changes were stimulated in large measure by the ability of China's national television audience to make its collective opinion heard.

The audience and technological change

The various streams of communication and cultural theory we have considered throughout this chapter clearly show that audiences indeed *are* active in key respects at the individual and collective levels.

Limited effects theory, uses and gratifications research, and cultural studies analyses all point in the same direction – human beings have the capacity to engage with, interpret, and use media technologies and texts in ways that advance their interests. This positive tendency has been shown to operate in capitalist contexts and in communist countries.

We must not be naive about this encouraging news, however. Audiences, like all categories of social actors, never operate with total freedom. They are subject to many suggestions, influences, and constraints.

By analyzing media audiences we can see how the crucial balance of the two main loci of power taken up in this book – the structured human environment, and the agency of persons and groups – takes form in real-world social communication. While the fundamental nature of the struggle between structure and agency seems to be a permanent state of affairs, the world in which the forces of structure and agency compete is constantly changing. But changes have emerged, and how do such changes influence the struggle?

Two main themes immediately come to mind. The first is the condition of everyday life and human communication in an increasingly fast and complex "postmodern" global reality. What does the concept "audience" mean in a world where social and cultural relations of all types are in such tremendous, dynamic flux? The meaning of gender, social class, age, sexual orientation, and education, for instance, interact dynamically with language, religion, family, rituals, and a wide range of everyday habits and customs to play crucial, but less and less predictable, roles in the ways audiences experience contemporary media.

Second is communications technology. Does the concept of audience, which we usually think of in terms of large groups attending to relatively few media forms and channels, still apply when the range of delivery systems, content, and user options is expanding so rapidly? What we want to know is *how much power and freedom do media consumers have in the complex and ever-changing social, cultural, and technological landscape of the early twenty-first century?*

A useful distinction can be made between "old media" and "new media" environments (Webster and Phalen 1997). Overall, the old media environment "is characterized by limited channels of communication that deliver content on a fixed timetable of the media's choosing." Old media content is quite uniform, is relatively constant across channels and media, and is commonly received by nearly everyone. The new media environment, on the other hand, "is distinguished by unlimited channels of communication offering content on a timetable of the individual's choosing." New media content is much more diverse, is associated with specialty channels, especially on cable and direct satellite TV, and is less universally received (Webster and Phalen 1997: 100–1).

Denis McQuail refers to the influence of such media environments in any given place and time as the *media structure* (McQuail 1997). How media factors help structure audience experience applies to any city or country. There is no cross-cultural uniformity, however. Despite certain homogenizing influences of "global television," for instance, media systems in various countries around the world still differ significantly (Lull 1988; 1990). National media systems reflect policies concerning the number of channels available, the technical reach and quality, broadcast schedules, policies on imported programming, and cultural values and priorities. British broadcasting, for example, was founded on a policy of limited domestic channels and public service. The same thinking was applied quite strictly in the Nordic countries, in most of Europe, and in many other countries around the world. The American commercial broadcasting system is unique in its relative lack of such social planning and regulation, and is much criticized globally for what is perceived as an attractive, but unhealthy, diet of programs. So, from the start we can see that "active audience" members are subject to varying media environments which help structure their experiences with media.

Audience activity therefore is not an open field, but operates within the confines of certain historical conditions. This dynamic relationship between media structure and the "active audience" brings us back again to the theoretical framework of "structuration" introduced in chapter 1. Webster and Phalen in fact conclude that "the mass audience concept, with its ability to accommodate notions of activity (such as individuals choosing preferred content), while still recognizing the power of structural factors to determine exposure [may provide a way to reason through the structuration quandary]" (Webster and Phalen 1997: 134).

Fragmentation and segmentation

Without question a general trend around the world today is a rapid expansion in the number of media channels, especially television, that are available to potential audience members. Not only is the total number of over-the-air broadcasting outlets becoming significantly greater worldwide, but cable and satellite communications systems are constantly being developed in new locations and vastly expanded where they are already established. More channels means more diverse content. More diverse content means more viewer options. More options means that the audience will divide into narrower and narrower viewing groups, based on differences in their preferences, for at least some of their viewing.

I've been describing fragmentation with special reference to television, but this trend applies to all forms of mediated communication including the Internet. Today's symbolic environment features many more technological options and content choices than ever before. The explosion in human migration patterns, together with the transnationalization of symbolic forms – programs, genres, styles, and stars – and the interactive qualities of many new media all help further divide the overall audience into niches. Such developments require that the niches become financially successful; there must be a demand for specialized programming, and program suppliers must be able to deliver the content. When advertisers and media executives conceptualize audiences as niche markets, they are thinking in terms of market "segmentation" or "hyper-segmentation" (Turow 1997). Driven by the potential for making lots of money, advertisers and media respond to the increasingly specific particular preferences of their audiences by providing content that satisfies those diverse interests.

Thinking this way, we could argue that the media give the people what they want in a kind of consumer-driven "marketplace democracy." But as the American communication researcher Joseph Turow argues, dividing up the audience according to typical demographic, taste, or lifestyle clusters is not the only way to conceptualize groups of people. The categories created by the advertising and media industries reflect a pure marketing logic. Turow points out, for instance, that "a television program could be geared toward 'those who went to Catholic schools' or 'those whose parents migrated from Eastern Europe' or 'those who somehow feel part of the Old South'." But, he says, these ways of grouping people don't appeal to advertisers or media executives because they don't "relate in any predictable way to the purchase of products" (Turow 1997: 200).

Dividing up the "mass audience" for profit can be traced in the United States to 1960s when advertisers started paying close attention to modern demographic categories and market segmentation. Even the revolutionary youth audience of the 1960s, embroiled in political and culture debates with their establishment elders, to some extent was created by advertising agencies who were trying desperately to appeal to the enormous baby-boom generation as an audience segment. By pitting youth against parents, advertisers tried to make certain products attractive to the lucrative youth market. The soft drink industry provides two good examples of what happened. Pepsi-Cola became the cola for the "Pepsi Generation" (later, "Generation Next"), and Seven-Up was marketed with psychedelic imagery as the "Un-Cola," in an effort to artificially separate beverage preferences, cultivate loyalties, and maximize profits according to different generational values (Frank 1998).

The advertising industries' attempts to compartmentalize the mass market depended on their ability to associate products with desirable demographic and lifestyle groups – what are called "quality audiences." In the United States this kind of industry research focused on "psychographic" and "lifestyle" clusters. Because marketplace competition was increasing, advertisers and media programmers determined that they needed to target their appeals and programs more and more specifically to audience subgroups that are large enough to produce significant ratings and revenues. The industries tried to identify who was available, what their values were, and how they lived. By tailoring ads, promotions, and programs to various lifestyle groups, the media attempted to enter, interact with, and influence the everyday lives of audiences by reinforcing and further conditioning certain lifestyles and patterns of consumption. In general, media preferences and the conditions and styles of everyday life resonate with each other: "media practices to a great extent attain their meanings in relation to, and together with, other practices. They are components in everyday life segments," according to communications researcher Bo Reimer, who has studied how media habits and lifestyles of audiences interact in Sweden (Reimer 1994: 207). Thus media researchers identify lifestyle groups by analyzing combinations of factors including audience members' age, education, gender, income, and living conditions (city, town, country), with their interests in leisure-time activities such as sports, gardening, reading, going to a dance club, and so on.

Polarization

We shall now raise the possibility that such *media audience fragmentation leads to fewer common experiences for any society, resulting in a harmful loss of commonality, and the creation of possible social polarization.* We continue with the example of Sweden in order to briefly explore this important possible consequence of media audience activity. Sweden and the other Nordic countries have only recently developed commercial and private television. Viewers can now tune in an abundance of cable and satellite channels. As a result, people have become far more selective in their viewing. Bo Reimer points out that audiences then "tend to watch more of their favorite genres, and less of other genres" (Reimer 1994: 205). For instance, one type of television program watched less by the overall population now is news, which "used to be a national genre [but] has become more a class-based genre now, related to 'high-brow' viewing patterns" (Reimer 1994: 205).[4]

What Bo Reimer observes in Sweden is symptomatic of a global tendency. As technology becomes more consumer-oriented and responsive to individual users, as content becomes more diverse, and as audiences become more fragmented, there will be systemic consequences. For one thing, traditional programming designed for large, anonymous, heterogeneous audiences gradually loses its dominance in the media system. This occurs whether it's the news on state television in Sweden or England, propaganda-driven news and entertainment on the Chinese television system, or prime-time situation comedies on the national commercial television networks in the United States. Not so many years ago the former "Big Three" American TV networks (ABC, CBS, NBC) almost totally dominated national viewing. But audience shares claimed by these networks fell from 90 percent in the 1960s to 45 percent by 1999. Some popular culture commentators believe that *Seinfeld* was the last blockbuster, mass-appeal, prime-time program that will ever appear on the American commercial television system.[5] Tremendous competition for audiences now comes from cable and satellite program services, VCRs, the Internet, and pay-per-view movies, sports, and specials. Even regular programming on the commercial TV networks now is more oriented toward particular audience segments. The rhythm of viewing has changed too. People used to watch entire programs, and sometimes spent an entire evening with one network channel. Now audiences use remote control devices to surf, graze, zip, and zap through their hyperactive viewing sessions.

As the number of viewing options expands, people who share geographic territory or nationality are less likely to attend to the same information or entertainment media forms and content. People view TV more privately and independently in a world of technological abundance and expanded cultural offerings. Rather than share common media experiences as any kind of symbolically united "mass audience," people occupy niches related to their various cultural orientations, lifestyles, languages, genders, ethnicities, sexual orientations, and technological literacies. Linguistic and ethnically based niche audiences are composed of "unusually loyal audiences who also consciously avoid other types of media content" (Webster and Phalen 1997: 110). Ironically, then, as the mediated "marketplace of ideas" becomes more robust, one strong tendency is for audiences to become more narrowly circumscribed by personal and cultural preference. While media events like major news stories, sporting championships, and political scandals continue to draw huge general audiences, more routine media content and experiences are becoming less and less commonly shared. It is a rather scary thought that what people today share most widely as television viewers is a shortlist of extremely famous personalities such as Michael Jordan, the late Princess Diana, Bart Simpson, and Monica Lewinsky.

The same tendency for any heterogeneous population to divide into fragmented, "niche" audiences for mass media appears in Internet-based communication too. Specialty or "vertical" portals and websites geared toward Hispanic, black, and Asian groups in the United States, for instance, are becoming very popular and profitable ventures.

The fragmentation and privatization of media and Internet experience may, in many respects, empower individual viewers because it gives them more of what they want. But from a societal standpoint, this contemporary phenomenon may be quite problematic. The tendencies of advertisers to create niche channels and sites, and for audience members to seek specialized content, "pushes groups away from one another rather than encouraging them to learn about the strengths of coming together to share experiences and discuss issues from different viewpoints" (Turow 1997: 199–200). Such differentiation may lead to greater "individualism, self-interest, impersonality, uncertainty, and flux than in the past," according to Denis McQuail (1997: 135), who also argues that while the balance of power between media institutions and media consumers seems on the face of it to be tipping more and more in favor of consumers, "there is no longer any mechanism for exercising this new-found power on the 'collective' behalf. The audience seems to have been transformed into a disparate set of consumers with no expressed common interest or institutionalized presence" (McQuail 1997: 134). And Joseph Turow, author of *Breaking Up America*, concludes his book with an even more ominous prediction: "Like heavy gates separating one community from another, the very structure of the (fragmented) American media world will drive people apart for a long time to come" (Turow 1997: 200).

These fears, it must be said, reflect a distinct bias emanating from relatively developed Western societies whose market structures have been operating for considerable time. Dividing up the market and threatening social unity in the process presume the prior existence of a large middle class of potential consumers, as well as a relatively well-functioning society. But in whose interest is it to maintain the social status quo? As the television audience began to fragment in the United States, Robert Johnson, chief executive officer of Black Entertainment Television (BET), a cable channel, told American media:

> People are a little bit more separate in their racial interaction now than they were in the 1970s and 1980s. People are identifying more with their own culture and ethnicity and feeling comfortable about doing so, without the pressure to integrate or amalgamate cultures. That's not necessarily a bad thing. (*Washington Post*, November 30, 1994)

And what about the world's less rich, developed, and unified countries? Do the same assumptions apply? Are these countries being carved up and polarized too?

This thorny issue is approached directly by the Mexican anthropologist Néstor García Canclini in a book whose title translates revealingly as *Consumers and Citizens* (García Canclini 1995). In the case of Mexico, *the market may do more to bring people together than tear them apart, at least in the short term.* Mexican people have been mightily disillusioned with their corrupt and inefficient state bureaucracies, their oppressive dominant political party (PRI), even the labor unions. They turn now to communications media, popular culture, and consumer goods for the attention, comfort, inspiration, and hope they can't get from civil institutions. García Canclini by no means endorses the market as the ultimate solution to such social problems; instead he recognizes the current widespread trend toward privatization of state industries and media, and the glittering attractiveness of the market in general, as a tendency that may offer some hope not only for individual consumers, but for Mexican society as a whole. Such hopes must not be cast to the wind, however. García Canclini offers a plan for development of Mexican and Latin America media and popular culture that responds to national and regional characteristics and interests because, he argues, the sources of international popular culture will otherwise move in even more strongly to respond to the people's demands for more and better information and entertainment.

Conclusion

Media sage Denis McQuail, whom we have quoted often in this chapter, reminds us that "the term *audience* has an abstract and debatable character, much as with other apparently simple concepts in the social sciences such as society or public opinion" (McQuail 1997: 77). Our discussions in this chapter have shown why the term "audience" is in fact so abstract and debatable. We began by interrogating the very concept of audience and its history, from direct effects to limited effects and the "active audience." We briefly reviewed uses and gratifications research, and offered an extended model based on "methods."

We then examined the connection between mass audience and mass society by exploring how media propaganda contributed to the rise of fascism in Europe in the first half of the twentieth century. Our case study of the People's Republic of China revealed that collective audience behavior need not be so destructive. Finally, we described how modern media audiences have become fragmented overall, and segmented into lifestyle groups. We ended the chapter by speculating on how changes in media technology and audience activity may polarize people culturally, at least in modern, Western societies.

Audience members' everyday experiences with media are first and foremost cultural experiences, but, like the concept of audience, culture is becoming increasingly abstract and debatable too, as we are about to find out.

6

Culture

Culture became an extremely fashionable buzzword inside and outside the academic world in the late twentieth century. Representatives of many different academic disciplines were laying claim to the term. Anthropology, of course, was founded on the integrity and usefulness of cultural analysis, and anthropologists sometimes make territorial claims to culture mainly on the basis of the discipline's long-term involvement with the concept.[1] British "cultural studies" became a separate academic discipline in the latter part of the past century, with American, Australian, and other regional and national varieties following close behind. American universities developed courses across a wide range of disciplines with titles such as intercultural communication, communication and culture, media and culture, culture and the arts, communication and world cultures, the sociology of culture, organizational culture, and cross-cultural psychology, among many, many others. The alert reader may have noticed that even *this* book uses the term culture in the title. Non-academic bookstores continue to stock volumes about culture too, from politically-motivated discussions of "culture wars" and multiculturalism to treatises on digital culture and ethnic cookbooks.

Ironically, at the very time culture was peaking in popularity, many scholars were arguing that the concept had outlived its usefulness. Because culture is used so broadly and easily now, some observers think the term simply no longer retains the degree of referential specificity that is required to make it analytically meaningful. For example, while culture traditionally has referred to human communities who occupy the same geographic territory, speak the same language, worship the same deity, and behave similarly across the spectrum of everyday activities, things are quite different today. In many ways the idea of "nation" as a geopolitical entity no longer works very well as a synonym for culture, however, because people who live inside any political state today represent an increasing variety of ethnic groups and lifestyle choices, and everybody now draws from a sprawling array of transnational cultural symbols and styles. Even those nation-states which are based on religion have not been able to avoid this global cultural trend.[2]

The symbolic and mediated nature of contemporary cultures, together with the unprecedented movement of human beings from one part of the world to another, have fractured the traditional pillars of culture. It has become more and more misleading to stereotype or "essentialize" people culturally. A fourth-generation British teenager with Asian features is not Chinese or Indian or Pakistani the way her great-grandparents were. In many respects culture is a far more complex, personalized matter today. Our objective in this chapter, then, is to begin to come to grips with what we mean by "culture," a project that will endure until the very last sentence of this book.

Years ago Raymond Williams (1962) succinctly defined culture as "a particular way of life" that is shared by a community and shaped by values, traditions, beliefs, material objects, and territory. From this perspective, culture is a complex and dynamic ecology of people, things, world views, rituals, daily activities, and settings. It's how we talk and dress, the food we eat and how we prepare and consume it, the gods we invent and the ways we worship them, how we divide up time and space, our sense of humor, how we dance, the way we work and play, how we make love, the values to which we socialize our children, and all the other many details that make up *everyday life*. Understood this way, culture is "our way of doing things" and it reveals "who we are" as well as "who we are not." Culture makes available the frames through which we know ourselves and others, providing coherence for cultural members while marking differences between groups.

Culture flows back and forth through the domains of collective consciousness, subconsciousness, memory, and social practice. It exists abstractly as a group's customs, mores, traditions, values, and institutionalized ideas, but it also takes form in how such abstractions materialize in routine social interaction. The meaning of culture emerges precisely in the dynamic nexus between abstraction and practice, between the pervasive and enduring mental structures of deep culture and the less entrenched surfaces of everyday life.

Though people and groups often regard their ways of life as superior or inferior to others, from a scholarly point of view culture as "everyday life" implies that everybody has culture, no culture is inherently superior to any other, and cultural richness by no means derives from economic standing only.

This perspective differs significantly from the "classical conception," for example, where culture is interchangeable with "civilization" or "high culture" (Thompson 1990). In the classical sense, culture is bestowed on some at birth, earned by others through some meritorious activity like completing higher education, or gained by making a pile of money or marrying into the right family. The classical definition refers to culture as a standard of intellectual and spiritual excellence, and discriminates between "cultured" and "uncultured" persons. We still frequently see the term used in this elitist fashion. A recent newspaper advertisement in California, for example, encouraged people to watch the public television channel, rather than the commercial stations, in order to "get a little culture." American Express offers its members a "culture pass" that admits them to museums, art galleries, and opera houses at reduced prices. In romance languages, to be "cultured" (*culto*) is to be well educated and well mannered. British Commonwealth citizens have no difficulty recognizing this discriminatory meaning of culture. Paul Willis (1990) stirred quite a bit of controversy in England when he made a policy recommendation to cultural authorities advocating recognition and financial support for the "common culture." Willis proposed that the ways of living, aesthetics, and cultural products of working-class youth should be given attention equal to that paid to the high-culture art forms and upper-class ideologies and lifestyles that British national cultural policy traditionally supports. He cites official statistics that clearly show how much more interest most people have in popular music, movies, television, and pub life, for example, than in "fine arts" like opera, theater, and ballet. Culture as "common" and as "everyday life" are steadfastly democratic ideas that disrupt any pretensions of cultural uniformity or superiority.

To speak of culture is, in many respects, to refer to rather stable biological, material, social, and spiritual forms that surround and influence us from birth. For a variety of reasons, most people tend not to stray far from "blood and belief, faith and family" (Huntington 1996: 126). We inherit language, nationality, religion, social class, family, and various habits composing everyday life such as the types of food we consume, and our basic patterns of verbal and nonverbal communication. As John B. Thompson points out, pre-existing cultural themes circulate in communicative activity, which then reinforce culture: "culture is the pattern of meanings embedded in symbolic forms, including actions, utterances and meaningful objects of various kinds, by virtue of which individuals communicate with one another and share their experiences, conceptions, and beliefs" (Thompson 1990: 132). We are born into expected ways of being, and into worlds of unique odors, sounds, sights, tastes, and other sensations. This is the "look and feel" of culture, which is related intimately to nature, emotion, and the human body. Culture may be essentially a social concept, but it is taken very personally. Culture is a medium that connects individual persons and small groups to larger communities through shared values, experience, and modes of expression.

Culture fuses places, persons, and styles of everyday life. The Mexican concept *del pueblo* is an excellent example of this. The *pueblo* in Mexico is the geographical place where men, women, and children live as a community, but it also refers to the people who reside there and how they live: place, people, style of life. To be *del pueblo*, thus, is to be *of* a cultural space, not just *from* a populated stop along the road.

What I have been describing so far are the *non-volitional* elements of culture – features of life over which we originally have little control and whose influence can never be completely extinguished, no matter how hard we may try later in life.

But culture is never a completely given or permanent state of affairs – not for collectivities, and not for individuals. We don't just inherit culture; we also invent, change, and transcend it. As we construct the material and discursive features of culture, we simultaneously construct ourselves and our social groups. This is particularly true today because cultural forms have become more and more symbolic, mediated, synthetic, and mobile, making certain cultural elements – especially those related to consumption and style – far more provisional and transitory than ever before. Furthermore, culture can no longer be considered a singular, unified social force. Groups and individuals today have polycultural profiles; "culture is not something that people inherit as an undifferentiated block of knowledge from their ancestors. Culture is a set of ideas, reactions, and expectations that is constantly changing as people and groups themselves change" (Watson 1997: 8).

The dynamic elements over which we exercise considerable control are the *volitional* aspects of culture. Human communication – the meaningful symbolic exchanges that constitute social interaction – is the means by which such changes take place.

Thinking about culture as communicative activity nicely blends the enduring aspects with the more dynamic, mediated elements. The meanings of ancestry, religion, tradition, language, marriage, family, work, leisure, neighborhood, social institutions, and so on are perpetually reproduced and modified through symbolic interaction. So is the way such elements are talked about and valued. Culture is not just things, values, and ways of being, but *how such things, values, and ways of being are interpreted and brought to conscious awareness through routine communication and social practice.* In this sense, culture is above all else *discursive*; culture has become "a general term for the sea of discourses and regimes of signification through which we constitute lived experience" (Chaney 1994: 191). Culture therefore functions simultaneously as *source* and *resource* because it provides "available meanings" that greatly influence "what can be expressed" by cultural members in order to fashion distinctive habits, skills, styles, and social strategies (Chaney 1994: 32).

Now more than ever before, constructing and organizing everyday life is highly complex, interpretative, symbolic activity. The particular ways of life and patterns of thought we encounter, and the lifestyles, identities, and social strategies we devise nowadays, are composed of an expansive and diverse pool of symbolic resources of cultural significance. The flood of symbolic imagery ushered in by telecommunications and information technology in the late twentieth century, and the extraordinary degree of global human mobility in effect during the same time period, have led to radical changes worldwide not only in the cultural syntheses people make, but in how they make them. Traditional resources ranging from food, language, and religion are combined with contemporary forms such as TV programs, sports teams and heroes, popular music, and websites to form the cultural styles and repertoires of groups and individuals.

If culture is something people continue to reproduce, adapt, and invent it must be useful. What purposes does culture serve for individuals and groups?

First and foremost is cognitive and social *stability*. Culture is a proven and powerful way we organize ourselves as individuals and as members of groups to create meaning, order, and safety. Culture "works on a number of levels and through a number of forms to give a structure of predictability to the practice of community life" (Chaney 1994: 139). In an increasingly individualistic and hedonistic world, culture remains fundamentally *relational*. The relational, communal quality of culture is what produces stability. Cultures are the frameworks through which we interpret ourselves and others. Cultures provide the matrices through which interpersonal knowledge is generated, giving coherence and consistency to our meaning systems and inspiring a sense of well-being. Culture organizes the way we distinguish between the known and the unknown, between friends and enemies, between the boring and the exciting. It guides relations with kin and with nature. Culture provides the grounds upon which we form our personal and collective identities, and facilitates a sense of belonging to wider social communities. Founded on a premise of sociality as a human requirement, culture also gives us opportunities to express individuality and personal style.

Cognitive and social stability can be constructed culturally in many different ways. For example, one person may choose to explore and combine a wide range of cultural elements and styles into an idiosyncratic synthesis – a *bricolage* of cultural significance that is subject to frequent review and modification. Imagine, for instance, a young Filipino-American man who attends a private, mainly white university, prefers rap and salsa music, is gay, and has just converted from Catholicism to Buddhism. Such a cultural synthesis – a highly personalized "way of being" – can inspire stability for certain persons. Other people, however, may find greater cognitive, emotional, and social comfort by retreating into more familiar, communal, conventional, rule-governed traditions, rituals, and social activities that are often based on religion, ethnicity, or nation, for example. The latter part of the twentieth century brought with it the "religious revolution," "multiculturalism," "nationalism," and "balkanization," which all exemplify this kind of cultural thinking.

The very label "culture" has symbolic power. People fear the loss of their culture. To invoke the term is to recognize, and give coherence and integrity, to a "way of life." This is what is generally meant by *cultural identity*. Ethnic groups who feel outside or unwanted by the "dominant culture" in any geographic locale are especially likely to cling tightly to their traditional culture, or invent new hybrids and subcultures. In the United States, the attention given to diverse cultures composed of "people of color" discomforts some mainstream, white Americans who notice that everybody but them seems to have the right to celebrate their ethnicity and culture. Of course the very foundation of mainstream North American life, especially the legal code, largely reflects "white" culture. Americans "celebrate" mainstream culture every day just by living it. But precisely because it has become so domestic and familiar, "white culture" hardly seems conspicuous or interesting to many people (unless, of course, you feel excluded or marginalized by it). In England, the punk movement of the 1970s has been described as an attempt by poor and working-class kids to create "white ethnicity" in an era when Jamaicans,

Indians, Chinese, Pakistanis, and others "of color" began to appear in great numbers and threaten the socioeconomic-cultural foundations of the United Kingdom (Hebdige 1979). Ethnic groups of all colors sometimes coalesce into modern-day "tribes," which provide solidarity for their members, but can also provoke "village racism and ostracism" as gangs or clans (Maffesoli 1996: 97).

Photo 6.1 Cultural identity. European American high-school girls found it difficult to determine what typical food could represent their ethnicity on "multicultural day" at school. They settled on pasta (*San José Mercury News* – Jim Gensheimer)

Ideology and culture

Culture is *redundant*. By "redundant," I mean that the clarity and force of culture derive from the extreme repetitiveness of everyday behavior. Cultural redundancy produces and reproduces *meanings* which form the bases of coordinated social interaction. As the Swedish anthropologist Ulf Hannerz has argued, "meanings develop and survive . . . through the redundancy of social life . . . societies and cultures emerge and cohere as results of the accumulation and aggregation of these [redundant] activities" (Hannerz 1992: 127, 15; insert mine). The American cultural studies theorist John Fiske calls culture "the production of continuities across domains of experience" (Fiske 1994: 194). Redundancies of thought and action across domains of experience, accumulated and aggregated over time, are perceived by members and non-members as meaningful cultural *patterns*. The patterns promote the interests of some social groups over others, which means that the patterns have profound ideological implications. Culture "generates meanings for ordinary experience; these meanings are ideological in that they serve to sustain forms of socially structured inequality" (Chaney 1994: 43). The purveyors of ideology depend on culture because ideology can only be effective when ideas circulate socially with great reach and repetition, a process which unfolds in the routine interactions of everyday life (see chapters 2 and 3).

Because culture is entangled with struggles over meaning and social power, it is ideological. Culture narrows down choices and prescribes behavior through formal and informal social rules (chapter 4). Ulf Hannerz's writing is concerned with just such crucial processes. He stresses three interrelated "dimensions" of culture. Hannerz says culture is (1) "ideas and modes of thought" that are (2) "made public" to the self and others through various "forms of externalization," including the mass media. This subsequently leads to (3) "social distribution – the ways in which the collective cultural inventory of meanings and meaningful external forms are spread over a population and its social relationships" (Hannerz 1992: 7). Ideas and modes of thought enter the public domain as cultural discourses, and then influence real human beings who live in unequal social worlds. Cultural analysis, then, cannot proceed as if everyone in a cultural community participates on equal footing. Hannerz points out that this disparity means that good cultural analysis always also requires a good sociology (Hannerz 1992: 10).

The *structural conception of culture* advanced by John B. Thompson echoes the same concern coming from the sociological side. Thompson argues that while culture has become more and more symbolic and interpretative in the era of mass communication, all symbolic forms exist in socially structured contexts which reflect, legitimate, and help reproduce relations of power and conflict (Thompson 1990). Cultural themes can be found in the way symbolic forms represent life, and in the contexts where such forms are interpreted and circulated socially. Cultural analysts therefore should "study symbolic forms in relation to the historically specific and socially structured contexts and processes within which, and by the means of which, these symbolic forms are produced, transmitted, and received" (Thompson 1990: 136).

But while culture *is* far-reaching, redundant, and ideological, it is not the sum of ideology itself, nor is culture simply a product of ideology. Ideology lives in culture, but *culture is more than ideology*. Our cultural lives, our human capacity for independent thought and creativity, our penchant for resistance, growth, and transcendence, embody much more potential than the reproduction or modification of patterns passed down from elites to everyone else in some determining process of social domination.

Emotion and culture

Common emotion causes us to recognize ourselves in communion with others.

Maffesoli 1996: 26

Culture is by no means influenced solely by the orderly domains of human cognition and rationality. Emotion, passion, fear, pleasure, and pain are foundational elements of culture too. These "structures of feeling," as Raymond Williams (1977) called them, saturate everyday life and are expressed by cultural members in routine communication. They are crucial to the construction of personal and collective meanings and identities. People don't just ask themselves, "Who am I?" or "Who are we?" They also want to know, "How do I feel?"

The sentiments that people share and communicate with each other form the emotional contours and structures of culture. They are the subjective conditions around which social life is organized and expressed. Such cultural domains include religion and spirituality, family and friendship, sex and romance, social festivals and rituals, as well as creative arts such as music, dance, literature, theater, fashion, painting, comedy, photography, and poetry.

Cultures differ in the way emotion is experienced and expressed. The term "Brazilian happiness" (*alegria Brasilera*), for example, refers explicitly and positively to the emotional orientation of people who live in the huge South American country. Many of these persons are objectively poor, but find real subjective happiness in the belief that they are lucky or "blessed" to live in such a beautiful place. These sentiments are commonly expressed in Brazilian popular culture, such as the odes to nature, life, and bodily pleasures found in the lyrics and melodies of the classic samba music of Jorge Ben and others. The emotional sides of culture can also be repressed. Wang Yi points out that in the official cultural development of the People's Republic of China, "feelings and passions" have long been ignored in discourses of Chinese culture and ideology. Recently, however, feelings and passions have been emphasized by the Chinese Communist Party – mainly through mass media entertainment – to connect emotionally with the people in order to maintain political control (Yi 1997).

Although some cultural groups express their emotions more openly than others, every person and group is motivated by the "feeling edge of culture," in the words of the American psychologist Edward Stewart (2000; see also Neiva 2000). Stewart and Neiva argue that the original development of cultures worldwide was based on physical and emotional vulnerability nested in fear. They say the reason primordial cultures formed as social groups was to protect themselves from environmental threats – to become "predators" instead of "prey."

Despite what may appear to be the obvious importance of emotion, it has not been theorized well in scholarly discussions of culture and society. Culture is by no means simply a detached, logical system of values and patterns of human behavior. The "cultural spheres" of life in many ways are worlds away from the "public sphere" of ideology, politics, and economics (Habermas 1989). Culture and emotion are certainly no less important than ideology and cognition as keys to understanding how, why, and in what ways we construct and interpret our "lifeworlds" and communities.

This is particularly true in the brave new world of twenty-first century media, communication, and culture. Passion, emotion, and sensation resonate sensually and link up smoothly with the richly symbolic, mobile qualities of postmodern cultures and peoples, deterritorialized as they are in time, space, and place, in search of signs of feeling, willing participants in a sensorium of electronic and virtual realities (see chapter 10). The "rationalized social" of modernity is being replaced by an "empathetic sociality, which is expressed by a succession of ambiances, feelings, and emotions" (Maffesoli 1996: 11) and given wide circulation by high technology. Riding the emotional tidal wave, a global pleasure principle is now in full force, with commerce and media influencing culture and community on an international scale today like never before.

Language and culture

> Culture is a conceptual system whose surface appears in the words of people's language.
>
> *Agar 1994: 79*

Anyone who speaks more than one language understands very well that language is much more than words. As the American anthropologist Michael Agar points out above, language is one surface of a deep and complex *system of concepts* we call culture. We cannot separate language from culture; they are intimately connected through meaning. Though language may be one surface of culture, personal interpretations and uses of language are by no means superficial; the most profound meanings are fashioned through language. We learn who "we" are, and who "they" are, largely through language. Agar defines culture as "something you make up to fill in the spaces between them and you" (Agar 1994: 128). Language is about differences in the way people live.

Cultural participation requires the observation, perception, interpretation, and learning of symbol systems. We come to know our cultures, and the cultures of others, through sensory perception of the self and the world (Stewart and Bennett 1991). Language is primary among the symbol systems of cultural representation that we encounter through our senses. As a symbol system, language is expressed and perceived primarily as an *audio code* (we first learn languages by hearing and repeating sounds and vocal inflections) and later, for literate peoples, as a *visual code* (through reading and writing). Other visual codes also help compose culture. Nonverbal gestures, facial expressions, spatial relationships, colors, art, and natural signs and symbols, for example, are all interpreted as visual code systems. Beginning in the mid-nineteenth century, an expansive new world of *mediated visual modes and codes* began to open up. Photography, film, television, video, and computer graphics all have their own modalities and codes which require special literacies. Mastering the various modes and codes of communication is how one becomes part of culture.

Language has boundaries and consistencies in its semantic elements and syntactic relationships; that's how we recognize and use languages to coordinate social activity. But these boundaries and consistencies are soft. Ultimately language is limitless. People play with language. They style it. Abuse it. Invent it. Give it accents. Sing it. So while language does indeed structure communication and consciousness, and serve as a glue that holds cultures together by providing common fields of meaning, it does not determine thought or behavior. Like all symbolic forms, language is a resource for the social construction and deconstruction of culture.

Let's examine one situation in which a struggle over language and culture played out in a national forum and became embroiled in political debates, policy disagreements, and charges of racism.

Box 6.1 Ebonics: A Link Between Language and Culture

"She BIN had dat 'han-made dress" (She's had that hand made dress for a long time, and she still does)

"Ah 'on know what homey be doin" (I don' know what my friend is usually doing)

"Can't nobody tink de way he do" (Nobody can think the way he does). (John R. Rickford 2000: www.stanford.edu/~Rickford/ebonics/ EbonicsExamples. html)

The Oakland, California, school board touched off a national debate in the late 1990s when it recommended that secondary schools in the area begin to teach children African-American Vernacular English, or *ebonics* (some examples of which you see above). Ebonics is a term for what many young, urban, black people speak. Some call it a language; others say it is a dialect of standard English. The argument in favor of ebonics made by the educational policy makers in California is that inner-city black children are systematically and unfairly disrespected by their teachers and administrators, and some of their fellow students, for the way they speak. This linguistic discrimination makes them feel inferior intellectually and culturally, and inhibits their learning. Ebonics, according to its supporters, can be a bridge. They claim it is not a lesser way to communicate verbally, just a different way. If teachers recognize and support ebonics by giving it a legitimate place in the curriculum, the argument goes, inner-city children will be more comfortable and able to learn standard English because they will feel respected for their "native" way of speaking and being.

The term "ebonics" is itself a play on standard English, as the word appears in no dictionaries. Ebonics fuses "ebony" (black) with "phonics" (the sounds of speech). It is a contemporary way to refer to "black speech" or "black dialect," a phenomenon which linguists have studied for years. Ebonics has its own rules and systems, so an argument can be made for its legitimacy as something more than "street slang." It is an oral, not written, form.

Ebonics may fail in the classroom, but it passes with honors where young people congregate, physically and symbolically. Ebonics mixes with other cultural elements — haircuts, body language, attitude —

to create an overall urban black style that is not only represented, but glamorized, by the mass media. Hip hop is the best example of the cultural mix. Popular music, contemporary hits and urban radio, music television, TV situation comedies, Hollywood films, advertising, mall culture, sports arenas and stadiums, and fast-food restaurants are among the venues where black English is used institutionally to create "cool" and make money.

But ebonics has not been cool in the classroom, at least not from most teachers' point of view. At the core of the ebonics debate have been the sensitive issues of culture, race, and class. Some linguists believe that ebonics can be traced to credible African languages and modes of expression. Others have argued that it is an American linguistic aberration. The famed black American economist and historian Thomas Sowell, whose work on race and culture we will look at closely in the next section of this chapter, suggests that the roots of ebonics are more in England and the United States than in Africa. He claims that ebonics is a contemporary version of the way uneducated white people talked in the American South; blacks learned it from them. Another view is that as lower-class blacks have become more and more isolated from mainstream society, they have simply developed their own systems and styles of communication and culture. Ebonics is a product of this social isolation.

Ebonics is ideological because it represents a deeper struggle related to race and social class. By speaking ebonics, young black people can refuse to participate and compete on the terms set by mainstream America – standard English and (northern European-derived) conventional culture. Ebonics is an alternative to the legitimizing function of standard language usage. It's perceived by many as an index to the inflection, history, and culture of black America. But, on the other hand, ebonics can also be used simply to excuse poor educational performance. In the midst of racial tensions and the furore over ebonics, research reported by the Associated Press in 1998 showed that some 86 percent of American blacks consider it "absolutely essential" that *all* children speak and write standard English, with "proper" pronunciation and grammar.

Whatever the position taken on the issue, the debate about ebonics is cultural. It represents one of the most evident and powerful "surfaces" of culture – language.

The struggle over ebonics pitted two forces against each other – conventional, standard English and a cultural (perceived as racial) adaptation of the language. The advocates of ebonics entered the debate on unequal terms. They had to fight against an official language that had been in place for years.

But English is no longer just the language of the United Kingdom and the United States. English has become the global language. As the British linguist David Crystal points out, nearly one-fourth of the *world's* population – some one and a half billion people – is now fluent or competent in English (Crystal 1997). How did this happen?

As Crystal explains, English began to spread all over the world because of Britain's vast colonial exploits in the seventeenth and eighteenth centuries which virtually installed the language in much of North America, Asia, Africa, and the South Pacific. The spread of English was backed up by Britain's superior naval and military forces, by the economic power it enjoyed as global leader of the industrial revolution in the eighteenth and nineteenth centuries, and by its position in that era as the world's great commercial trader. The United States of America continued to spread English throughout the world in the late nineteenth and twentieth centuries when it assumed superior transnational military and economic power.

Later, world systems of political, economic, and cultural management such as the United Nations, the International Telecommunications Union, the Organization of Petroleum Exporting Countries, and the International Civil Aviation Organization adopted English as the the common language in order to facilitate efficient and safe communication. It is generally agreed that the world needs a common language for certain purposes. That language is English, a fact that may change in the future, but not in our lifetime, and not without some radical, if gradual, realignment of world economic, political, and military influence.[3]

Culture "wars" are commonly fought. These wars often take shape in battles over language. The fierce debates over the "English only" principle in the United States, for instance, is a struggle familiar to Americans who live in areas with large Hispanic populations. Language battles are familiar all over the world. English competes with French in Canada, and with dozens of regional languages in India. Russian has contended with languages in all the European and Middle Eastern states of the former Soviet Union. Tribal languages compete with colonial languages in Africa. The cultural standoff between Mandarin and Cantonese in China may never be resolved.

When non-English-speaking first-generation immigrants are required to speak English at school or work, the apprehension they feel is not just about language and communication, but about culture. Even when a language is spoken with perfect clarity and skill, a slight foreign accent can raise questions for some about the speaker's intentions and loyalties. Furthermore, the language–culture relationship is not limited to vocabulary, grammar, and pronunciation. Institutions also try to regulate when people can speak, to whom, about what, and at what volume level. Bilingual and multilingual immigrants, however, do have one tremendous advantage. While the dominant language may make them feel uncomfortable or excluded in many settings, they can use their native language to gain certain advantages in many social situations. Indeed, linguistic "code switching" has become a common characteristic and desirable skill of life in postmodernity. Moreover, while the children of immigrants to the United States say they suffer discrimination because of their linguistic and cultural differences from the mainstream, they nonetheless greatly prefer English over their parents' languages.

The cultural impact of English is no longer made primarily by word of mouth. The United States developed the communications and entertainment industries – from the telegraph and telephone to satellite TV and computer software – which for more than 100 years have steadily spread English all over the world. The most recent and most influential technological development is the Internet, of course, where the vast majority of international/intercultural communication is carried out in English. Nothing in world history has accelerated the use of one language as much as the Internet. Originally, America Online, the world's largest Internet service provider, wouldn't even allow chat rooms to be conducted in any language other than English, "in order to insure that there is a comfortable community for all members."

The pervasive presence of English on a global scale has a host of ideological, political, and cultural meanings, not all of them favorable to the language or to the countries where it is spoken natively. To people outside the United Kingdom and the United States, English represents progress and modernity, but also dominance and dependence. English is colonialism, imperialism, militarism, First World, old world, modern world, postmodern world, BBC, Hollywood, McDonald's, rock and roll, Star Wars, Gulf Wars, Internet, Disney, CNN, Michael Jordan, Microsoft. The global ascent of a language signifies the global ascent of a culture, which implies a hierarchy of cultures, which, if you don't speak English natively, means that your culture is not on top in global terms. The consequences are conflictual.

Race and culture

The bottom line is we are African . . . we need to meditate on the messages
our ancestors are telling us.
Ji Jaga, formerly known as Geronimo Pratt, an ex-Black Panther recently freed
from jail, at the 1998 World African Unity Festival held in Compton, California

Do you see why I hate white people? Asians too.
Charles Barkely, African-American professional basketball player jokingly
responding to a white journalist during a post-game press conference

I was never a very threatening kind of black man.
Colin Powell, former possible USA presidential candidate
and retired chief of American military forces

Black Americans who thought O. J. Simpson was guilty of murder: 25%
White Americans who thought O. J. Simpson was guilty of murder: 75%
USA Today, October 9, 1995

The very words we use and the framework within which we think are
shaped by cultural patterns spread by force in centuries past.
Thomas Sowell, African-American historian, 1994: 62

That's just the way it is. Some things will never change.
Tupac Shakur, slain African-American rap artist, from Changes

Perhaps nothing pushes people's buttons as much as discussions
about race. The United States is quite the laboratory for studying
racial and cultural relations. The country is composed of an extremely complex mixture of peoples who almost all came from some
other place. Indeed, if we consider "native Americans" – the indigenous tribes who occupied mainland America prior to the arrival of
the Europeans in 1492 – to be the only people truly "of this place,"
then we are speaking of but about 1 percent of the present USA
population. Even the belief in the "indigenous" people as the original inhabitants of North America is itself now subject to considerable scientific controversy. It may be that Euro-Asian Caucasians
were physically present in North America long before the "native
Americans" appeared. The skull of a "Kennewick Man" found in
Washington state in 1996 long pre-dates and is physically unrelated
to "native" Americans (*Wall Street Journal*, January 8, 1999).[4] Subsequent recent archeological discoveries in Brazil, Chile, and several
eastern states in the United States have cast even more doubt on the
theory that Native Americans, who trace their roots to northern Asia,
are the original inhabitants of North America. Physically distinct

from Native Americans, the indigenous ancestors of the Western hemisphere may have immigrated from north central Europe, the Iberian Peninsula, or Southeast Asia.

Racial discussions in North America almost always revolve around the black–white issue. The government-appointed Kerner Commission in the late 1960s concluded that the United States was moving toward two societies – "one black, one white – separate and unequal." In 1998, a report from a similar commission – the Milton S. Eisenhower Foundation – said the Kerner report had come true thirty years later. Although more blacks have entered the middle class and been elected to political posts in the United States recently, wage inequality between rich and poor (the poor are disproportionately black) leaves a large proportion of the American black population behind. The causes of the socioeconomic gap and other racial problems in the United States are complex, and some think they are unsolvable. Some 55 percent of all Americans say "race will always be a problem," and half the black population believes "racial discrimination is a very serious problem," according to a 1997 Gallup poll. Young, well-educated, high-achieving blacks are the most pessimistic.

Consider these reasons for alarm: young black males go to prison in numbers that far outweigh any other racial group. Unemployment among blacks is higher than other racial groups. Blacks are far more likely than whites to be on government welfare. Blacks file many more complaints about discrimination in housing than any other group. Black youth now distance themselves from their previous stabilizing influences – family, church, and community – have become more isolated generally, and are more likely to commit suicide than ever before. One-third of black church members surveyed by the University of North Carolina believe that the AIDS virus was produced by the American government as genocide against African Americans. Another third think it "might" be true, leaving only a third who don't think so. Black sports coaches and other educators claim the rules and tests for college eligibility are biased against young men and women of African heritage, thereby limiting their opportunities in higher education. *New Yorker* magazine reports that in the late 1990s nearly 60 percent of American blacks believed things were steadily getting worse for them.

Yet at the same time, we see contradictory trends. The racial gap has blurred in many respects. Middle-class blacks are moving to the suburbs. Interracial dating and marriage between blacks and whites are way up. And, as we will explore at length in the next chapter, the black presence in American popular culture has climbed to astounding proportions, and is replete with extraordinary implications of cultural empowerment.

Culture and race are not the same thing, but they are often associated or confused with one another. This is understandable because, particularly in premodern times, characteristic ways of living reflected shared, relatively exclusive geographic territories traceable to racial origins. When we say, for example, "Chinese culture," we refer to an imagined people and way of life originating in race and geography. Europeans have long marked cultural differences according to geographic (national) boundaries. Today, however, racial and geopolitical definitions of culture, while they still strongly persist, are becoming far more complex and ambiguous.

The ability to isolate race as a genetically derived, distinct characteristic of a human being or social group is clouded by two scientific principles. First, racial purity cannot be claimed legitimately in any scientifically precise sense simply because of centuries of global genetic intermixing. The accelerated patterns of human migration and integration we observe in the world today only extend genetic mixing that pre-dates recorded history. Second, as the work of Italian population geneticists Luca Cavalli-Sforza, Paolo Menozzi, and Alberto Piazza (1996) concludes, the races are basically alike genetically anyway. Variation *within* racial groups is much greater than differences *between* groups, and no race is genetically superior to another. They argue that race is basically meaningless at the genetic level. Genetically speaking, then we are all much more alike than we are different.

Does this mean that there is no such thing as different races? In genetic terms, apparently so. Yet we still often hear expressions such as "racial discrimination," "racism," "race relations," and so on. This is because in the popular consciousness, physical signs such as skin color, eye color, hair color and texture, facial features, and body type continue to be perceived, categorized, evaluated, and judged as racial. And, of course, these signs *are* racial in the sense that some people have more African blood, or more Nordic blood, or more Japanese blood than other people and look different because of it, even if they are not "pure" African, Nordic, or Japanese.

Race is sometimes asserted as an index of legitimacy and authenticity by groups who hope to find political solutions to what they consider past racial discrimination. The "indigenous" Maoris' claim against white settlers in New Zealand for land rights, for example, and similar claims by "ethnic Hawaiins" on the island state are based on "blood quantum" to prove racially based qualifications for financial and other forms of legal compensation (Halualani *in press*).

The mixing of races through marriage and procreation is clearly one of the signal tendencies of world history at the dawn of the twenty-first century. This fact, however, has yet to be accommodated by many official agencies and institutions. The 2000 census in the United States, for example, had no "multiracial" category for respondents to select.[5] Government forms of all types force mixed-race people to choose one parent over the other – as in the case of the son or daughter of an African-American father and northern European mother having to choose "African American" or "black" as the self-identifying racial category. The reasons for this curious situation can be found in cultural history, one example of which we are about to consider.

Box 6.2 Culture mediates race: Brazil and the United States

There are only two qualities in the US racial pattern: white and black. A person is one or the other; there is no intermediate position. Although all Americans, white and black, grow up and accept without question that definition of a Negro, there is no logic in it. There is no reason why a person with half his ancestry white and half black should be defined as a Negro.

Degler 1971: 102

It's impossible to talk about Brazilian music without talking about variety, diversity. That's what Brazilian music is all about because it reflects our people. We are mixed people of different races and religions so it's very natural to create original things, different things, new things.

Famous contemporary Brazilian pop singer Marisa Monte interviewed by the San José Mercury News, 1997

While a person with just "one drop" of African blood may be considered "black" in the United States, a person of seven-eighths African heritage in Brazil would not, in most cases, be considered African or black, but *mulato*. A Brazilian with one "black" (African) parent and one "white" (European) parent would most likely be thought of as *moreno* (brown). But these are just the basic categories. Degler discusses the following racial distinctions made in parts of Brazil: *preto retinto* (dark black), *preto* (black), *cabra* (slightly less black), *cabo verde* (black, but with straight hair, thin lips, narrow and straight nose), *mulato escuro* (dark, but mixed race, African part obvious), *mulato claro* (lighter skin, mixed race, less African looking), *pardo* (light-skinned *mulato*), *sarara* (light skin, red or brown hair which is kinky or curled), *moreno* (light skin, straight hair, but not considered white), *branco de terra* (white, but with a trace of African features), and *branco* (white, of European ancestry, but also divided into blondes and brunettes by hair color). All this can become very confusing for a light-skinned, green-eyed, light-haired, "brown" Brazilian, for example, when he or she moves to the United States only to find that his or her "race" has suddenly changed!

Race, as we know, is genetically imprecise. Perceptions of race also vary widely. We can use the cultural contexts of Brazil and the United States to explore how culture mediates perceptions of race. Much of the analysis given below is drawn from the book *Neither Black nor White: Slavery and Race Relations in Brazil and the United States*, a Pulitzer prize-winning volume written by the American historian Carl Degler (1971).

The two major importers of African slaves to the Americas were colonial Brazil and the United States. Now, several generations after the abolition of slavery in both countries, the United States and Brazil have the largest populations of African descendants living outside Africa. What can be said about the descendants of African peoples living in these two countries today? How do they live and how are they are perceived?

While many cultural patterns originating centuries ago in Africa can be seen in the way the descendants of slaves live and are perceived in Brazil and in the United States today, significant differences have also been produced by the social history African people have had with the dominant national and regional cultures of the two countries. On the surface at least, African-Brazilians seem to get along much better with persons of other racial groups compared to African-Americans in the United States. For instance, I once watched a female African-Brazilian college student before my class there one evening lovingly stroke the hair of a blonde female colleague and commented that she "loved" the texture and color of the blonde's hair. I thought to myself, this interaction would not likely happen in the United States, not even in California. Such friendliness by African-Brazilians (a term *not* used in Brazil, by the way) is reciprocated by European-Brazilians (also not used). Groups of friends in Brazil nearly always make up a rainbow of skin colors.

Students and workers don't divide up by color and sit together in segregated groups in the cafeteria. There are no "black neighborhoods." Brazil may be "the most racially tolerant nation in the world" (Degler 1971: 96).

Photo 6.2 Racial tolerance in Brazil. National culture greatly influences race relations, as Daniela Mercury, one of Brazil's most popular singers, and her friend demonstrate

How did these different perceptions of race in the United States and in Brazil come about historically and culturally? Were African slaves treated much more harshly in the United States than in Brazil so that racial animosities in North America persist while they have faded in South America? That has been the conclusion of some scholars. Carl Degler, however, offers another well-documented explanation. To briefly summarize his very complex argument, discrimination between black and white, slave and free, was embedded in the legal codes of both Brazil and the United States from the beginning of the colonial period. But in Brazil such laws were abandoned or never strictly enforced. Legal definitions of who is racially African or "black" and who isn't were never precisely drawn in Brazil, so racial boundaries were never clearly constructed. In the

United States, on the other hand, "blood quantum" distinctions about what defines a "Negro" were much more plain, referring to anyone of African ancestry.

In Brazil, the Portuguese immigrants were males who arrived in South America single or without their wives. Conditions for open miscegenation were ripe. In the United States, most immigrants of the colonial period arrived as intact families. Sexual unions between Europeans and Africans in colonial North America were comparatively few and clandestine. Furthermore, the Portuguese immigrants to Brazil differed greatly in the sexual aspects of culture from their English and other northern European counterparts in the United States. Sexual autonomy for Portuguese males contrasts sharply with the restrictive Protestantism of the British and other northern groups: "Even in Brazil today . . . the family is still dominated by the father, who is in complete control and independent control of his own sexual activities; his wife simply ignores his mistress or extramarital escapades. He, in turn, is careful not to neglect the welfare of his family" (Degler 1971: 232).

Ideological differences between English and Portuguese articulated into colonial realities in other ways too. Most important may be the northern emphasis on individual rights and on the definition of freedom as an absolute cultural value. This created a clear and necessary social distinction between slavery and freedom in the United States. Portuguese culture, on the other hand, was (and remains) far more hierarchical, traditional, and Catholic, so that "no pretense was made that all men were free and equal; each man had his place in the social hierarchy, some high, some low, some in between. In such a scheme there was a place for white, black, brown; for free, half-free, and slave" (Degler 1971: 263).

Economics also played a crucial role in the differences. Although slavery was abolished in Brazil later than it was in the United States (1888 in Brazil, 1863 in the United States), the Brazilian economy in the latter half of the nineteenth century and the beginning of the twentieth provided greater economic opportunities for former slaves than were available to emancipated blacks in the United States. In stark comparison to the United States, Brazil was very sparsely populated overall when slavery was abolished, and the majority of people living in the country were either black or of mixed race. In the United States, blacks had to compete with whites for semi-skilled jobs in an overcrowded labor market. The former slave, thus, was often feared by whites in the United States, but not in Brazil.

Another crucial factor was the close relationship African slaves in Brazil maintained with Africa, compared to the lack of such ties on the part of slaves sent to the United States. Not only is Brazil much closer than the United States to Africa geographically, Brazilian blacks – slaves and free – maintained much closer economic and cultural ties to mother Africa. Many former Brazilian slaves moved back to Africa, and some even participated in the slave trade, which endured until nearly the twentieth century. Such an intercontinental connection was not maintained between North American blacks and Africa. One can see the legacy of this profound difference today, especially in the former slave-importing land of Bahia, where African food, religion, music, and many other cultural elements remain in place. Many Brazilians feel genuinely connected to, and drawn to, Africa today. Few blacks in North America hold such sentiments.

All these historical, cultural developments contribute to the divergent racial and cultural relations characteristic of Brazil and the United States. The way people are perceived racially is largely an artifact of economic, cultural, and geographical history, and greatly influences social perception today. Because Brazilians are categorized across a range of statuses related to physical characteristics and social class, the South American nation does not suffer the "us" versus "them" racial mentality operating in the United States – what Degler calls American's "compulsive concern with racial purity" (p. 189). In Brazil, the mixed-race person can take advantage of the "mulatto escape hatch," while the mixed-race person in the United States stays black. This difference between the racial politics of the two countries, however, should not be interpreted necessarily as more favorable for African descendants in Brazil. Because race has never been much of an issue in Brazil, racism often simply takes a less explicit form. Consequently, there has been little consciousness raising about racial problems per se, and very little political activity directed against problems of racial discrimination.

We all have brown eyes, brown hair, brown skin. Why are we killing each other?

> Mother of a 13-year-old Latina girl killed in
> gang violence in the San Francisco bay area

While not genetically viable in any absolute sense, race nonetheless does function in various discursive modes. In fact, "race" is a term that is frequently used when "culture" would actually be more correct. Race is a convenient physical index. The physical signs, however, can be very weak and misleading cultural indicators. We identify ourselves and others by observing patterned, characteristic ways of thinking and behaving, and we look for physical signs to guide our categorizations. Such acts of stereotyping at once function to help us make sense of the world and protect ourselves, but at the same time they can create unwarranted cultural conclusions. Africans from Somalia and from Nigeria may both be black, but they are very, very different culturally. Japanese and Vietnamese may share some physical resemblances, but they, too, differ greatly. Germans and French are classified as (mainly) white Europeans. Same for Norwegians and Italians. Argentinians and Guatemalans are Spanish-speaking Latinos, but manifest tremendous cultural differences.

Internal cultural patterns

If cultural patterns are not genetically or racially determined, where do they come from? In light of the evidence showing that genetics does little to explain human difference, then the logical conclusion is that people differ from each other culturally because of *environmental* factors that affect social groups. Given this, a central question is of the longevity of environmental influence. Are cultural patterns relatively short-term, or do they evolve over long periods of time? Do cultural groups think and act in characteristic ways mainly because of the situations they are in today, or are behavioral predispositions conditioned by environmental influences that span many generations? Answers to this question come from many places, and are often inspired by blatantly biased political motives. For example, those who argue that cultural patterns, especially among "underachieving" groups, are responses to repressive, local, relatively short-term conditions often believe that government or other institutional interventions can be applied to fix the problem. Affirmative action programs that accelerate access to jobs and education by lowering standards or establishing quotas for "underrepresented minorities" are a prime example of this.

Others argue that the cultural patterns of today developed long ago and have endured for centuries. The patterns are not determined, not hereditary, and not permanent, but they nonetheless last for generations, and stay relatively intact even when cultural members move from place to place geographically. This perspective is considered wrong or "politically incorrect" in many academic quarters, however, because while it dismisses genetic or racial explanations, it still recognizes that groups of people who are generally perceived along racial lines have extremely durable values and behaviors which may or may not serve them well in their reterritorialized environments.

The most convicing spokesperson for the "long-term" view is the black American historian Thomas Sowell, a senior fellow at the Hoover Institute of Stanford University. Sowell has travelled the world for years in order to study the complex and sensitive relationship between race and culture. He believes that cultural consistency and endurance can be explained largely by what he calls *internal cultural patterns*, which precede the immediate environment:

> Group cultural patterns may indeed be products of environments – but often of environments that existed on the other side of an ocean, in the lives of ancestors long forgotten, yet transmitted over the generations as distilled values, preferences and habits . . . Peoples whose skills and values have been shaped by different external factors in the past tend today to have different internal cultural patterns with which to confront the opportunities and challenges presented by the external conditions of the present. (Sowell 1994: x, 229)

Where do the internal cultural patterns come from? Sowell argues that crucial factors in cultural formation and continuity are related largely to the social consequences of geography. Cultures differ in part because of "the mere fact that different peoples and cultures have evolved in radically different geographical settings" (Sowell 1994: 13). Access to usable waterways, he says, may be most important. Efficient access for ocean-going vessels permits interchange with other cultural groups. In a discussion of the advantages that "coastal peoples" have had through the ages, Sowell points out that the waterways of the nations of black Africa have been particularly limiting: "Geography is not all-determining, but it can set the limits of human possibilities narrowly or widely. For much of sub-Saharan Africa, it has set those limits narrowly" (Sowell 1994: 237). China, as I pointed out in the last chapter, has suffered from a similar inward orientation.

Internal cultural patterns reside and persist in the deep recesses of the collective consciousness and the collective memory. They are not absolute or determining, and they do not pertain to the same degree to everyone in any cultural group. They are reinforced continually through the routines of everyday life. The patterns are very resistant to change, particularly, as Sowell points out, for groups that live relatively isolated from other cultural groups. Consider the case of the

Mixtec indigenous people from the high interior plateaus of the southern state of Oaxaca, Mexico. A United States religious charity recently built a medical clinic in Oaxaca to help the Mixtec fight their high level of serious illness and premature death. The modern clinic, its doctors and medicines were rejected by the Mixtec, however, who prefer to walk uphill, past the clinic, to a natural water spring where they pray for good health instead. The Mixtec believe that any sickness they develop is God's punishment for failing to carry out spiritual requirements, not what the North American doctors believe to be the preventable consequences of bad hygiene.

Does Sowell's notion of "internal cultural patterns" mean that cultural groups are forever inscribed into particular roles and statuses? Do the internal cultural patterns and their consequences change? Is there a permanent global cultural hierarchy? According to Sowell, "it is not necessary to claim that particular people or a particular culture is superior in all things or for all time. To the contrary, world leadership in science, technology, and organization has passed from one civilization to another over the centuries and millennia of world history" (Sowell 1994: 6). Sowell makes the striking observation, for example, that Britain was thoroughly undistinguished culturally at the time the Romans arrived: "Before ancient Britain was invaded and conquered by the Roman legions, not a single Briton had ever done anything to leave his name in the pages of history" (Sowell 1994: 63). He says that after the Romans withdrew from the British Isles in the fifth century AD, Britain regressed to its barbarous social practices. The Romans found the culture that would later become the world's first industrialized nation to be the most backward of all European peoples at the time.

Cultural traits or qualities, then, are by no means predetermined, inevitable, or permanent. This is an extremely important point because it means that the notion of internal cultural patterns must not be confused with any deterministic genetic or racial explanation.

Still, Thomas Sowell is not interested in serving any politically correct interests with his work on race and culture. To the contrary, he is often criticized for espousing what some scholars consider to be conservative, even reactionary, views on culture. This reflects the extreme sensitivity people have about race. Some critics are especially incredulous about Sowell's perspective because he is black. Despite his impeccable credentials, Thomas Sowell was conspicuously left off a much-ballyhooed commission on race relations in the United States appointed by former President Clinton in the late 1990s. As an historian, economist, and advocate of the "free market," Sowell says he examines facts and trends as objectively as he can, and then tries to explain how culture works, particularly in terms of the varying cultural capacity for economic productivity. Sowell wants to know, for example, why Jewish, Chinese, and Lebanese people do so well economically wherever they go. Furthermore, he points out, it is exactly their persistence and success that are sometimes held against immigrants: "many people in many lands have recognized the capabilities of the Jews, the Chinese, the Lebanese, and others as reasons to discriminate against them" (Sowell 1994: 155). The horrific abuse of Chinese by Indonesians in Indonesia right up to this day is but one particularly troublesome example of this destructive cultural tendency.

Cultural groups that are "deterritorialized" (for example, former African slaves in Brazil, Algerian laborers in France, Mexican farm workers in the United States, Indian professionals in England, Filipino domestic workers in Hong Kong, Chilean refugees in Sweden) always face discrimination in their new lands. The forms of discrimination differ in ways related to culture and class, and are not always consciously given or mean-spirited. Present-day cultural patterns of deterritorialized peoples reflect their enduring internal cultural patterns, *and* how they are treated and respond to local conditions in recent history. Despite some characterizations to the contrary, one reason why the United States is such an attractive place for immigrants from all over the world is because people are relatively free to be themselves culturally. The rights that Americans hold so dear – especially those of religion and expression – are really guarantees of a kind of cultural freedom that are found in very few places on earth.

Social class and culture

Culture is grounded not only in race, but in social class. Race and class are intimately intertwined, but their linkage is often overlooked in cultural analysis. Thus to speak of, say, Korean culture might bring to mind a stereotypical or idealized image that can easily obscure how differently rich Koreans live from poor Koreans in many respects. If culture takes shape in everyday life, and if the everyday lives of the rich and poor differ – even among people who descend from the same racial lines and live close to one another – then culture is differentiated meaningfully by social class. Said another way, a person or family's ranking in the socioeconomic hierarchy is not just a financial status, but a cultural demarcation as well.

This relationship between social structure and culture has been well recognized in various streams of academic critical theory.

However, the typical argument made by these scholars is that culture should not be granted much status as an analytical concept. They say that culture does not exist independent of political economic forces. In fact, culture is created by these forces. Culture is a kind of political-economic "effect." How people live depends mainly on where they rank in terms of income and social prestige.

We should not accept this argument. Culture is indeed structured in various ways, some of them owing to differences in social class, but *culture certainly is not determined by material relations or social class positions*. Nor is culture of secondary importance. Those who view culture as a product of social class fail to take into account culture's variety, power, and scope, including its brazen contradictions. Any theory of culture as determined by political-economic forces fails to recognize the vital, creative ways people produce culture in the routine and not-so-routine undertakings of their daily lives. Culture, therefore, should not be considered something "simply derived from class, as if it were a crude form of ideology" (Rowe and Schelling 1991: 9). Cultural differences are not the same as class differences. We need a less parochial critical perspective.

Social theorists and researchers have wrestled with the complex connection between social structure and culture for years. In the disciplines of sociology and communication, for example, some scholars have tried to explain why people of various social classes prefer different genres of art and music. Why, for instance, does one young Brazilian prefer samba music while another would rather listen to hard rock? To explain such differences, the American sociologist Herbert Gans (1974) tried to accommodate both social class and culture within a concept he calls "taste culture." Taste culture refers to *cultural strata* in a society that approximate the *social class strata* of that society. While Gans does not equate the two, he finds significant parallels between taste and social class position. A simple illustration is that people from the upper socioeconomic classes prefer classical music more than do members of the lower classes. Such relationships between social class and taste, however, rarely correspond as neatly as they do in this example. Although they may have more in common culturally than just musical taste, fans of heavy metal, rap, rock, punk, jazz, and even country and western music, for instance, cannot easily be grouped socioeconomically. And to return to the samba/hard rock example: in Brazil, samba is identified with youth from the lower socioeconomic classes and hard rock with the upper classes, while in Europe and North America (where samba music has been appropriated as an exotic cultural form) just the opposite is true. George H. Lewis (1992) has productively elaborated

Gans's ideas by explaining taste cultures in terms that are grounded not solely in social class positions. Lewis shows how the preferences people have for types of music ranging from rap to country and western link up with their demographics, aesthetic orientations, and political leanings too.

Habitus

Certainly one of the most systematic and well-known attempts to come to grips theoretically with the relationship between culture and social structure is the research and writing of the French sociologist Pierre Bourdieu (1984; 1990a; 1990b; 1993). Bourdieu studied the cultural values and activities of people in differing social positions of French society, mainly in the 1960s. He tried to find a way to describe and explain the lifestyles of French people who differ by factors such as where they live, their professions and vocations, financial status and education, artistic preferences and aesthetic tastes, and other aspects of everyday life. Bourdieu resurrected and reworked the concept of *habitus* to bring all the lifestyle factors into one explanatory paradigm based on situated social interaction. This encompassing theoretical concept is the habitus – *a system of socially learned cultural predispositions and activities that differentiate people by their lifestyles.* While habitus is claimed to account for cultural taste, it is not simply a cold system of aesthetics detached from the sensate world. Habitus is how we live. It pervades our bodies and our minds, our emotions and our logics.

Habitus is learned through social experience. Social class organizes social experience in key ways because people are greatly influenced by the social and economic conditions of their immediate environment. They "internalize their position in social space" (Bourdieu 1990a: 110). But Bourdieu and other theorists point out that *social experience does not simply reflect one's slot on a socioeconomic scale. What a person learns culturally is influenced by, but not limited to, the tastes and everyday activities of people who occupy the same social class.* The diversity of cultural styles we see in France or anywhere else is thus organized in ways that are shaped in part by socioeconomic factors, but also develop from other less structured and predictable influences, especially in an era of mass media and the wide circulation of symbolic cultural forms (Hannerz 1992: 13–14; Thompson 1995).

How then do we develop our cultural styles, our habitus? Bourdieu describes the process of cultural learning with a well-known metaphor from the world of sports. He believes habitus develops in a manner similar to the way athletes acquire knowledge and strategies in sport by means of their "feel for the game." Especially in constant-action sports such as football (soccer) or basketball, veteran players know what to do almost instinctively. Like playing a sport competently, cultural skills and styles become second nature. You know what to do, even without thinking about it, based on accumulated knowledge. The feel for the cultural game develops from motivated, strategic, repeated, practical experience. In this way habitus becomes "a system of acquired dispositions" and an "organizing principle of action" (Bourdieu 1990a: 13).

Sport serves not only as a good example of how habitus is learned, but also how it is displayed. The Olympics and the World Cup provide excellent opportunities to view how competitors and teams from different cultures around the world play different sports. For example, while both teams are playing football on the same field and by the same rules, consider how differently the squads from Germany and Nigeria approach the game. Brazil is known throughout the world not just for its unsurpassed winning record, but for the "beautiful" way it plays the game, a style that reflects the creativity and sensuality of Brazilian culture generally.

Photo 6.3 The beautiful game. Sport is one visible surface of culture, and the Brazilian football team is known worldwide for a style of play that resembles dance. Star player Roberto Carlos is featured in a TV commercial during the 1998 World Cup (reprinted with permission of Nike, Inc.)

The system of dispositions which makes up the habitus has a generative quality in much the same way as language does (Chomsky 1972). Cultural orientations, like languages, are open systems whose particular forms, styles, and meanings are constantly created, reinforced, and transcended (i.e. "generated") in actual use. The generative nature of habitus underscores several key theoretical assertions Bourdieu offers: social actors are purposive, active agents who do not blindly reproduce culture; modes of behavior making up the habitus are patterned but not finely regular or lawful; and part of the system of dispositions and practical logic of habitus is "vagueness," which insures that spontaneity and improvisation will characterize people's "ordinary relations to the world" (Bourdieu 1990a: 78). The indeterminate, generative, and vague qualities of habitus reflect its contingent nature. Habitus is not a person's or a group's unified cultural style that applies uniformly in all situations, but is instead acquired and exercised uniquely in relation to different cultural territories, domains, or "fields" (Bourdieu 1993).

Conclusion

Pierre Bourdieu's theoretical work is particularly significant because it attempts to develop an appropriately complex and dynamic theory of culture and society. Today's globalized cultural realities, however, don't have much in common with the old world contours of the socially stratified, relatively homogenous mid-twentieth-century France that Bourdieu analyzed. France today has a much larger immigrant population, especially North Africans. And most important, communications and entertainment media of that era differ greatly from those which French citizens have access to today. The very nature and dynamics of cultural life have changed. In theoretical terms, culture as a relatively long-term totality has given way in many respects to short-term *lifestyles* fueled by the hedonism of commercial media. Culture in many parts of the world has become less collective, more individualistic, less related to group identities, more related to personalized styles. Human needs for sociality, community, and identity may not have changed much over the years. What has changed is the human, technological, and symbolic landscape, provoking new cultural formations and modalities. Central to culture at the dawn of the twenty-first century is the subject of the next chapter – the popular.

7

Symbolic Power and Popular Culture

Admiring Friend: "My, that's a beautiful baby you have there!"

Mother: "Oh, that's nothing – you should see his photograph!"

Daniel J. Boorstin, The Image

Significantly the villain in *Tomorrow Never Dies*, the James Bond film released at the close of last century, wasn't an operative for a reneg-ade government, a corrupt industrialist, or a religious terrorist, but a media mogul in the mode of a Rupert Murdoch, Ted Turner, or Silvio Belusconi. Bond's cinematic antagonist not only reported the news, he tried to manufacture and control it through hegemonic manipulation of a global satellite TV system and hundreds of daily newspapers. The film was a thrilling and bitingly critical testament to how the instruments and terms of social power have changed in the age of information and high-tech communication.

Power takes many forms. As John B. Thompson (1995) points out, *economic power* is institutionalized in industry and commerce; *political power* is institutionalized in the state apparatus; *coercive power* is institutionalized in military, police, and incarcerating organiza-tions. But *symbolic power*, which is of great importance today, is far more ephemeral, flexible, and democratic. Symbolic power is defined as "the capacity to use symbolic forms to intervene in the course of events, to influence the actions of others and indeed to create events, by means of the production and transmission of symbolic forms" (Thompson 1995: 17).

A "symbolic form" can be thought of as something as simple as a physical gesture, verbal utterance, or cave painting. But for our purposes, symbolic form refers mainly to the content of human communication mediated by print, photographic, filmic, audio, televisual, or digital technologies of reproduction and transmission.

Symbolic forms don't appear randomly or in isolation. They constitute codes, require literacies, and promote some interpretations over others. They are choreographed to serve the purposes of their authors and sponsors. Although the meanings of symbolic forms can never be completely fixed, they reflect certain social, cultural, and ideological themes and biases. Symbolic forms are shaped into *narratives*, *genres*, and *discourses* by communications media and by audiences. That is an important part of the way symbolic forms assume their character and force.

Like political, economic, and coercive power, symbolic power is often institutionalized and functions to promote the interests of the socioeconomic elite. The obvious example is mass media organizations whose very products are symbolic forms, as was depicted so disturbingly in *Tomorrow Never Dies*. For centuries symbolic power has also propelled the interests of the church, which is "concerned primarily with the production and diffusion of symbolic forms pertaining to salvation, spiritual values and other-worldly beliefs," as well as schools and universities which are "concerned with the transmission of acquired symbolic content (or knowledge) and the inculcation of skills and competencies" (Thompson 1995: 17). All sources of social influence depend on symbolic forms to leverage their power in today's mass-mediated world. Political candidates require careful image making in an age of television, voter disaffection, and the turning away from political parties. Advertising companies and public relations firms orchestrate symbolic campaigns for their corporate clients. Governments drill their subjects with propaganda. The travel industry stimulates island fantasies. Even government military forces try to glamorize unglamorous jobs with dreamy recruitment advertising.

The list of social power agents who depend on symbolic power to intensify and make their messages relevant excludes no one. But symbolic power does not just extend the vested interests and objectives of those who already benefit from other forms of institutionalized power. Far more accessible and usable than the "hard" power resources of politics, economics, and coercion, symbolic power connects with and activates the "soft" domains of ideology, art, and culture. These domains are ultimately uncontrollable by elite social forces. Though symbolic power can be generated by money and authority, it requires no financial investments or supervision. Symbolic power reinforces hard power, but it also reduces, ridicules, and relativizes it. Symbolic power can be used creatively in daily life by everyone on earth, helping individuals and groups cope with, adapt to, create, and transform environments structured by the forces of economic, political, and coercive influence.

This is because the raw materials of symbolic power – symbolic forms – are not limited the way political, economic, and coercive resources are. The amount of political candidates, parties, and campaign monies is finite. Economic institutions have budgets and bottom lines. Military arsenals can be counted. Symbolism, on the other hand, functions in the boundless and vital realm of the human imagination. Symbolic forms can never be used up. They are inherently open to an infinite, diverse progression of possible interpretations, a condition which encourages people to use symbolic forms creatively.

Symbolic forms are *polysemic*. They mean different things to different people. They are *multisemic* because they can mean different things to the same person at different times, places, and situations, and in different moods. Symbolic forms are *combinatory* because they can be creatively synthesized, altered, recontextualized, divided, and added to other forms. Meaning is never self-evident. Meaning construction is processual and highly subjective. Symbolic power, thus, is exercised by message senders and by message interpreters and users in the relatively open field of signification.

Box 7.1 The Sixties and Symbolic Power

Come you masters of war
You that build all the guns
You that build the death planes
You that build the big bombs
You that hide behind walls
You that hide behind desks
I just want you to know
I can see through your masks

Bob Dylan, "Masters of War," 1963

Feed your head

Jefferson Airplane, "White Rabbit," 1967

Symbolic power has long been used by religious organizations, governments, corporations, educational institutions, political parties, and mainstream culture and media industries to advance their interests. But in the 1960s in the United States and elsewhere, symbolic power flourished in ways that did much more than reinforce society's entrenched institutions, its dominant ideology and culture. To the contrary, it was used to wage ideological and cultural warfare against the power bloc. The "Sixties" provides a striking historical example of how the pervasive, expansive, and ultimately uncontrollable nature of symbolic power can relativize traditional forms of social power and change the cultural landscape for ever.

Several historical factors set the stage for the explosion of symbolic power during the 1960s. Americans were torn by the Vietnam War, the civil rights and "black power" movements, the "credibility gap" and the "generation gap," a forceful rekindling of feminism, the sexual revolution, a sharp increase in drug use among middle- and upper-class youth, the assassination of John F. Kennedy, Martin Luther King, Robert Kennedy, and Malcolm X, allegations of illegal CIA involvement in foreign countries (particularly the assassination of Chilean president Salvador Allende), a new awareness of environmental issues and the destructive potential of nuclear power, the consumer movement, the resignation of President Richard Nixon under threat of impeachment for "high crimes," and an overall rethinking of "establishment" values, mores, and lifestyles by American youth.

The political and cultural chaos of the Sixties (which actually extends at least until the frenetic withdrawal of American military forces from Vietnam in 1975) was fueled mainly by rapid development of alternative communications media, and by the provocative symbolic content they transmitted to rapidly growing audiences. Symbolic power requires circulation of symbolic forms. The revolutionary atmosphere of the Sixties and all that followed in its wake could not have happened without such developments.

Even the most mainstream and commercial mass medium, television, played a revolutionary role in politics and culture by bringing the war home in a way no society had ever experienced. More than 90 percent of American homes had television by the time the war began. Televised reports from Southeast Asia became increasingly critical of the US involvement. Images of the war appeared on the nightly news and shocked the public.

Radio became a particularly potent medium for exercising symbolic power in the Sixties. Frequency modulated (FM) stations changed their formats from classical and elevator music to progressive rock (originally "underground") to appeal to the rapidly emerging "baby-boom" generation consumer market. Prior to the mid-1960s, FM radios were few; listening to FM was the province of "high-fi" buffs. But when a few progressive rock FM stations broke out in markets such as San Francisco, New York, and Los Angeles, young people started to buy FM radios en masse, transforming the radio and music industries. With their superior fidelity, greater range of audio representation, stereo capability, and alternative music and culture, FM stations began to dominate listener ratings. Conservative station owners hired long-haired, hippie announcers because the "freaks," their rap, and their music were generating more money than previous staffs and formats could. The deejays encouraged listeners to stop the war, integrate the races, get off the commercial treadmill, take drugs, question authority, break away from their parents, and generally just drop out of the establishment.

Progressive rock radio's popularity exposed a whole new generation of musicians and music types — extremely powerful symbolic forms — ranging from Jimi Hendrix, the Doors, and Cream to Joan Baez, Ravi Shankar, and Pharoh Sanders. The Monterey Pop Festival in California and Woodstock in New York further ritualized, reinforced, and promoted the alternative consciousness that progressive music and media advocated.

Other alternative media including underground newspapers, *Rolling Stone Magazine*, independent and foreign film, even radical comic books contributed to the revolutionary symbolic environment.

No doubt the Sixties was an extraordinary period in American and world history. Political battles raged over war, race, gender, the body, and the very core of American values and policies. The terms of social power were in flux. While the government and the big corporations exercised their political, economic, and coercive power to the maximum during the Sixties, even the most disenfranchised hippie felt that "power to the people," "flower power," "make love, not war," and other symbolic movements and expressions of the time had great persuasive impact too. In situations like the cultural upheaval of the Sixties, symbolic power does more than compensate for a lack of political, economic, and coercive power. It provokes cultural reflection and changes of consciousness. Because symbolic power operates in the mysterious realm of the human imagination and consciousness, the psychological, social, and cultural influence it stimulates can only be estimated, never measured precisely. Moreover the Sixties never died symbolically. Its social, political, and cultural consequences remain in the collective memory of people all over the world.

Popular culture

While some follow Brahms, Sting, and Carlos Fuentes, others prefer Julio Iglesias, Alejandra Guzman, and Venezuelan soap operas . . . the idols of Hollywood and of pop music, designer jeans and credit cards, sports heroes of various countries . . . make up a repertoire of constantly available signs.

García Canclini 1995: 51

The play of signifiers becomes the domain of experience.

Chaney 1994: 213

The term "popular culture" (*cultura popular*) in Latin languages refers literally to "the culture of the people." Popular, in this sense, does not simply mean widespread, mainstream, dominant, or commercially successful, as it is often understood. Instead, popular culture means that *artifacts and styles of human expression develop from the creativity of ordinary people, and circulate among people according to their interests, preferences, and tastes.* Popular culture thus comes from people; it is not just given to them. This perspective tears away at distinctions typically made between producers and consumers of cultural materials – between the culture industries and contexts of reception. By interpreting and using popular symbolic forms, everyone helps produce popular culture.

One question that college teachers like to ask their students is, "Do the mass media reflect social reality or do they create it?" Without doubt, the best answer is "both." More interesting questions might be "*How* do the media reflect and create social reality, who benefits, and in what ways?" or "How do the media help facilitate the social construction of cultural reality?" Technically, of course, the mass media can neither reflect nor construct "sociocultural reality" as no such pure or permanent thing exists anyway. Furthermore, media programmers have no interest in reflecting or creating reality. What they do is piece together symbolic fragments to produce images and stories that resemble our surroundings in some ways and not in others.

There is no commitment to faithfully produce anything except that which quickly catches the public's fancy and turns at least a short-term profit. In developing prime-time commercial television programs, for instance, producers, network officials, station executives, and advertisers all research and ultimately guess what the audience will watch.[1] Similarly, artist and repertoire agents from the popular music industries scour the streets for marketable talent. The chosen content of all the culture industries is packaged, put on trial, and the crapshoot begins. The popular culture marketplace is extremely unpredictable. Certain themes, genres, sounds, styles, and stars strike a responsive chord, resonating with audience members' identities, emotions, opinions, tastes, and ambitions. The vast majority of television programs, rock and rap music, novels, computer software, and all other cultural offerings, however, fail to turn a profit.

The role of the culture industries, therefore, is to solicit, select, sort, market, and distribute certain symbolic resources with the hope of appealing to a viable market. These resources take the form of persons – writers, actors, singers, and so on – and the scripts, scenes, songs, and other symbolic forms they create. Most executives of the culture industries are in the business strictly for the bread. They don't care about what they sell, so long as it makes money. Even the most threatening and anarchistic cultural materials and political statements are shamelessly packaged and sold. This was the famous case of rap singer Ice T's "Cop Killer" song, for example, which, until its eventual removal from the album, made hundreds of thousands of dollars for Warner Communications. Original rock and roll, acid rock, folk rock, punk, heavy metal, and rap all have served the cultural and political ambitions of their originating artists while they simultaneously generated enormous revenues for the culture industries. Most mainstream trends in fashion, music, language, and dance, in fact, begin as "radical" forms of expression originating in "people's culture."

Popular culture (1)	Culture industries	Popular culture (2)
Folk origins, *vox populi*	Combing and sorting system; high technology	Interpretations, personal and social uses; fans, consumers
Symbolic forms created by popular classes; common culture	Selects, amplifies, modifies, enhances, packages, distributes, markets, promotes symbolic forms	Cognitive coherence, personal and collective identities; sense making, social interaction and influence
Art, deviance; youth-oriented	Economic risks and profits; mainstream and niche markets	Active audience; meanings, pleasures; symbolic power

Figure 7.1 The process of popular culture

Popular reception

Even if one feels alienated from the distant economic-political order, one can assert sovereignty over one's near existence.

Maffesoli 1996: 44

The culture industries draw from, feed, reinforce, and challenge the whims, preferences, and loyalties of pop culture fans. Without question, the social circulation of media images brings about commercial success and helps make the spread of the dominant ideology possible (see chapter 2). Images appearing on the commercial mass media promote particular products, help create communities of consumption for product groups and brand names, and generally reinforce a consumerist atmosphere.

Such institutional priorities, however, do not simply reproduce the dominant ideology and culture while earning money for the culture industries. Nor does the culture industries' packaging of popular symbolic forms stifle the creativity of audience members. Just the opposite is true. First, what catches on in television, film, music, and the rest of commercial culture must appeal to audiences. Audiences' criteria for acceptance cannot be dictated, and their tastes are in constant motion. Second, popular symbolic forms become widely recognized and accessible resources used by audiences in a wide variety of ways. That's partly how cultural materials become popular. Such preferences, interpretations, and uses are not just a matter of ideological and cultural reproduction. Many of the most profound consequences of popular culture – both in favor of and resistant to dominant modes of thought – lie precisely in how people engage with media imagery to express themselves, feel stable, construct their identities, and influence others. So, for symbolic forms to become popular, audiences must play an active role at every stage. Because audiences act mainly in their own interests, they exercise tremendous influence over the entire process.

In recent years John Fiske has been the most outspoken of cultural studies theorists to argue that audience members are by no means hopelessly dominated by mass media and the culture industries. Fiske tries to show how symbolic forms ranging from torn blue jeans to pop singers and songs are used creatively by fans to promote their interests (1989; 1993; 1996). But Fiske carries this argument about people's ability to manage their cultural experiences one controversial step further. Popular culture, according to Fiske, is serious social struggle. Contrary to the frequently heard criticism that popular culture is nothing but capitalistic commercial exploitation or "mass culture," Fiske argues that *making popular culture by everyday people is actually resistance to and evasion of dominant ideological and cultural forces.* Completely in opposition to any theory of ideological hegemony, Fiske believes that people exercise symbolic power to win battles against their "oppressors" from the political-economic-cultural "power bloc." Winning such symbolic struggles gives "pleasure" to those who resist hegemony. Pleasure is a key idea in this way of thinking. In Fiske's words, "Popular pleasures must always be those of the oppressed, they must contain elements of the oppositional, the evasive, the scandalous, the offensive, the vulgar, the resistant" (Fiske 1989: 127).

Popular culture according to this view is empowering. The mass media actually contribute to the empowerment by distributing cultural resources to subordinated individuals and groups who then use these symbolic forms to construct tactics of resistance against hegemonic, corporate strategies of containment. One of Fiske's sharpest examples is that of young Australian Aborigines who watch old American TV westerns and ally themselves not with the "heroic" white cowboys, but with the Indians. The Aboriginal viewers "cheer them on as they attack the wagon train or homestead, killing the white men and carrying off the white women" (Fiske 1989: 25).

John Fiske's optimism about the freedom and creativity he believes audience members exercise in the "struggles against the power bloc" is legendary. His confidence that media audiences successfully subvert the forces of ideological and cultural control has certainly helped dispel the idea that audiences are nothing but passive consumers or victims of media. Giving audiences such credit was an important theoretical move in the history of media, communication, and cultural studies, which in the past had focused too much on the negative, manipulative "effects" of mass communication.

But let's not go too far. Many scholars believe that Fiske hopelessly romanticizes the role of audience members in meaning construction, and that his theoretical claims are not well supported by empirical evidence. The British sociologist Keith Tester is among Fiske's critics. He argues that "Fiske's work confuses the possibility that the audience *might* carry out oppositional readings of media texts with the claim that they actually *do* carry out such readings. Fiske is guilty of confusing what *could* happen with another claim about what *does* happen" (Tester 1994: 70).

Another serious theoretical problem is an oversimplified conceptualization of "pleasure" as it has been used by Fiske and other cultural studies researchers and writers (Condit 1989). For example, the feelings of people in totalitarian political states as they resist dominant ideological and cultural messages can hardly be called "pleasures." We must be careful not to equate, for example, an American girl's fascination with the rebelliousness of Courtney Love, Alanis Morisette, or Madonna with the feelings of young female workers in China as they critically interpret government propaganda transmitted by state-operated television.

To conclude this section, the "popular" in popular culture really means that cultural themes and styles originate in everyday environments, and are later attended to, interpreted, and used by ordinary people – sometimes, but not always, in very resistant ways – after being commodified and circulated by the culture industries and mass media. The media routinely stimulate the imagination of audiences who put symbolic representations to work in their everyday living situations. So while the sights and sounds of mass-mediated popular culture may be first produced and distributed by commercial enterprises headquartered in the entertainment capitals of the world, such symbolic forms are routinely evaluated, interpreted, and used by non-specialist culture producers living in even the most remote provinces.

Popular emotions

Laughter and irony are an explosion of life, even and especially if this life is exploited and dominated.

Maffesoli 1996: 51

I hate you.

Popular heavy metal song by Slayer

A fascinating side story to one of the most captivating media attractions of recent years – the O. J. Simpson scandal – concerns tensions that developed among the jurors who served for nearly a year at the televised criminal trial of the famous black American football player accused of killing his wife and her male friend. The racially mixed group of jurors was required to live in a hotel together, eat meals together, and socialize together – but to never talk about the trial, and to never watch television (in order to avoid media commentaries about the famous courtroom proceedings). How were they to pass their time? They were allowed to watch video movies together. If it is indeed true that the jurors – and the American public at large – were to finally judge the guilt or innocence of O. J. Simpson largely on the basis of his race – and by implication, his culture – then the world could have had a preview of just how deep racial and cultural differences can run by examining what happened when the jury selected movies for group viewing. A serious problem arose when the jurors couldn't agree about what movies to watch. According to one juror who had been dismissed for arguing too much with the others, members of the group differed markedly about what videos they thought were funny. The beleaguered jurors apparently wanted to spend their free time being entertained by their preferred style of humor – one of the most important features of culture.

By wanting to laugh and loosen up after a hard day of serious work, the jurors demanded a satisfying *emotional* experience. Cultural media routinely try to stimulate human emotion, sometimes relentlessly so. Through various narratives, some scripted, some not, culture industry producers desperately try to provoke emotional responses from their audiences, and very often succeed. People never just "watch" television, as mass communication theorists might suggest, nor do they simply "read" television, as semioticians like to say. More than anything else, audiences "feel" television and other popular media, often quite deeply. We may be speeding along smoothly in the fast lanes of the logic-driven "information age" these days, but we also routinely take slow, less predictable excursions on the bumpy side-roads of emotion for other kinds of pleasure.

Crying, laughing, and screaming at the movies and falling in love with stars of the silver screen have been passions for people the world over since cinema began. Some women savor their daily crying sessions as they privately watch "a nice weepie" TV soap opera (Morley 1986: 159). Music provokes the full range of emotion – from speed-metal headbanging anger to saccharine sentiments inspired by romance ballads. Some men cheer televised sports triumphs, and slump in despair at the losses. Television evangelists excite religious fervor and financial donations. Political candidates woo voters' hearts.

Charismatic heroes of the culture industries and popular media succeed when they are able to effectively connect symbolic imagery to human emotion and experience. Love, hate, fear, hope, joy, sadness, disgust: all the emotions play well on the electronic media.

Emotional "branding"

Advertisers try to associate the commodities and services they sell with the profound subjectivities of everyday life too. They believe that consumers develop relationships with products based more on emotional involvement than on any rational comparison of the goods' more objective features. Functionaries in the advertising world straightforwardly refer to use of emotional appeals for trying to "addict" consumers to their products as "branding."

Global advertising executives believe emotional branding works best to influence middle-class consumers in developing countries, and relatively poor people in the more developed countries. Fantasies promised by advertising and dreams of obtaining more material goods become even more salient and persuasive for people with little discretionary income because advertising can stimulate the imagination of a "better life." By competing in the realm of emotion, product quality and price become remarkably unimportant.

Mediated feelings

Does media content really matter? Doesn't everybody know what the media gives them isn't real? Don't people keep a critical distance from movies, television, websites, and other media? Empirical studies done by two American communication researchers show that it certainly does matter what people see at the movies and watch on television, and that people do not, perhaps cannot, maintain much distance from their mediated communicative interactions. Human beings physiologically, cognitively, and emotionally experience a wide range of common orientations, feelings, and communicative behaviors mediated by visual communications technologies as if they were "real" (Reeves and Nass 1996).

Indeed, the producers, writers, and financial backers of television, video, and film *depend* on just such deep-felt parasocial, para-emotional interactions and consciously try to excite the affective capacities of their viewers. They meet little resistance from audiences. In fact, television, video, and film viewers *demand* that media evoke feelings that are more extreme than those to which they are accustomed. For example, successful action adventure movies and horror films must provoke extreme emotional responses from their male-dominated audiences.

Video pornography has become a particularly popular middle-class genre that can excite viewers' involvements even to the point of ecstasy and orgasm. Pornography is routinely used to provoke, complement, or substitute for "real" sexual contact, or stimulate interaction between real partners through vicarious shared sexual experience. Symbolic interaction with pornography requires skills that simultaneously link imaginative insertion into the contrived sexual scene with technical abilities to operate video equipment (slow motion, slow rewind) in order to produce maximum physical pleasure.

Soap operas, especially the Latin American variety known as *telenovelas*, invite viewers to swim for months, sometimes years, in a sensorium of emotional experience. Such an invitation often seems nearly impossible for people to decline. Latin American *telenovelas* are shown during prime-time viewing hours, and have enormous social and cultural significance (Martín-Barbero 1993; González 1998). To be successful, the *telenovela* must regularly provoke peak emotional experiences through its narratives and visuals. Intense emotional realism is what counts. Such emotional connections compose the "tragic structure of feeling" that soap-opera viewers and media consumers in general want to experience (Ang 1985).

Racial, generational, gender, and social class differences frequently wash away in front of emotional experience. For example, poor, racially-diverse Brazilian women eagerly watch lush prime-time national soap operas that feature upper-class settings and stories and light-skinned actors. The viewers ignore class discrepancies between themselves and the mediated realities, focusing instead on the emotionality, intimacy, and social usefulness of these extremely popular shows (Tufte 2000). Soap operas remind us of our emotional vulnerability. One of the most famous Mexican soap operas, which became a global phenomenon stretching from Latin America to China, reveals this idea well by its title – *The Rich Cry Too* (*Tambien Los Ricos Lloran*). Far from discouraging viewing and viewer involvement, emotional vulnerability encourages it. Indeed, emotional imperfection is a "sign of life" (Maffesoli 1996: 38).

Television and other media disembed, recontextualize, and compress not just information, but emotion, and by doing so connect vitally with their audiences. The experiences of fear, romance, anger, passion, joy, sadness, and pain, for example, are all enhanced today by the superior technical quality of digital audio and video technology. Mediated emotional involvements arriving via "global" technologies of communication may be perceived as even more intense than local, unmediated feelings.

Story, genre, discourse

Virtually all media programming, even unscripted sporting events, consists of stories. Narratives are basic to culture. They help people make sense of their environments. Stories symbolize cultural values and provide cultural continuity. But stories don't just function instrumentally as cultural devices; they are extremely pleasurable. Stories provoke the imagination, connect to emotion, and stimulate fantasies. Readers, listeners, and viewers enjoy speculating about the outcome of stories, particularly soap operas (Zermeño 1998) and scandalous news (Bird 1997).

Stories compose genres, which are the categories of media content such as action movies, romance novels, or situation comedies. Genres can be recognized by their conventions. The "western," for example, features a typical setting (nineteenth-century American West), stock characters (hero-gunfighter, bad-guy cowboys, threatening Indians, saloon girl) and characteristic events (gunfight, card game, swindle, saloon brawl) (Grossberg, Wartella, and Whitney 1998: 160). Some stories and genres appeal more to men, others to women, across cultures (Lull 1988; 1990).

Discourses are the patterned ideological and cultural themes that symbolic forms, stories, and genres represent and reproduce. A discourse is the way objects or ideas are talked about publicly that gives rise to widespread perceptions and understandings. Discourses help organize ideology and culture. Keeping with the main theme of this book, however, we know that such structuring tendencies do not determine audience response: "Popular entertainment may be structured by the reiteration of certain formulas and genres which provide staple narrative forms . . . but even so there will be an overwhelming need for novelty in performances [and] styles" (Chaney 1994: 210).

Cultural uses of symbolic power

How symbolic power is applied is what makes it significant. *Symbolic power articulates into historically specific cultural situations.* Symbols are given meaning by interpretation, and every interpretation takes place in a cultural context and serves a cultural purpose. People use symbolic power to achieve individual and collective objectives. This is what I mean by the cultural uses of symbolic power – the specific, contextualized employment of symbolic forms to construct cognitive coherence, assure ontological security, bring about social influence, and help develop or reinforce collective and individual identities. Culture interacts with and assimilates symbolic power now more than ever because culture is made up of not only the traditional values, durable features, and routine activities that form local living environments, but also a broad and attractive array of symbolic resources expressed by the mass media and other social institutions. People routinely select and weave mediated, publicly available symbolic representations and discourses into the particular cultural conditions and discourses of their everyday lives, producing "cultural conversations . . . particular modes of social organization" (Jensen 1990: 182).

Cultural influence can be exercised when people use symbolic displays – including the systemic ideological and cultural associations, structures of authority, and rules that underlie them – in their cultural interactions and strategies of action. True, mediated symbolic forms are made culturally powerful initially by the way their sponsoring institutions frame, organize, and present them. But, ultimately, cultural uses of symbolic power reflect how, in the situated realms of everyday life, groups and individuals construct, declare, and enact their cultural identities and activities, and how those expressions and behaviors influence others.

Symbolic power and popular culture combine to play a central role in the formation of contemporary "cultural capital" (Bourdieu 1984). This notion of *cultural capital* is very important in our discussion of symbolic power. The term "capital," of course, is a synonym for money. We use economic capital to purchase things and to win various kinds of social status and influence. Same with cultural capital, which refers to cultural knowledge and style. Like money, cultural knowledge and style can be shown or "spent" in social interaction. Because contemporary forms of culture have become more and more symbolic, cultural "transactions" are exercises of symbolic power.

The commercial mass media have greatly accelerated and diversified the nature and influence of symbolic power. Symbolic power enables individuals and groups to produce meanings and construct (usually partial and temporary) ways of life (or constellations of cultural zones). These symbolic spaces and mediated homelands appeal to the senses, emotions, and thoughts of the self and others. Patterned cultural exercises of symbolic power resemble what Anthony Giddens calls "life politics . . . a politics of choice . . . of lifestyle . . . of life decisions" (1991: 214). Although symbolic power has certain deep-felt economic and political origins, dimensions, and consequences, it is not the same as political, economic, or coercive power, nor it is produced only by the already powerful. Political power begets administrative and legal authority and influence. Economic power can be cashed in for material advantage. Coercive power threatens genocide and global destruction. Being a successful "cultural programmer" in the competitive cultural marketplace engenders other unique roles, statuses, and achievements.

Unlike previous eras where human experience was limited mainly to local environments and influences, culture today is much more symbolic, diverse, and dynamic. Values, beliefs, and lifestyles are far less fixed in time and space. People create, interpret, and use a range of symbols and symbol-producing technologies to fashion multiple cultural styles and identities. Unprecedented access to mass and micro communication technologies, and the robust nature of the symbolic popular cultures the technologies embrace and promote, allow construction of highly personalized identities, and the formation of specialized interpretative communities.

The ability to define a situation culturally is one extraordinary application of symbolic power. This can be done in a restrictive or permissive way. For example, controlling a decision about which language will be used in a particular context is one fundamental way to define the situation culturally. Institutionalized cultural management also shows up regularly in rule structures such as school dress codes that tell students what clothing and hairstyles are culturally acceptable. These codes are meant not only to standardize appearance and conduct, but to allow authorities to demarcate social power differences between themselves and their culturally unmanageable subjects.[2]

But language, hairstyles, clothes, and virtually all other cultural features can be used in permissive, creative ways too. Such symbolic exploration and assertion are basic to how youth communicate and construct their cultural styles and identities. Many American schools have instigated school dress codes lately, for instance, to fight back against students' "distracting" individual modes of dress (haircuts, jewelry, clothing styles) and their use of colors for gang identities. Young people on the margins of society are particularly active cultural scavengers and *bricoleurs*, combing their environments – especially the symbolic arenas – in search of materials with which to assemble their identities and express their beliefs and values as cultural style, sometimes as subcultures (Hebdige 1979; Willis 1990; Lull 1992a).

Music is a domain of popular culture where we can easily find many striking examples of how symbolic power is exercised culturally. We've already discussed the Sixties at some length. But consider the cultural dimensions and potentialities of the Sixties precursor – 1950s rock and roll. The Fifties is much more than an era in the history of popular music. It is a widely recognized, distinct, and romanticized cultural space. Characteristic styles of dress, dance, language, and gender relations are among the cultural features associated with the original rock-and-roll era. For many middle-aged baby-boomers, invoking cultural style by using Fifties rock-and-roll music is a way to reclaim one's youth and display cultural competence to others. Doing so temporarily privileges a (partial) way of life – in this case teen rebelliousness, the quest for fun, and feeling sexy. The Fifties rock-and-roll images will be with us forever. Audio and visual recordings make it possible for symbolic representations of this and other popular cultures to be preserved and put to use by people decades after a cultural moment has completed its original cycle. Indeed, the "swing" craze of the late 1990s was a particularly successful recycling of musical style and cultural nostalgia. Communications technology makes it possible for people to live inside a wide range not only of *cultural space*, but also of *cultural time*.

All popular music forms have specific cultural associations and implications. America's contemporary hip-hop culture has become a dominant symbolic space for developing cultural identity and influencing society. Rap speaks matter-of-factly to the everyday circumstances of many urban black young people while it simultaneously serves the fashion needs and cultural interests of other listeners living light years away from the inner cities.

Music-based subcultural groups express themselves through distinctive styles such as those we associate with hip hop, grunge, punk, reggae, and heavy metal. Subcultures often form, develop, and ascend with the times politically, as was the case in the hippie era of the 1960s. In Algeria today political and cultural resistance is expressed in the underground *rai* ("thought" or "will") music. Chinese pop singer Cui Jan was a strong cultural force in the student–worker rebellion there in the late 1980s. The list of examples where music has been used in political and cultural struggle is endless. Because of its accessibility and flexibility, music may be the perfect form of expression for alternative political and cultural groups and movements (Lull 1992a).

Box 7.2 Symbolic Power, Cultural Space, and "Time" in Lithuania

(This case study is based in part on personal correspondence with Justas Mamontovas, managing director of KOJA Records Group, Vilnius, Lithuania. Mamontovas is also author of the lyrics to "Time".)

Southernmost of the three Baltic nations (Estonia and Latvia being the others), Lithuania was under the control of Russia for most of the twentieth century. With nearly four million inhabitants, Lithuania is the largest of the Baltic states. All the states were crucial parts of the former Soviet empire because they gave Russia, which is nearly landlocked to the west, access to the Baltic Sea and to the Atlantic Ocean.

By satellite television in 1990 the world watched incredulously as Lithuanians, Estonians, and Latvians stood up courageously to Russian hegemony to declare their independence from Soviet occupation. Later that year the Berlin Wall fell, uniting East and West Germany. The brave actions of people in the Baltics led to the eventual crumbling of the entire Soviet empire.

Popular music played a central role throughout the shocking political-cultural transformation. Rock music had been a major form of resistance in the struggle against the former Soviet empire in all its satellite nations (Wicke 1992). And when Estonians united to declare their independence from Russia, nearly the entire population of 1.5 million people gathered in the huge amphitheater outside the capital of Tallinn to join hands and sing pre-communist-era national songs.

But this brief analysis focuses on a specific musical development *after* Lithuania and the other Baltic nations became independent in 1990. This case study reflects the extraordinary symbolic value of popular music.

A 20-year-old rap singer from Vilnius, Lithuania's capital city, working with the manager of KOJA Records Group, also in Vilnius, got the idea of creating a cultural duet with the famous Lithuanian opera tenor Virgilijus Noreika. The idea for the song had been inspired by the Rhapsody Overture compilation released by Polygram in 1997, where famous rap singers recorded duets with famous opera singers. The young Lithuanian rapper, Lukas, asked his sister, whose schoolmate is Noreika's son, to propose the idea to the renowned singer.

The hybrid concept was accepted enthusiastically by Noreika. Lukas proposed to get Lithuania's top producers involved, and Justas Mamontovas volunteered to write the lyrics for a song titled "Time." The song became the chart-topper in Lithuania, selling more than 17,000 copies. Dance and classical remixes of the track were also made and released on compact disc and tape as an extended play (EP) album.

On New Year's Eve 1998 the song was performed live for more than 10,000 people in Vilnius's central square. A video clip was

Photo 7.1 The symbolic power of popular music, Lukas (left) and Noreika join forces to transcend generational differences (reprinted with permission of KOJA Records Group, Vilnius, Lithuania)

made of the event, and has been repeatedly broadcast throughout Lithuania on national television.

A pop music success story, to be sure. But why are this particular song and fusion of artistic forces so important? The answer lies in the cultural and historical specificity of its production.

These men represent two generations of Lithuanians who passed through the historic struggle for independence from very different perspectives. Lukas, the rapper, was but 11 years old when the Russians left. Noreika had spent his entire adult life under the communist regime. Lithuanians of different generations in the past often struggled over political and cultural issues. The older generation was much more conservative, fearing change; the younger generation demanded change. Now that the Russians are gone, people from different generations in Lithuania can come together under much less divisive circumstances. The joining of Lukas and Noreika in song symbolizes this positive political and cultural change.

Here are the lyrics to their extraordinary song:

"Time"

It might be hard for you to understand us
We were born in different times
Decades separate two generations
Time had cut the relations
We had evolved all
Into eternal Children–Parents' War

But I do believe in the power of Time
I do feel that history's wheels will soon turn 'round
Walls of Time will collapse
Generations will come together

Chorus: You can't stop the Time
         You can't turn back the Time
         We are all equal to the Time
         The Time is almighty

Time is running fast
We and our parents start singing the same song
Nobody would have trusted it not long ago
That we will lose ambition to change their world
Please open the door
To the adult people's world

I have already thrown away my pink glasses
I'm ready to obey the Law of Time
        *(permission to publish lyrics and photo granted by
             KOJA Records Group, Vilnius, Lithuania.
        Additional information available at headq@koja.lt)*

This case study represents not only the potency of symbolic power, but also the creativity and impact of the "cultural hybrid," which will be taken up at length in chapter 9.

Culture and the material world

Michael Jordan's impact on US economy in his last year as a basketball player with Chicago Bulls: $10 billion.

Fortune *magazine, 1999*

I want to come in and do for Reebok what Michael Jordan did for Nike.

*Stephon Marbury on the day he was drafted by the
Minnesota Timberwolves professional basketball team*

You don't win silver. You lose gold.

Nike billboard advertisement campaign during the 1996 Olympics in Atlanta

One compelling motivation behind certain human behavior is the desire for material goods. This may seem to be an obvious point, but its importance cannot be overstated. People everywhere want "stuff." The post-Cold War triumph of a hypercompetitive, global, capitalist economic system is a fact of life. Consumer goods and media imagery are fundamental to the system.

Such goods and images can be viewed as nothing but material and ideological components of global economic and cultural domination by the world's more developed countries, especially the United States, the members of European Union, and Japan. But there is much more to the story than that. No doubt the global circulation of goods and images benefit their producers, but material goods also challenge and change culture in positive ways. As Paul Willis points out, the market stimulates a "permanent and contradictory revolution in every culture which sweeps away old limits and dependencies" (1990: 26). Ideological predispositions and social practices that make up styles and lifestyles are constructed in large measure from symbolic and material resources of the commercial market. These resources are not shapeless, but they are not determining either. In forming preferences, opinions, and tastes, social actors discover that "the world is not presented as pure chaos, totally devoid of necessity and capable of being constructed in any old way. But this world does not present itself as totally structured either, or as capable of imposing on every perceiving subject the principles of its own construction" (Bourdieu 1990a: 132). Thus, we cannot reasonably view people simply as victims of their materialist tendencies. Consumption is an undetermined cultural process, not just an effect.

An extraordinary example of the correspondence between production and consumption, between ideological representation and social interpretation, between symbolic power and cultural usage is the American athletic shoe phenomenon. By blending themes of empowerment, transcendence, and irreverence, Nike had become a stunning economic, symbolic, and cultural success of worldwide proportions by the 1990s (Goldman and Papson 1999). Many American athletes, especially professional basketball stars such as Michael Jordan, Stephon Marbury, and Allan Iverson, have been recruited to hype the expensive shoes for Nike, Reebok, Fila, and others.

Marbury's comments quoted at the beginning of this section reveal an incredible transformation of priorities brought on by the economic impact of popular culture. Rather than worry about how he might help his new professional basketball team win more games, Marbury worried more about The Other Game. He wants to stimulate sales for his shoe company. That's because Marbury and his agent know where the money is. Michael Jordan's income as spokesperson for sports gear and consumer goods greatly exceeded his player salary, sometimes by a ratio of 10:1. The money he raised for Nike, MCI Worldcom, Gatorade, Wheaties, and the rest far outdistanced revenues generated from tickets sold and TV rights for the games in which he played.[3]

But profits generated from the commercials are not all institutional, and not all paid in dollars or pounds. The symbolic aspects of the athletic shoe phenomenon are in many ways far more important than its economic consequences. Inner-city black culture is intensely glorified in many advertising campaigns, especially the athletic shoe commercials. The inner-city playground, rough as it is, has become a cultural reference point indicating where the really good basketball players come from. Some of the commercials are filmed in black and white to further accent the stark quality of the "hood." The marketing technique is to transfer images of the culturally constituted world, the ghetto playground, to the consumer product, the shoes. The commodity is resignified through cultural space. Grant McCracken argues that:

> The creative director of an advertising agency seeks to join [the culturally constituted world and the consumer product] in such a way that the viewer/reader glimpses an essential similarity between them. When this symbolic equivalence is successfully established, the viewer/reader attributes certain properties he or she knows to exist in the culturally constituted world to the consumer good. The known properties of the world thus come to be resident in the unknown properties of the consumer good. The transfer of meaning from world to good is accomplished. (1990: 77)

The athletic shoe commercials represent, commodify, and extend culture. The vast majority of people who admire and identify with Michael Jordan, for instance, never saw him play basketball in person. But Jordan is not a media creation; he was strategically re-created for commercial purposes. The media made much more of him than he, or anyone, ever could be as a flesh-and-blood human being. Every detail was managed to perfection – from the slow-motion, high-flying slam-dunks on Nike TV commercials to the wiping-of-the-brow Gatorade spots ("If I could be like Mike!") and the broad, disarming smile staring at us from the Wheaties box. Because of his basketball talent, personal charm, and extraordinary media exposure, Jordan reached iconic status in Anglo-American popular culture. He joins a very select group of cultural superstars at the highest level – Elvis, the Beatles, Martin Luther King, Marilyn Monroe, James Dean, Princess Diana, John F. Kennedy, and Babe Ruth among them.

Now, some years after retirement from basketball, Jordan's bigger-than-life media persona remains part of an inviting pool of contem-porary symbolic resources used culturally. The basketball shoes and the competitive advertising campaigns behind them not only turn culture into a commodity, they also extend the culture. But while only industry can sell the shoes, the culture is packaged and sold by a wide range of everyday vendors. These cultural agents range from inner-city black boys whose lifestyle is glorified by the commercial media to suburban white girls who high-five and call each other homegirls. They all use the symbolic potential of this variety of popular cul-ture to advance their interests. The principle applies to virtually all popular culture forms.

Popular cultural capital: black gold

We should have gotten our freedom much sooner;
You ain't never seen a black man on *The Honeymooners*

Quincy Jones, Back on the Block. The Honeymooners is
a famous 1950s American TV serial

Is it coincidence that the fields dominated by black Americans – basket-ball, jazz, running backs in football – all have improvisational decision making, with numerous factors being decided in an instant under emo-tional pressure?

Sowell 1994: 184

I love this game!

Black American jazz musician Winton Marsalis in a promotional
announcement for America's National Basketball Association

Hip-hop is where the cultural excitement rests.

Los Angeles Times, *January 1, 1999*

One of America's most respected pop music critics, Robert Hilburn of the *Los Angeles Times*, proclaimed in his first column of 1999 that "rock and roll has died (again)." Reflecting on the decades when bands such as the Byrds, the Doors, the Eagles, Van Halen, and Guns "N" Roses ruled Hollywood, the Sunset Strip, and the American music industry, Hilburn finds current rock groups like Sugar Ray, Matchbox 20, Korn, and the Cherry Poppin' Daddies to be "tired . . . dead end." Hilburn says "now the sound you are most likely to hear on the Strip and the streets of Hollywood . . . is the hip-hop of Master P, DMX, Wyclef Jean or Busta Rhymes." For the first time a hip-hop record (*The Mis-Education of Lauryn Hill*) was Grammy Award winner for Album of the Year in 1999.[4] Hilburn believes rock music may not recover this time because "for the first time in its four decade history, rock and roll has lost the allegiance of its young target audience as well as its all-meaningful contact with the over-30 constituency that championed it for years" (*Los Angeles Times*, January 1, 1999). Although rock CDs still outsell rap albums overall in the USA, rap's sales are growing at a much faster rate and its cultural implications are even greater.

Rock music represents white America and northern Europe. Even the term "rock" signifies "not black" to many people inside and outside the music industry. Rap music and hip-hop culture, on the other hand, originated in urban black American neighborhoods and represent one highly-visible variety of black American culture. The hip-hop scene embraces African-American influences ranging from Malcolm X and Louis Farrakhan to Muhammed Ali and Shaquille O'Neal. Some varieties of rap music, most notably "gangsta' rap," are blatant social critiques, not just dance music. Rap has a more authentic raw energy and radical edge than contemporary rock and roll. What was once considered a passing fad akin to disco, rap and hip hop have persisted to the point where the music of Dr Dre, Will Smith, LL Cool J, Grandmaster Flash, and Tupac Shakur are now considered classic pop music oldies.

The mass media, especially television, have been accused over the years of blatantly stereotyping racial groups, particularly African-Americans. Certainly to dismiss blacks with the age-old stereotype of "singers, dancers, and athletes" is an incomplete, misleading, and racist evaluation. But such a dismissal also grossly misunderstands the power of popular culture. Today's pop music trends are part of a sea change in American and global popular culture, a virtual takeover of youth culture by black stars. The strength and gracefulness of black athletes, the majestic tones of black singers, the attitude and cultural appeal of rap artists, and the quick, fluid movement of black dance styles are among the most tantalizing forms of contemporary popular culture. Singers, dancers, and athletes are cultural heroes of the first order whose symbolic power is immeasurable. Although the media continue to concentrate on stereotypical aspects of American black (and other) cultures in pursuit of corporate profits by keeping characters and stories predictable, they also single out and glamorize images that many people, especially youth, find extremely attractive.

Ironically, then, the mainly white-owned commercial mass media and culture industries, including sports franchises, are largely responsible for promoting black popular culture to the celebrated status it has attained worldwide. This didn't happen overnight. Black musicians, for instance, were not given recording contracts by the music industry until well into the twentieth century. Black athletes were banned from the professional leagues. Black actors rarely found regular work in American television and film until the 1970s. The reluctance to feature black entertainers was eventually overcome when industry realized the extent to which black culture is marketable. Now, black presence in popular culture far exceeds the size of the African-American population, and not just in the music scene. By the late 1990s, for instance, representation of black Americans on commercial TV more than doubled the proportion of blacks in American society, according to the Nielsen television ratings company.

African Americans are themselves extremely active consumers of pop culture products, especially black pop culture. The Nielsen company reports that black households in the United States watch television on average 70 hours per week, about half again as much as other viewers. Black children watch nearly two-thirds more TV than other viewers. Furthermore, black viewers much prefer programs with black casts, stories, and culture. For example, *Seinfeld* and *Home Improvement*, programs which feature white stars, stories, and culture, ranked at the very top of national TV ratings in America for years but never attracted large black audiences. Asked which media personalities they most admire, black children aged 10–17 ranked Michael Jordan, Moesha, Will Smith, Martin Lawrence, LL Cool J, and Oprah Winfrey – all black stars – as their favorites in the 1998 annual survey by Children Now.

The electronic media and the sounds and images they produce resonate sensuously with the orality of black styles of communication and culture. But people of all colors, races, and cultures eagerly buy black music, cheer on black athletes, and regularly tune in black television programs. The same 1998 Children Now survey, for instance, shows that white, Latino, and Asian children also rate black stars –

especially Michael Jordan, Will Smith, and Oprah Winfrey – among their favorites. The cultural crossover converges from all ethnicities toward black popular culture, but not the other direction. The tendencies are most pronounced among youth.

The $3.2-billion US Tommy Hilfiger fashion empire became so successful because, according to *New Yorker* magazine, he was the first white designer to realize that white kids – not to mention Asians, Latinos, and youth from other ethnic groups too – would buy what black youth buy, not the other way around.

We can use the case of black popular culture to help illustrate the relationship between race and culture as well. Let me once again use an example from American media. The comedian Sinbad, former host of *Showtime at the Apollo*, a popular late-night weekend TV program originating from the famous theater in Harlem, paid the highest compliment he could one week when he introduced a talent contest entrant as "the blackest white man I ever met!" Every non-black guest on this lively show must be able to do one thing: be black. They don't have to *be* black, but they must be *black* – American black, that is. The racially-black audience at the Apollo doesn't mind if white, Asian, or other singers, dancers, or comedians compete by copying black style. In fact, they applaud wildly when it is done successfully. But the point is you better get it right! You better be (American) black *culturally*. Those who are black racially have an inside track on being black culturally. White rap singers more than anyone these days feel pressure to prove they are black enough to perform a style of popular music so clearly associated with black culture.

By their tendencies to focus on certain marketable characteristics, mass media and popular culture tend to turn racial groups into predictable cultural phenomena. By acquiring the black cultural look, for example, people of all races consequently acquire something of the black "race" too.

The popular culture marketplace certainly doesn't eradicate racism – some critics claim it only exploits minority groups even more – but it undeniably provides unprecedented access to black cultural space. This is true not only in the domains of athletics, music, and television. By the mid-1990s, pop music radio stations in many major American urban markets had been given over almost exclusively to contemporary black musical forms including rap, house, acid jazz, and techno often combined with rhythm and blues, soul, funk, and disco oldies. But just as important, those top-rated stations – whose listeners come from all racial and cultural groups – feature young black male deejays who talk to each other, and to telephone callers, between and over the songs. Listeners can easily drop in on and participate in black culture via FM radio stations. And, after a rough beginning, where black musical groups were largely excluded from the playlists, MTV Music Television and other music video channels have also widely exposed black youth culture, especially hip hop. By the early 1990s, an all-rap program (*Yo! MTV Raps*) had become the music channel's hottest cultural property and highest-rated show. Black veejays routinely engage black artists and fans in conversation on MTV. Nationally-syndicated talk shows hosted by African Americans such as Arsenio Hall and Keenan Wynans, where black vernacular, subjects, and styles of discussion also dominate, have been other wide avenues into everyday black culture. Scandalous American talk-show host Jerry Springer says his program, and others like it, are another mediated space where black people can be themselves. In the midst of the controversy about whether or not the often violent actions of guests on his show are authentic, Springer told MSNBC that "normally black people have to dress white and talk white. On our show they don't have to do that."[5]

Popular culture can help reverse patterns of race-based social influence. Such is the potential of symbolic power. The "black power" and "black is beautiful" social movements originating in the 1960s, for example, spoke to much more than color, race, and politics. These were cultural primal screams: "Say it Loud! I'm Black and I'm Proud!" Black power is symbolic power, which is now widely appropriated by media institutions of all types, and by audiences of all colors and cultures. Rather than consider the spectacular images of American black popular culture that appear on the mass media only as exploitative, I suggest we look at the issue from another perspective too, taking into account the extraordinary force of symbolic power and the cultural capital it creates.

Carnival culture

> Soccer, television, and Carnival are alike in that each creates a democracy missing in most areas of Brazilian life.
>
> *Kottak 1990: 43*

The success of black popular culture is by no means limited to developments in the United States or the United Kingdom. And while transnational commercial media and culture industries are largely responsible for the effective spread of black popular culture to most parts of the world, this is not the only vehicle for its success. Brazil, like America, has a large black population (though as we have seen in chapter 6, "black" is largely a northern way of categorizing people racially). The Brazilian government decided as part of domestic policy in the 1930s to make black culture an important part of national identity. The element of black culture selected to accomplish this task was samba music and dance. Media designated to spread the influence of samba were radio and the record industry (Rowe and Schelling 1991). This historical development did not help Brazil's black community very much economically, politically, or socially, but it did generate extraordinary cultural capital for blacks in Brazil, and for all Brazilians as they are perceived by people living outside the huge South American country. As Colombian Jesús Martín-Barbero observed about his neighboring national culture: "The black physical gesture became the heart of the popular . . . the passage which started from the *candomble* [an Afro-Brazilian religion] and followed a winding path, twisted and overlaid with other meanings, finally brought music to the record and the radio" (1993: 174).

Samba is the "official" music of Brazil, and Carnival is the official party (see also chapter 4, "Rules and culture"). Every Brazilian city has its own Carnival celebration. Carnival is one of the Brazilian sensations – a cultural ritual that has become mediated, commercialized, and globalized by the culture industries and news organizations. Television images of Carnival are contemporary Brazilian cultural icons. In fact the highlight of Carnival – the parade of the samba schools – can only be experienced via television for the vast majority of people in Brazil's big cities because the cost of tickets for the live event has escalated well beyond a common worker's monthly salary. Furthermore, while the famous Carnival ritual integrates many features of Afro-Brazilian culture into what was originally a Portuguese festival – changing the whole look and atmosphere of the national party – dark-skinned Brazilians are excluded from their own party in many ways. Few of them can afford tickets to watch the parade in person, and many of the parade's featured personalities are light-skinned stars of Brazilian television and other media.

On the other hand, television does bring the parade and the Carnival experience into the homes of all but the very poorest Brazilians. Carnival, thus, originates in the poor neighborhoods, passes through the elite and upper middle classes on the parade grounds, and returns to the poor on television. Television coverage may miss the grandeur and ambiance of the live celebration, but it adds its own production touches to enhance the ceremony's impact. Cameras focus on the featured media stars, the undulating hips of the beautiful *morenas*, the spinning *Bahianas*, the lightning-fast samba dancers, commentary by experts, and replays of the parade's best moments.

Conclusion

Fears were rampant when the old mass media were new. Mass media and mass entertainment terrified some academic theorists (especially in Europe) in the early part of last century because acceptable cultural styles and standards appeared vulnerable to the ravages of popular taste. The expanding, unknown "urban mob" (Pearson 1983) seemed to be taking over society by dictating "vulgar" preferences in the commercial popular culture marketplace:

> In the most forceful version of these concerns it was feared that the new culture industries could be used to so stultify the tastes of mass audiences that not only would [the masses] be incapable of appreciating the emancipatory potential of cultural innovation, but they could also be enslaved by new forms of charismatic leadership. (Chaney 1994: 14)

Today's "urban mobs" and other societal non-elites not only consume, but help produce, popular culture as sources and receivers in mediated communication. They are themselves among the new charismatic leaders. Cultural realities today are grounded more and more in symbolic milieus of mediated experience. Symbolic spheres manifest cultural appearances. Symbolic power and popular culture constitute and reinforce each other in media content and in the routine social exchanges that compose everyday life. And while the kinds of cultural innovation being invented today may not conform to the elite standards of taste preferred by some early twentieth-century European critical theorists, other cultural innovations have emerged. Furthermore, the symbolic weight of new cultural styles and statements does help counterbalance the more predictable and often repressive effects of traditional forms of power, and the institutions and persons behind them.

8

Meaning in Motion

People do not live without constraints or always act in ways that best serve their interests. The economic elite labor overtime to maintain their power. Dominant ideologies are extremely potent social influences. But staying with a central theme of this book, communication and culture can never be fully managed by society's political-economic power brokers, including its mass media image makers. Ideological discontinuities and social disruptions are especially evident in today's fast-paced, contradictory, conflictive world. Although social institutions and information technology clearly serve their managers and backers in certain ways, they also sometimes combine to shake dominant political visions and cultural traditions to the core. Such processes are the subject of this chapter and the next. But before we discuss how these complex and dynamic forces take form, let's examine some of the ways industrialization and modernity influence the production of commodities, information, and entertainment, using political-economic theory as our critical framework.

Media and cultural imperialism: a brief review

Industrialized capitalist societies produce mass-mediated messages in much the same way they produce commodities. Historical parallels between the two domains of production are striking (figure 8.1).[1] In pre-industrial societies people had to be extremely self-reliant – raising food, constructing and maintaining living spaces, making and repairing clothes, and so on. Because some persons were more skilled at certain tasks than others, pre-industrial specialization, the

age of the artisan, emerged. The earliest forms of organized industrial activity, the manufacturing stage, soon followed. Men and
women with various talents applied their trade for bosses who
managed production, cultivated markets, and sold the first mass-
produced goods. Full-blown Western, capitalist industrialization
grew rapidly from the manufacturing stage. Assembly lines accelerated the speed and efficiency of production, corporate structures
mushroomed, and marketing and advertising developed as essential
related industries.

Such frenetic industrial growth, however, brought with it a heavy
social price. Workers were forced to unionize to protect their right to
health, safety, job security, reasonable working conditions, and a
living wage. But labor unions couldn't solve all the social problems
that came with industrialization. The overall effect on the human
psyche was profound. Anthony Giddens summarizes the classic
Marxist and mass society critique of industrialization this way:

> As the forces of production develop, particularly under the aegis of
> capitalistic production, the individual cedes control of his life circum-
> stances to the dominating influences of machines and markets. What
> is originally human becomes alien; human powers are experienced as
> forces emanating from an objectified social environment. (1991: 191)

Commodities	Messages
Self-sufficiency	Interpersonal communication
Artisan	Artist
Manufacturing	Independent producer and agent
Industrialization	Network

Figure 8.1 Stages of capitalist production

A similar historical trajectory can be traced in the production of
public information and entertainment. The earliest forms of communication, of course, were unmediated interactions taking place in
families, neighborhoods, and communities. But, like the production
of commodities, some people became information and entertainment
specialists – storytellers, musicians, artists, writers, orators. Development of communications technology in capitalist societies led to

the mass production of public messages in much the same way as sophisticated tools and machines, and the profit-driven organization of labor and industrial production behind them, made the expanded manufacture of commodities possible. Public communicators of all types began to depend on business agents and independent producers (to negotiate contracts with publishers or arrange musical or theatrical tours, for instance). Artistic control and integrity eroded as public information and entertainment became institutionalized, commodified, and commercialized.

Production and sale of popular culture quickly became a major industry, especially in the United States. This development is represented by the last stage of message production in figure 8.1 – network, which corresponds to the industrialization of goods. By "network," I mean the complex of culture industries overall, not just the television networks. In the network, information specialists and entertainers lose much control over their work. Business decisions persistently overrule artistic choices in the never-ending quest for financial gain.

Throughout most of the twentieth century the trend in culture-industry ownership was toward concentration in the hands of fewer and fewer multinational corporations (Bagdikian 1997). Furthermore, the culture industries became part of a vast system of inter-related agencies. In the United States, for example, this includes government offices (e.g. Federal Communications Commission, Federal Trade Commission, press secretaries); industry lobbying groups (e.g. American Newspaper Publishing Association, National Association of Broadcasters, Motion Picture Producers and Distributors Association of America, Magazine Publishers Association); national and international information suppliers such as wire services, television program production companies and syndicators, the music industry, and radio and television networks; advertising companies and the clients they represent; as well as individual publishing houses, radio and television stations, cable outlets, satellite systems and programming distributors, computer hardware and software producers, Internet service providers, even local telephone companies which during the past decade have branched into many commercial communications services. All these agencies have a vested interest in maintaining the political-economic-cultural system. It is today an industrial collectivity and basic ideological mindset with worldwide implications.

Signature trends in today's communication industries began to emerge more than 500 years ago. The origin of modern Western media can be traced to the invention of the first mass communications technology, the manual printing press, in mid-fifteenth-century Europe. The social implications were dramatic and long-lasting. Development of the Gutenberg printing press stimulated a shift in institutional power away from the church, which previously controlled the flow of ideas and information through public channels, to new symbolic and cultural centers and networks (Thompson 1995). The first major social consequence of modern communications technology, therefore, was to challenge established lines of institutional authority. With the advent of the printing press, "for what may have been the first time in history, a human community willingly harbored a nonreligious agent of social change, and permitted it to transform on a continual and systematic basis virtually every feature of social life" (McCracken 1990: 29–30).

Further development of communication technology and the shift of symbolic power from one institution to another fostered new ideological priorities. From the very beginning, media industries were "commercial enterprises organized along capitalist lines" (Thompson 1994: 33). This was true not only of the printing press in late medieval and early modern Europe, but also of film, radio, and television in the United States centuries later. Like their counterparts in England and many other European nations, American law makers tried at first to ensure that the awesome communicative capabilities of the new electronic media would be used for humanitarian and artistic purposes. Legislation drawn up by United States congressmen in the 1920s, for instance, demanded that the new medium of the day, radio, should not become solely a commercial instrument. But just as marketplace forces subverted social utopian visions in other public spheres in America, expectations of media performance died out too. Just a few decades after the first AM radio station crackled through the airwaves, the fundamental mandate of commercial electronic media – to broadcast as a "public resource" and in the "public interest, convenience, and necessity" – was virtually forgotten. Today, American media regulatory agencies such as the Federal Communications Commission and the Federal Trade Commission are far more likely to represent industry interests than they are to protect citizens' rights. Commissioners are routinely recruited from, and return to, the very industries they are supposed to monitor. The market has replaced government as the regulator of media.

Economic realities greatly influence the international flow of news and entertainment too. News and entertainment combine with America's highly effective industrial, military, transportation, and technological presence worldwide to create and sustain favorable conditions for maintaining its national interests. All the relatively developed nations (the "core" countries) use modern communications technology to conduct business and represent their economic priorities and cultural values globally. The major Western international news agencies – Associated Press, United Press International, Reuters, and Agence France Presse – have spread culturally-biased journalistic reports throughout the world (Smith 1980). Domination of global news reporting and the continued spread of the English language were made possible by developments in communications technology. As Finnish communications researcher Terhi Rantanen points out, "the United States became the only country in the world to have two international news agencies and thus a dominant position in the world news market. This development took place simultaneously with the United States' expansion in cable communications, radio, and motion pictures" (Rantanen 1994: 34). And in the entertainment industries, the United States' pop cultural products are rivaled only by aircraft manufacturing as the nation's most profitable exports. American popular music, TV serials, video games, books, computer software, and the like sell extremely well all over the world. American popular culture industries depend on such profits. For example, more than 60 percent of Hollywood's film revenues now comes from overseas.

For many years, American political economist Herb Schiller has been one of the world's most outspoken and eloquent critics of the grim scenario described in this chapter so far. The kind of domination we have talked about here is sometimes referred to as *media imperialism* or *cultural imperialism*. Schiller blames such imperialist exploits mainly on the domestic and international political-military-industrial ambitions of the United States (1969; 1973; 1976; 1991; 1996). He claims that American citizens themselves were the first to be trapped in the "corporate-message cocoon . . . [but] what is now happening is the creation and global extension of a near total corporate informational-cultural environment" (Schiller 1989: 168, 128). Consequently, according to Schiller, American cultural images and commodities have "overwhelmed a good part of the world" by "smothering the senses" with a "consumerist virus" (Schiller 1991). Media and cultural imperialism is now thought of more as a corporate than a political force.

Worldwide hegemony of corporate ideology, speech, and cultural activity is, according to Schiller and his sympathizers, made possible by communications technology interacting with the "enormous expansion of scientific and technical information, computerization, and the preeminence of the transnational corporation." This further combines with a "marketing ideological atmosphere" steadfastly supported by an American military–industrial partnership in place since the end of World War II (Schiller 1989: 69, 33–4). Since World War II the power of multinational corporations from the United States, Europe, and Japan have come to dominate much of world trade. The Multilateral Agreement on Investment (MAI) together with the General Agreement on Tariffs and Trade (GATT) and the formation of the World Trade Organization (WTO) further contribute to an increasingly singular world economy.

Herb Schiller is right that communications technology historically had been developed and used by the military and economic power centers of capitalist societies. Such was the case, for instance, with radio in World War I, television in World War II, and information technologies in the Cold War, Vietnam War, Gulf War, and Yugoslavian War. Allocation of the first satellite channels was supervised by the American-dominated and American-housed Communications Satellite (COMSAT) and International Telecommunications Satellite (INTELSAT) which both generously accommodated their first clients – American businesses. From their inception to the present day, satellite channels have been used primarily for transnational corporate communications.

By the mid-1990s advances in communications technology had become truly mindboggling. Again, the immediate beneficiaries were those who could gain the most materially by an increased capacity to gather, store, manage, and send information. Transnational corporations gobbled up everything from satellite channels, powerful mainframe computers, and multimedia configurations to fax machines, voice mail systems, and cellular phones. Technology provided a competitive edge for relatively small businesses too. Telemarketers, for instance, used computer-generated voices to make endless sales pitches directly into people's homes, hawking everything from magazine subscriptions to real estate.

The satellite/cable television combination became so significant that in 1991 entrepreneur Ted Turner was *Time* magazine's "Man of the Year." By 1998 the crown jewel of Turner's former cable empire, CNN Cable News Network, had three times turned the human drama and technological glitz and glamour of the Gulf War into a surreal and sterile video-game simulacrum. Years earlier former US president George Bush admitted that CNN news reports routinely became crucial sources of intelligence that directly influenced his policy decisions, including the official response to China during the

1989 student–worker uprising. When Iran's president Mohammed Khatami wanted to reduce political tensions with the United States and open possible trade negotiations, he skirted around the US government's filter by addressing the American public directly in a CNN interview from Tehran. Former American president Bill Clinton pointed out that the American public had no real idea of where Kosovo is "until CNN started talking about it." Then he counted on CNN and the other news channels to educate the American public about the target of NATO military aggression. The "CNN effect" is unquestionably a central part of contemporary global politics, but we are beginning to see that contemporary news-gathering and disseminating activities have diverse consequences, not all of them hegemonic.

CNN's influence was part of an incredible expansion of commercial telecommunications generally throughout the world during the 1990s. Viewers in the former communist Eastern and Central European nations erected satellite dishes to pull in signals from the West, contributing greatly to the overthrow of repressive political structures. In Scandinavia and Western Europe the treasured commitment to broadcast public service, firmly in place since the introduction of electronic media, gave way to competitive market realities facilitated by satellite and cable systems. Public sector television channels all over Latin America were rapidly privatized. The Chinese TV system became more and more commercial every year, and satellite television began to cover all of Asia. And while audience shares for the commercial networks in the United States continued to decline, hundreds of satellite and cable channels now compete for a slice of the still overall television viewer base.

Critics like Herb Schiller believe that communications activity driven by the interests of multinational corporations brings about systemic, negative cultural consequences on a global scale. Some national governments apparently feel the same way. In the late 1990s, for instance, Canada removed all USA-made television programs from its prime-time schedule. Headed by the fiercely protectionist French delegation in 1996, the European parliament voted to limit non-European films to be shown on European television, pay TV, video on demand, and on-line services. Such limits and bans are common in many other parts of the world, especially in developing countries. The Islamic Taliban government of Afghanistan is the most extreme, having banned all television sets, VCRs, videos, and satellite dishes beginning in 1998.

The zones of indeterminacy

We will now question and qualify many of the assumptions and
claims laid out in the preceding pages. So far I have painted a rather
depressing picture of mass-mediated communication. Through
processes of industrialization and networking, media institutions
dominate artisans and artists, depersonalize their work, and exploit
their labor and creativity. Institutional infrastructure and technology
combine to overrepresent the interests of capitalist owners and managers. Using advanced communications technology, Western transnational businesses monopolize the international flow of information,
debasing and colonizing world cultures along the way.

Although I firmly believe there is more than a grain of truth to
each of these claims, and to their cumulative weight and logic, we
cannot leave our analysis at that. We cannot assume, for instance,
that industrialization is inherently imprisoning and that institutions
are monolithic instruments of political, economic, and cultural
control. Communications technology never serves only its institutional creators, developers, and managers. Symbolic forms are not
interpreted uniformly.

British critical theorist John Tomlinson (1991; 1999) has made
a particularly well-reasoned case against the common media and
cultural imperialism argument put forward by Schiller and others.
Tomlinson shows why such imperialism theories mislead because they
are overly (1) *functionalist* (as if communications were a closed
system); (2) *deterministic* (as if ideological "effects" are consistent
and predictable); (3) *unempirical* (these theories lack real-world evidence, especially about how audiences interpret and use symbolic
forms); (4) *atheoretical* (communication processes are not sufficiently
explained or located within broad social theory); (5) *reductionist*
(complex social phenomena are reduced to simple models of human
behavior); (6) *pessimistic* (an unjustifiable gloom-and-doom "victim-
ization" theme pervades the work); and (7) *paternalistic* (an elitist,
scolding, authoritative tone characterizes the writing, and compliance
with the authors' "superior" views is demanded with no room for
debate or discussion).

I agree wholeheartedly with Tomlinson, and set out here to make
a far more sophisticated assessment of media and cultural imperialism by first questioning the classical critique of capitalist industrialization and modernization, a brief version of which I presented at the
beginning of this chapter. To begin with, some commentators believe
that many critical theories romantically misinterpret history, especially when it comes to accounts of social power:

> In many pre-modern contexts, individuals (and humanity as a whole) were more powerless than they are in modern settings. People typically lived in smaller groups and communities; but smallness is not the same as power. In many small-group settings individuals were relatively powerless to alter or escape from their surrounding social circumstances. The hold of tradition, for example, was often more or less unchallengeable ... Pre-modern kinship systems ... were often quite rigid and offered the individual little scope for independent action. We would be hard pressed to substantiate an overall generalization that, with the coming of modern institutions, most individuals either are (or feel) more powerless than in preceding times. (Giddens 1991: 192)

Giddens's perspective may reflect a cultural bias in its core assumptions about the desirability of personal freedom and independence, but it does rightfully tear away at a romanticized and misleading account of Western social history. And it is true that today some long-standing cultural traditions in the East are, in fact, changing. Western individualism has greatly influenced life in Japan, South Korea, Taiwan, Hong Kong, Singapore, even China and Vietnam, for example. In any event, we should not accept at face value the idea that industrialization, modernization, and globalization somehow forcefully destroy cultures against their collective will.

Why is it that the consequences of global communication and commerce cannot be confidently predicted? I have labeled this section of the chapter, "zones of indeterminacy." This means that all four major components of any communication system – source, channel, message, and receiver – are ultimately uncontrollable by any political-economic-cultural force. The components, or zones, are not determined.

The remainder of this chapter will focus on the first three components of communication systems – sources, channels, and messages. Our goal is to demonstrate that by looking closely at actual processes of communication, we shall see that particular consequences are indeed not determined nor necessary. This means that the apocalyptic pessimism of the media and cultural imperialism theses are simply not supportable. We shall continue to deconstruct imperialism by taking up the fourth component of the system – receivers – in chapter 9.

Communication sources: institutional diversity

The first assumption of the imperialism thesis that should be put to rest is the idea that institutional infrastructure and technology work together in some uniform way to benefit only their owners and managers. In reality mass media often do just the opposite; they stimulate ideological and cultural diversity, sometimes precisely by contradicting their owners' and managers' intentions. Media institutions are, after all, *social* institutions. They are made up of human beings. So, just as the memberships, agendas, and activities of any social group change over time, whatever ideological structures social institutions articulate are inventions which, like their authors and interpreters, are not static. The "social construction of reality" must be understood as a process that applies as much to the nature of institutions, including media institutions, as it does to the dynamics of daily life anywhere else.

No single institution can ever articulate but one ideology. Certainly no media institution can. In fact, diversity and contradiction are fundamental themes that emerge when we closely examine what is presented on the mass media throughout the world. This is because institutions all have multiple authors each with their own identities, values, and points of view who are trying to attract and please equally diverse and demanding audiences. Furthermore, the mass media professions often attract very independent, creative, critical, even rebellious personalities as employees. Many years ago the American sociologist Herbert Gans pointed out that creators of commercial media programming in the United States constantly "fight to express their personal values and tastes . . . and to be free from control by the audience and media executives" (1974: 23). Basing their argument on textual analyses of programs and on interviews conducted with American TV producers and writers, Horace Newcomb and Paul Hirsch support Gans's point. They argue that television is certainly as much a forum for the expression of ideas as it is an ideological weapon of any controlling or dominant political-economic group or class. They claim that the television system as a whole produces a "multiplicity of meanings" and emphasizes "discussion rather than indoctrination . . . contradiction rather than coherence" (1987: 459). Television programs, therefore, ultimately reflect the range of values, beliefs, and opinions held by people who make up the industry. This is what the "cultural forum" means.

The principle of the cultural forum applies broadly. For example, although American and Chinese media institutions operate within very different political and bureaucratic systems, the media function as a forum in both contexts. Unofficial ideological and cultural visions held by Chinese media specialists – journalists, TV writers and producers, and film directors, for example – are expressed in Chinese media as an inevitable consequence of multifarious media professionals carrying out their workplace routines. We have already discussed one historically significant example of how this works in the case of politically-charged domestic Chinese television programs (see chapter 5). Because Chinese media are operated by the government, messages authored by journalists, editors, and entertainers are supposed to represent official positions. However, many media professionals have their own ideas about the direction China should be headed and how to get there:

> many of the ideological twists and turns that have come from the national government itself in China have been influenced by nuances originating with workers in television and the other mass media who have dared to author unofficial ideas, accounts, and explanations. By invoking the government's own rhetoric and rationale of openness and reform, China's change agents in the media have actually been able to do their oppositional work in the guise of sanctioned national interest. (Lull 1991: 213)

Several factors interact to destroy the omnipotence of any presumed official ideology in China: the diversity of perspectives held by influential workers in the nation's media industries; the inability of the state to manage and control its cultural policy in any consistent or uniform way; contradictory values expressed within the totality of domestic and foreign programs and commercial advertisements; a desire on the part of TV station managers to attract and please large audiences; and the rapidly increasing number of television stations, each with its own requirement to fill airtime. These conditions contributed to an ideological chorus that stimulated a profound cultural reflection and political crisis in the late 1980s, and the influence is today being felt even more strongly, especially in the economic and cultural areas.

Even where media institutions are ostensibly used by the official controllers to foster ideological and social unity, diversity and disunity can arise instead. An isomorphic relationship develops between institutions and their ideological structures: as institutions change, their structures change too, leading to the further adaptation of institutions, and so on. Beyond this, institutions not only constantly change internally, their positions relative to each other also fluctuate. For example, during China's official modernization period, from 1979 to the present, the overriding characteristic of Chinese society, which at one level may be the most planned and prescriptive nation in the world, has been profound disorganization and contradiction within its major institutions and policies – the Communist Party, the political apparatus more broadly, the economic program, the system of jurisprudence, and the culture industries (especially television, but also newspapers, film, Internet, and the other mass and micro media).

Another good example of the inability of China to define and carry out any singular cultural policy can be seen in the country's negotiations with the Disney Corporation over establishing a Chinese Disneyland. The *New York Times* reported in late 1996 that "Although China's government often looks monolithic from the outside, the mixed signals that Disney received [from different official sectors each with a role in bringing Disneyland to China] illustrate how rivalries between leaders and interest groups can flare, particularly between Beijing, the capital, and Shanghai, the financial center."

Similar developments were taking place in many of the former Soviet-bloc nations of Eastern and Central Europe in the late 1980s and early 1990s. The remarkable thing about all the rebellions against communist authority is that they were made possible in part by the same state-owned-and-operated media organizations that were designed to prevent just such ideological disputes and social crises. International media reports of turmoil spread from one country to another, further fueling the flames of resistance. Consider the following events that took place as the Soviet Union fell apart:

- Fearing the political influence of rock music, the former East German government called mandatory meetings of the country's pop musicians to announce strict rules for writing and performing music. Designed to shackle the growing East German pop music movement, the government meetings provided instead an opportunity for musicians to meet and talk. On these occasions musicians organized resistance to the very government that called the meetings to quell the cultural uprising (Wicke 1992).
- An alternative to the official television news source in Hungary, the Black Box Network, forced the government system to become less propagandistic and more objective in its news reporting. The relatively progressive official Hungarian service then influenced viewers in the former Czechoslovakia and Romania who were able to receive TV signals from their less repressive communist neighbor.
- Liberal professionals inside the print and broadcast journalism industries in the former Czechoslovakia exercised unprecedented

freedom during the crucial weeks leading up to the "Velvet Revolution" (the nonviolent overthrow of Russia's control of the country in 1989).

■ Former Romanian dictator Nicolae Ceauşescu cut back TV transmission as part of his austerity program, leading angry viewers to try harder than ever to pick up foreign signals. Videotape trafficking also increased as even the poorest Romanian families managed to gain access to VCRs. Later, when gun battles raged between revolutionary forces and state soldiers in Bucharest, the fiercest fighting took place at the Romanian National Television facilities. After ruling officials were ousted, the new leader, Ion Iliescu, was sworn into office in the government television studio. Legitimacy of the new government was established by humiliating the captured Ceauşescu and his family on state television.

More recent ideological and cultural struggles in communist nations reveal the same institutional tendencies:

■ In Cuba the government-sponsored national film industry produced the award-winning *Strawberries and Chocolate*, which debuted before an international audience at the country's annual film festival in Havana in 1994. The film depicts a passionate struggle between the forces of communist hegemony and resistance to that hegemony by exposing how Cuba's government has oppressed homosexuality specifically, and ideological and cultural openness in general. The film became a monumental symbol for social change in Cuba.

■ In order to earn considerable foreign currency, China cooperated with the American film industry in the late 1990s to produce *Seven Years in Tibet*, *Red Corner*, and *Kundun*, all of which harshly criticize the Chinese government.

■ Chinese leader Jiang Zemin and former US president Bill Clinton held a joint press conference in Washington in 1997, and the following year debated each other at a televised news conference in Beijing. In the live broadcast Clinton talked about individual rights, freedom of speech, and the Tiananmen Square crackdown. Clinton said protesters had "raised their voices for democracy" and that "the use of force and the tragic loss of life was wrong." Later, he said many of the same things during a live radio talk show in Shanghai.

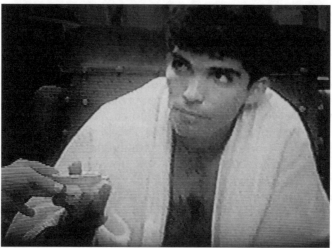

Photo 8.1, 8.2 In a poignant scene from the Cuban film *Strawberries and Chocolate*, the cosmopolitan character Diego offers Communist Youth loyalist David a taste of the outside world (reprinted courtesy of Miramax Films)

    Mass media outlets are multivocal. The symbolic weight of subtle subversive messages can be far greater than often-repeated representations of the dominant ideology. What appears on the mass media frequently contradicts the ideological articulations of other social institutions. Unofficial, underfinanced media can have greater social impact than official, well-financed channels. When conditions are right, institutional and ideological diversity can burst to the forefront in sensational ways capable of changing the course of history.

The market

Television can become an unparalleled agent of resistance to authority when the imagery it presents interacts with troubling local conditions. Let's reflect for a moment on one of those symbolically heavy media moments – the televised beating of black motorist Rodney King in Los Angeles, California, in 1992. Can it reasonably be argued that repeated showings of this videotape on television helped maintain the hegemony of America's power elite? Or did this highly symbolic event – the white power structure mercilessly beating down a helpless person of color – actually undermine the special interests of the powerful? In effect, the Rodney King video became a one-minute commercial exposing racial discrimination. The horrific images coincided with conditions experienced personally by many disenfranchised Americans, especially poor blacks and Latinos. Later, when the first "not guilty" verdict for police brutality was announced by the media, two news stories – the King beating and the verdict – interacted to spark the South Central Los Angeles riot. Media coverage of the riot then exacerbated the violence.

What motivated television and the other mass media to pay so much attention to the Rodney King saga? Surely it was the marketplace value of the incident, owing more in journalistic practice to its sensationalism than to any moral responsibility assumed by the profession that produced such a fierce counter-hegemonic barrage. News reports of the verdict were played up sensationally too, especially on TV where the King videotape was almost always shown again. But no one, including journalists, owners, and managers of media properties, could have predicted the startling consequences. The impact ranged from the immediate burning of hundreds of businesses during the riot itself to George Bush's inability later to explain away the problem during his unsuccessful 1992 presidential re-election campaign. The Los Angeles riots became a known-in-common political and cultural resource dramatically symbolizing "what's wrong with America." To the degree that the original video, the riots, and the media coverage helped run Bush out of office, American business interests, which are typically much more comfortable with a Republican president, were damaged as well. For those at the other end of the socioeconomic spectrum, one major effect of the King video was to give apparent undeniable credibility to the often-made claim that the American criminal justice system does not treat ethnic minorities fairly. In the public mind, a courtroom conviction of the police officers was not necessary to determine the truth of the situation. The King tape was self-evidently persuasive. In the popular mind, any legal interpretation finding the police not guilty could only be further evidence of blatant racism and a corrupt criminal justice system. The Los Angeles violence was a different kind of vote cast by an angry jury at large.

Worldwide circulation of the videotaped Rodney King incident and all that it symbolizes was made possible by a key element of capitalist economic and cultural relations – the market. Television news directors all over the world rushed frantically to put a copy of the tape on the air. Furthermore, the endless showings of the King tape certainly did not require a particularly clever or resistant reading by audiences in order to get the full impact. The evidence was right there in front of all us, displayed and discussed sympathetically by the major media themselves. The power of the market had worked to inform and inflame relatively powerless people rather than deceive or repress them.

The market drives the entertainment side of media and popular culture even more than the news and information side. The entertainment industry searches frantically for the next big money-making thing. It's tricky, of course, because culture-industry moguls don't want to invest large sums of money in unproven ideas. It's best to come in strong right behind the cutting edge. What is put up for sale must be bought. Then, anything goes. The popular culture marketplace ultimately disrupts any pretense of an imposed or unified dominant ideology. As Matt Johnson, singer for the pop band The The, once told attendees of the New Music Seminar in New York, "The record companies don't care if you're Buddhist, communist, or capitalist so long as you make money for them." Even Herbert Schiller's caustic books, which blatantly criticize capitalism, multinational corporations, and media imperialism, are published and distributed worldwide by multinational corporations, profiting everyone, including the author.

Box 8.1 The Privatization of Public Media

A phenomenon of major significance in the current era is the privatization of public media channels, especially television stations, in many parts of the world. Privatization has been particularly rampant in Latin America, where state-supported "public" media systems have steadily lost audiences to commercial competitors, especially satellite systems.

Privatization is a particularly sensitive matter. State-supported, usually non-commercial media channels in many countries have been considered (especially by intellectuals and political liberals) to be untouchable, precious societal institutions that are dedicated to preserving cultural traditions, values, and priorities. The privatization and commercialization of such channels are sometimes regarded as an unconscionable surrender to capitalism and foreign influence. The Norwegian media studies scholar Jostein Gripsrud has been one of the most outspoken advocates of the role of state media in the face of global competition (1999). Gripsrud believes that public media can respond more responsibly to the needs of national populations, such as that of Norway (where but one or two television channels has been the norm over the years), than imported or highly commercialized media can. Such an argument is not completely without merit.

But let's consider the other side of the story for a moment, using Mexico as our case in point. In 1993 a Mexican state television channel was privatized, becoming the commercial channel TV Azteca. Programming changed decidedly, and some would argue not for the better. Many Mexicans, however, enjoy the culturally provocative programming strategy of the privatized channels.

The best example may be the now-famous Mexican soap opera, A Woman's Glance (Mirada Mujer), which appeared on TV Azteca. In this sensational series, a 50-year-old woman suffering from unbearable Mexican machismo strikes back.[2] When her husband repeatedly abuses her and leaves her for a mistress, the program's heroine does not do what a traditional Mexican woman is expected to do – wait patiently and non-judgmentally for her husband's eventual return – but instead falls in love with a handsome, caring man nearly twenty years her junior. This shocking turn of events on TV publicly ridiculed the taken-for-granted marital double standard of Mexican culture, empowered Mexican women generally, and sparked a fiery national debate not only about the state of marriage, but about many gender-based cultural assumptions.

The program also took up other issues usually typically ignored by Mexican media: abortion, sexual harassment, and alcoholism, for instance. Women and younger viewers were extremely enthusiastic viewers of A Woman's Glance.

Rather than turn people off by its controversies, the fresh programming policy of TV Azteca has made the channel very competitive in the ratings with long-time favorite Televisa. The ratings success has also provided a financial basis for expansion of such programming into other nations in the Latin American market including Guatemala, El Salvador, and Chile. Such positive transnational cultural influences can be made possible by privatization and the lure of the market.

We have concentrated mainly on the established mass media and culture industries in this analysis of institutional diversity. Media and popular culture institutions have become so global, diverse, and commercial that – in contradiction to most critical perspectives – they defy ideological and cultural control. If we bring the Internet and today's wildly-expanding array of digitally-based information technology industries into the discussion, then we move from our central theme, indeterminacy, to near-chaos. Among the most intriguing questions that face national and international policy makers in the early twenty-first century is what to do about this growing communications beast, the Internet. Even more than mass media and the familiar array of culture industries, the Internet is truly outside institutional management, regulation, or control.

Communication channels: unmanageable technology

Just as institutions have diverse and ultimately uncontrollable lives of their own, technology also cannot be completely managed by individual or corporate design. We discussed at some length in chapter 5 how the video, cable, and satellite technologies of the late twentieth century decentered and expanded consumer options, fragmenting audiences into various niches. Here we will explore how communications hardware contributes to this overall process.

The aforementioned Rodney King incident can be summoned again to illustrate how technology does much more than extend and amplify the reach and influence of big media institutions. The Rodney King beating was videotaped by a man learning to use his new camcorder. He released the tape to the national television networks who circulated it worldwide. Two vehicles of ideological control – large capitalistic corporations and telecommunications technology – combined to circulate an unmistakable, unforgettable, unconscionable image. The result can hardly be considered the imposition of dominant ideology or a technological manifestation of media or cultural imperialism.

The Rodney King story is a striking example of how technology can work to represent the interests of relatively invisible people and stimulate social change. Not long after the King story had died down, a similar incident took place when television news cameras on a helicopter captured southern California police chasing and beating a truckload of illegal Mexican immigrants. The immigrants sued the state of California and, like Rodney King, received a huge financial settlement. And what about the O.J. Simpson murder trial which was going on during roughly the same time period? A former Los Angeles police officer who had investigated the crime scene, Mark Fuhrman, was confronted during the trial with an old audiotape of him boasting of how he and other police routinely abuse the rights of black citizens. The officer also used an unmistakable racial slur in his taped remarks. The infamous "Fuhrman tapes" then became primary evidence in Simpson's successful defense that the police were biased against him simply because of his race. The Texaco oil company suffered tremendous embarrassment last decade too when some of its chief executives were exposed on tape making racist remarks.

Visibility and accountability

Not only were audio and videotape recordings crucial pieces of evidence in the King and Simpson trials, the trials themselves were televised live to national audiences in the United States, and to other countries as well, creating maximum *visibility*. Along with the visibility comes *accountability*, the responsibility that powerful people have to their constituents or fans, as we saw in the case of media scandals (see chapter 4 and Thompson 1995; 1997). One significant consequence of the Rodney King and O.J. Simpson trials, for instance, is that fewer criminal arrests have been made in Los Angeles since, particularly when white officers are dealing with black suspects. Police departments now equip their own vehicles with video cameras ostensibly in order to protect citizens' rights, but also to shield officers against claims of Rodney King-inspired police brutality charges. Many experts praised television's role in the Simpson legal proceedings especially because it held lawyers, judges, and witnesses publicly accountable. The American public would not let the Simpson scandal disappear until some measure of justice was extracted from the man legally ruled "not guilty" but found

culpable by the population overall, a judgment which had been facilitated by a national audience who watched the trial on TV and still
held Simpson responsible for the deaths.

Video cameras have become commonplace in convenience stores,
fast-food restaurants, banks, gas stations, drug stores, department
stores, and many other places as anti-crime devices. Cameras
have been used in hospitals and mental institutions to discourage
staff members from mistreating patients. The man found guilty for
bombing the United States federal building in Oklahoma City was
seen on videotape at a McDonalds just before he rented the truck
used in the bombing, evidence which linked him to the crime. Tiny
cameras have even been placed in the masks of Mickey Mouse,
Minnie Mouse, Donald Duck, and the other cartoon characters at
Disney World in order to identify teens who make sport out of pum-
meling the famous figures and running away.

Global visibility and accountability

Today we are accustomed to thinking of the individuals who appear before
us on our television screens as belonging to a public world which is open
for all to see.

Thompson 1995: 119

Before television, two world wars. After TV, zero. We Love TV!
Promotional campaign for ABC-TV, USA, 1998

Since television arrived they can't fool us anymore.
24-year-old college student, Beijing, China,
talking about the communist government; Lull 1991

Television and the other electronic media have made the Vietnam
War, Watergate, the Gulf War(s), the 1989 *Exxon-Valdez* oil spill in
Alaska, nuclear power plant accidents at Three Mile Island, Pennsylvania, in 1979 and at Chernobyl, Ukraine (formerly the USSR), in
1986, Tiananmen Square, Rodney King, the O.J. Simpson trial,
Princess Diana's death, the Clinton scandal, and the Yugoslavian War
among other media events all strikingly visible to a global audience.
Electronic media can instantly inform the world and implicitly hold
powerful people responsible for their actions. They can also prevent
certain actions. Military troop and equipment movements, for
instance, are visible not only to governments by means of espi-
onage and high-tech surveillance, but to the entire world via the
technologically-enhanced capacity of international news-gathering
companies. During the Yugoslavian War in 1999, for instance, tele-

vision stations all over the world aired satellite-transmitted video footage of a train full of innocent passengers that had been destroyed by an American warplane, and of the mistakenly bombed Chinese embassy in Belgrade, before NATO and US officials admitted that the accidents had occurred.

The result of all this is sometimes known as the "chilling effect" – the ability of media to intimidate and limit activity – which is by no means always a bad thing. The self-congratulating, promotional rhetoric of the ABC-TV network above may oversimplify television's role as a global peacekeeper, but it is not a completely unfounded claim.

Television does not require print literacy, thereby widening greatly the potential of the medium to expose many things. The Clinton–Lewinsky affair in 1998, for example, seemed more than plausible long before Monica's stained blue dress emerged from the closet and the legal judgments were made. TV viewers worldwide could see the physical comfort and sexual energy between Clinton and Lewinsky simply by viewing the repeated showings of the reception lines where they embraced. Those famous visuals were shown *ad nauseam* for more than a year, their sheer repetition suggesting mutual culpability. Most information communicated in interpersonal interaction is nonverbal – visual cues that are revealed quite explicitly by television.

Visibility and accountability are generated not just by the technical audiovisual qualities of global media. Adoption of international standards of journalistic practice also contribute. The demanding, intrusive Anglo-American journalism style often breaks through local barriers reinforced by language and cultural customs to uncover hidden truths and expose those responsible (Agar 1994: 194–206). American-trained reporters at the young Mexican newspaper *Reforma*, for example, have exposed widespread government corruption, greatly curtailed the tradition of payoffs to journalists for favorable reporting (*el embute*; see Riding 1984: 124–6), and conditioned increased expectations of honesty and fairness among readers. Vigorous journalism thus protects the people's "right to know." Even the dreaded paparazzi can play a positive role in media scrutiny. While any one instance of paparazzi behavior may seem despicable, the scandals they help produce can also balance the sociocultural power equation (Lull and Hinerman 1997). From news, radio talk shows, TV comedy shows, and Internet chat rooms, the lurid details of crimes of desire travel fast, amplifying and reinforcing the original story with incredible symbolic impact. The global visibility of electronic media therefore exposes and deters potential abuses on the part of those who hold traditional forms of social power.

Visibility or surveillance?

Communications technology helps society in many respects. But what about the other side of the story? Is it really a good idea for government or economic institutions to watch us so closely? Whose interests are served by such surveillance? Herbert Schiller (1996), Oscar Gandy (1993), and others have cautioned that constant social surveillance using communications technology works against the social good, and serves mainly to protect society's political-economic power holders. Technologies become policing devices used by powerful persons and institutions to reinforce social norms and maintain control. According to this view, the threatening "Big Brother" scenario has not only become technically possible, but put into practice, and threatens us all.

Concerns expressed by academic critics about the negative consequences of surveillance often spring from or coincide with the writing of the famous late French social theorist Michel Foucault, especially his analysis of prisons, *Discipline and Punish* (1977). Since the sixteenth century, armies, schools, hospitals, and prisons in Western societies have used close observation and documentation among other strategies to create what Foucault argued have become controlling "disciplinary societies" (see Thompson 1995: 119–48).

But is this truly the case? John B. Thompson points out that Foucault's reference to the "Panopticon," a prison surveillance system that keeps a watchful and punishing eye on everyone (pan-optic), is "not convincing" as a "generalizable model for the exercise of power in modern societies" (Thompson 1995: 134). He explains:

> Whereas the Panopticon renders many people visible to a few and enables power to be exercised over the many by subjecting them to a state of permanent visibility, the development of communication media provides a means by which many people can gather information about a few . . . thanks to the media, it is primarily those who exercise power, rather than those over whom power is exercised, who are subjected to a certain kind of visibility. (Thompson 1995: 134)

That certain kind of visibility can serve as a neutralizing force in the global mix of social influences, holding persons from football hooligans and police officers to presidents and members of the royal family more accountable for their actions than ever before. Telecommunications also inspire a general "cultural visibility." That was a big part of the restlessness of communist cultures over the years, contributing greatly to their general decline worldwide, as populations in those countries were able to see images from the more developed capitalist nations. Currents of mainstream American culture, complete with their vivid representations of freedom, rights, democracy, and fun lifestyles, are particularly visible on a global scale. Such seductive images provoke no uniform response, however. Admiration, disgust, joy, jealousy, and resentment are common reactions. Nonetheless, sheer presence on the media bespeaks a nearly incomprehensible form of social influence. Thus *visibility in and of itself is an extraordinary kind of power*. We have more information about all nations and cultures now, making perceived cultural similarities and differences more apparent worldwide, while concealing the great range of internal variety that all nations and cultures manifest.

Unforeseen consequences

Although the global telecommunications industry has realized much of its intended marketplace potential, history is full of examples where communications hardware is appropriated in unforeseen, unwanted, and even illegal ways. Satellite-transmitted TV signals, for instance, can be picked off relatively easily. A favorite hobby among technology-oriented consumers in developed countries is finding ways to watch satellite TV programming without paying the subscription fees. Creative techno-theft takes place at the institutional level too. As one example, American TV networks and programs, including Spanish-language channels, are intercepted, amplified, and sent through cable television systems making huge profits for entrepreneurs in Mexico and the Caribbean. During the 1989 civil unrest in China, the Chinese government took satellite signals being beamed out of Beijing by Western news organizations, put a completely different narration on the images, and transmitted the revisionist reports back to their own people as part of an impromptu propaganda assault. At the same time, American news agencies were stealing satellite-transmitted national news reports of dissidents being arrested by the communist authorities from the Chinese national television system. The images were then used by American broadcasters to inform and influence their audiences by selectively showing what was happening inside China. By the mid-1990s, some Chinese families had obtained satellite receiver dishes and were regularly watching Rupert Murdoch's Star TV transmissions and other international channels. Government coordination and control was so weak during the economic frenzy of China in the 1990s that the military and the national Ministry of Radio, Film, and Television had even sold satellite-receiving equipment to individual consumers, further under-mining ideological and cultural control.

The conclusions British sociologist and music critic Simon Frith reached about technological development of the music industry apply broadly to communication and culture:

> If there's one thing to be learned from twentieth century pop music history, it is that technological innovations have unexpected conse-quences. The industrialization of music has changed what we do when we play or listen to music . . . but these changes aren't just the result of producers' decisions and control. They also reflect musicians' and consumers' responses. (1992: 69)

To elaborate Frith's point, a familiar texture of 1960s rock music was ear-shattering feedback intentionally produced by guitarists who banged their instruments against high-volume loudspeakers. Years later hip-hop deejays created a radical new sound by rhythmically "scratching" the grooves of vinyl recordings back and forth. Con-sumers play their part in the mix too. The first phonographs, which were marketed as dictating machines, could not be sold for the intended purpose. Eight-track audio cassette players stalled. Audio compact disc players became the industry standard while digital audio tape (DAT) machines never captured much consumer interest. Consumer technologies such as car phones, pagers, and cellular phones, even touch-tone telephones, have been appropriated by drug dealers as sales tools and police alert devices. Home copying of audio and videotapes and compact discs has significantly reduced profits that were supposed to accrue to the transnational music and film industries.[3]

Some consumer technologies alter or downgrade the social effects of the original technology. Television remote control units, for instance, make it easy to mute or avoid commercials. Inexpensive devices that block certain TV channels or permit only a preset amount of viewing time are available, and can even be built into the TV set itself. VCRs equipped with the "Commercial Free" feature automatically "fast forward" through commercials when viewers watch recorded tapes. At times the social consequences of com-munications technology are quite subtle. For instance, telephone answering machine messages can be saved not for the institutionally intended reason of preserving information, but for the emotional experience of hearing the voices again and again. Indeed, "techno-logical change is not something that occurs independently of the uses to which [social] agents put technology" (Giddens 1984: 178).

Internet: the push and pull of on-line cultures

The eureka moment for most of us came when we first clicked on a link
and found ourselves jettisoned across the planet. The freedom and imme-
diacy of that movement – shuttling from site to site across the infosphere,
following trails of thought wherever they led us – was genuinely unlike
anything before it.

Johnson 1997: 110

Information technology cannot simply be lumped together with
other technological devices in any discussion about communication
and culture. By now everyone understands that new technologies
have radically transformed the way we create and communicate. The
big, multinational corporations and other large businesses benefit
tremendously from information technology, just as they have from
all previous technological advances. From intranet communication
and international data storage and transfer to increasingly-profitable
e-commerce ventures and high-tech advertising, imaging, and marketing, the corporate world has found very sophisticated ways to
take advantage of the most recent developments in information
technology.

The culture industries are among the corporate entities that benefit
the most. Websites for every imaginable cultural product have been
launched. The Internet itself has become an alternative broadcasting
system capable of transmitting digital sound and video around the
world. The fabulous success of Amazon.com reflects consumers' willingness to spend enormous amounts of money on books, music, and
videos by means of Internet transactions. Major communications
media companies such as commercial television networks and
cable channels have diversified into Internet images and properties,
complementing and extending their influence as sources of news
and information (see chapter 2). Entertainment corporations invest
greatly in Internet-based projects to exhibit, promote, and sell their
products in cyberspace. Innovative pop culture artists such as David
Bowie have even become Internet Service Providers (ISPs). Information technology companies sell shares of their own stock for unheard-
of profits.

But the power of information technology rests not only in the
hands of big companies. It didn't start there either. Histories of
the invention of the personal computer and its software document
the accomplishments of creative, independent-minded individual
entrepreneurs including long-haired Steve Jobs who designed the first
Apple Computer in his Silicon Valley garage, and nerdy, bored Bill

Gates who dropped out of Harvard to found Microsoft. That independent, inventive spirit continues to characterize how the information technology industries operate, and how their products are used by consumers.

Information technology is far more accessible and user-friendly than traditional communications technologies and media for consumers too. For individuals with sufficient resources and motivation, computers, email, Internet access, and other information technologies and services offer truly exciting possibilities in the digital age. From instant international email, chat rooms on every imaginable subject, and access to millions of information sources, to the capacity to develop a website and start a one-person global business for very little money, even the most critical observer of current trends would have to admit that information technology can be used productively by many people who would otherwise be left out. Information technology remarkably expands the range of communication options, styles, and discourses. The possibilities will continue to grow as telecommunications and Internet technology and connectivity become more integrated. Interactive communications such as family video conferencing, video email, and videotaping without a VCR will be more common. Downloading, storing, and retrieving data of all kinds will be much more user-friendly, giving non-specialists many more options for managing their time, money, and experience to advantage.

The MP3 Internet audio format, for example, has given consumers a technical way to obtain music tracks without having to pay for overpriced compact discs in record stores. Not only can consumers avoid contributing to unwarranted industry profits, they can pick and choose which musical tracks they want – another instance of "cultural programming" by non-specialists (see chapter 6). The digital alternative gives small record producers and distributors a chance to compete with the major international record companies for attention to their products too.

Developments like this reflect how the Internet has "leveled the playing field" in the ideological, economic, and cultural spheres. Websites and email are widely used by individuals and groups as an inexpensive global "soapbox" to criticize, resist, neutralize, avoid, and make fun of institutional structures, forms, and persons of authority:

▪ A website hosted in the USA serves as a place for gays in Singapore to meet. Gay websites cannot be registered or operate in Singapore itself, but Singaporian gays can easily contact each other and arrange to meet by exchanging messages on the USA-based site.

▓ Players dropped from the 1998 Iranian national Olympic football team were reinstated after an Internet-organized protest of Iranians all over the world put pressure on Iran's government to reverse the decision.

▓ Ultra-conservative, punishing, moralizing (but *very* popular) radio talk-show hostess "Dr Laura" (Schlessinger), one of the richest entertainers in America, is literally exposed on a website by a jilted ex-boyfriend. The former boyfriend said he wanted the world see the X-rated pictures so they could learn what a hypocrite she is. Dr Laura could not legally recover damages.

Dr. Laura

The notorious photos of Dr. Laura Schlessinger, the popular radio talk show host.See related news article.

[Index | 1 | 2 | 3 | 4 | 5 | 6 | 7 | 8 | 9 | 10]

Vote for you favorite Dr. Laura photo:

Sele[ ]

Leave a brief comment for the next voter to see (optional):

[   ]

[Cast Vote]

[Home | Splash Mountain | Airport Girl | Monorail Girl|]
[Backyard Flasher | In the News | Your Mountain | Feedback]

Photo 8.3 Exposing Dr Laura "for who she really is" on the Internet

A phone sales representative from Adobe Systems, Inc., in San José insults a Vietnamese-American caller by saying "You Orientals are cheap!" The caller emails friends who post a description of the incident on an Asian community website, reaching 15,000 people within hours. Community members bombard Adobe with email messages that prompt the employee to admit the racial slur and resign from his job.

A student-led Internet protest in Indonesia prompts the resignation of President Suharto and inspires a friendly political intervention from the United States.

Indigenous rebels in the southern state of Chiapas, Mexico, send out email messages to world humanitarian leaders condemning the bloody invasion of federal troops into the area, bringing about tremendous international attention and condemnation. A website established by Canadian sympathizers to the Mexican rebel movement continues to post the latest news and comments, helping maintain global visibility for the otherwise relatively powerless indigenous people.

The American-based Environmental Defense Fund brings together environmental databases from all over the world to a single website "in order to harness the information revolution and empower citizens" as environmental activists.

The limitation in China on the number of foreign films that can be shown in cinemas every year has sparked much home viewing of pirated movie videos, particularly because China offers few entertainment alternatives. Video cassette recorders (VCR), video compact disc players (VCD), and digital video disc players (DVD) have become very popular home appliances for urban families, particularly those who benefit from China's liberalized economic policies or have extended families and friends in Hong Kong, England, the United States and elsewhere who bring them equipment.[4]

Although China has imposed strict rules about the Internet "to safeguard national security and social stability," people creatively use it for a wide range of alternative and subversive purposes. For example, political resistance groups inside China develop a controversial message about a current situation and send it to friends and relatives outside the country, who then "spam" it back all over the People's Republic, thereby limiting the potential for tracing the source. A Chinese language on-line journal of dissent, *Tunnel*, is managed and edited in China. When ready for electronic publication, it is delivered secretly to the United States, then emailed back to China from an anonymous "nobody@usa-net" source. Web surfers inside China easily avoid censorship by linking to computers outside China to exchange political information, entertainment fare, and pornography, and for official and unofficial business transactions.

The downside

The freedom that Internet communication offers individuals and groups has tremendous advantages, but precisely because it is so unregulated and unmanageable some profoundly negative consequences occur as well. Email and chat rooms, for instance, permit anonymous participation that can range from the poetic and playfully erotic to the abusive and hateful. Besides all the creative and positive uses of the Internet, information technology has also been used to distribute anonymous racist and sexist messages, to organize hate crimes, and to exploit children sexually. Such morally bankrupt actions and crimes on the Internet are hard to police. Indeed, we are just beginning to comprehend the full gamut of consequences of life where virtual representations, conversations, and discourses compete with more traditional forms of mediated and unmediated communicative interaction and dialogue in a fundamentally unregulated, global environment.

Communication messages: shades of significance

We've explored the first two "zones of indeterminacy," institutions and technology. We have found institutions to be diverse, and technology to be ultimately unmanageable. Now we shall concentrate on the third zone of indeterminacy – messages. We focus briefly on two important concepts from semiotics, psychology, and communication theory to demonstrate that the meaning of messages cannot be imposed by their authors on readers, listeners, or viewers in mediated or unmediated settings. These concepts are *polysemy* and *selectivity*.

Polysemy and selectivity

Brahma: to Spaniards, a bull; to Brazilians, a beer; to Americans, a recreational road vehicle; to Indians, God.

Polysemy in particular and semiotics in general have become very important study areas in communication. But analyses of how symbolic imagery is variously interpreted and used long predate the recent trends in cultural analysis. The early work on these subjects was done mainly by American social psychologists and sociologists. In a classic study (Cooper and Jahoda 1947), researchers found that a cartoon series designed to reduce racial prejudice ("Mr Bigot") actually did more to reinforce than diminish it. Years later other researchers observed the same effect with the famous American television series, *All in the Family* (Vidmar and Rokeach 1974). The series's executive producer, Norman Lear, tried to make the lead character, Archie Bunker, look like a bigoted fool. Lear reasoned that prejudiced viewers would recognize themselves in Archie's doltish antics and would change their ways as a result. *All in the Family* became enormously popular and it did stir controversy. But just like the "Mr Bigot" cartoon strip, it did something the producer had not anticipated. Instead of being repulsed by Archie, TV viewers with predispositions like his found him likable, even heroic. They perceived him to be down-to-earth, honest, hardworking, and kind. On the other hand, viewers opposed to Archie's values thought he was bigoted, loud, rigid, domineering, and mistreating of his TV wife. How Mr Bigot and Archie Bunker were interpreted was framed by readers' and viewers' values and orientations. These predispositions cannot be altered easily.[5]

These examples demonstrate that symbolic forms are open to multiple, diverse, contradictory interpretations. Messages are *polysemic* – they contain many (poly) possible meanings (semic). What they signify to different people depends on how they are interpreted. The interpretative process is the *selectivity* aspect of meaning construction.

Let's continue to clarify polysemy and selectivity by referring to another early empirical study in social science. In this case, researchers analyzed how students from two American colleges interpreted a film of a football game played between the schools. Accounts of the game varied wildly. The researchers concluded that "the 'game' was actually many different games and each version of the events was just as 'real' to a particular person as other versions were to other people" (Hastorf and Cantril 1954: 134). They explained that "there is no such thing as a 'game' existing 'out there' in its own right which people merely 'observe.' The game exists for a person and is experienced by him only in so far as certain happenings have significance in terms of his purpose" (p. 133).

These early studies in social psychology and communication reveal two fundamental principles that are now being addressed from a different perspective in semiotic analysis and cultural studies research: nothing is interpreted neutrally, and meaning cannot be imposed. It's clear from either perspective that people interpret and use cultural phenomena such as pop music stars, television programs, and sporting games in ways they find reinforcing, stimulating, or otherwise rewarding. Popular culture is not an independent force that works against the will of a person or a society. It originates in and resonates with society at large. When the media and popular culture contribute to social change, this occurs because represented ideas appeal to predispositions and intentions people already hold. The media primarily provide examples and give specific suggestions (Gans 1974: 57).[6]

Interpretative systems of meaning

Meaning is not something assigned only to external objects. Interpretative work is also a process of self-discovery and understanding. Every interpretation of a sign is simultaneously an interpretation and transformation of the imagined self. The teenage girl who thinks about Canadian rock music phenomenon Alanis Morissette, for example, at the same time takes stock of herself. When a young man in Helsinki tries on a pair of jeans for the first time, he conjures up an image of America and of himself too – perhaps of himself in America. In England, "young women use their preferences for one [pop] star over another to help delineate the criteria they consider important in relationships and to see how they differ from their peers in their 'taste' in men" (Willis 1990: 57). Chinese viewers of imported Japanese TV soap operas interpret their own situations along with the stories. The immense popularity of Brazilian talk-show host Silvio Santos can be traced to the way his personality and image resonate with key axes of Brazilian culture, especially paternalism, religion, class, and family (Uribe 1995).

All semiotic activity therefore is made up of complex associations that flow back and forth between external and internal worlds. Such subjective involvements and relationships constitute profoundly dense and dynamic processes of meaning construction.

People choose, combine, and circulate media representations and other symbolic cultural forms in their everyday communicative interactions and in doing so produce meaning and popular culture (chapter 7). The meanings all have social and cultural origins, interpretations, and uses. The significance and degree of acceptance that TV actors and actresses, pop stars, sports heroes and the like ultimately receive is produced by fans, not by stars. People pick and choose from the symbolic field in front of them, interpreting and using such resources in ways that reward them, and so doing they exercise one variety of symbolic power.

Box 8.2 Queens of Polysemy

Now we will call out the case of two extraordinary media stars from the history of American popular culture – Mary Tyler Moore and Madonna – to demonstrate concretely how polysemy and selectivity work.

Mary Tyler Moore is a true icon of American popular culture. The beloved actress and television producer has been successful in many

Photo 8.4 Mary Tyler Moore. The star of the *Mary Tyler Moore Show* (center) appealed to a wide range of viewers (reprinted with permission of Fox Family Channel)

endeavors, but is still best known as lovable television news reporter Mary Richards in the *Mary Tyler Moore Show*. What made it possible for Mary Tyler Moore to become such a superstar? Why did she attract such an enormous audience for so many years? And what about Madonna, who not only made it very big in popular culture, but became a celebrated and controversial personality in academic circles too? College courses have analyzed the Madonna phenomenon. Scientific journals display statistical data about her and scholarly books still debate her psycho-sociocultural-sexual significance. Who adores Madonna and why?

By trying to answer these questions about Mary Tyler Moore and Madonna we can begin to understand how people construct the meaning of their popular culture experiences. Let's first consider the case of Mary Tyler Moore. I conducted an empirical study exploring why female TV stars in America achieve their success during the time when Mary Tyler Moore was very popular (Lull 1980). Female viewers were asked to give their reasons for liking the best-known "TV women" of the time. Mary Tyler Moore emerged from the research in a category of her own. She was ranked by viewers at or near the top of the list of female TV stars for a broad spectrum of reasons. She was perceived to be the "typical American female," "someone like me," "someone I want to be like," "someone I would want as a friend," and "someone I would like to have for a mother." No other female star came close to Mary Tyler Moore's diverse appeal. She was a character for all needs and perceptions twenty years ago, and her satellite and cable reruns today attract older fans and a whole new generation of admirers.

Oprah Winfrey explained on her talk show that she got the courage to pursue a career as a broadcast journalist because she admired Mary Tyler Moore so much in her role as reporter Mary Richards. When Moore appeared many years later as a guest on Oprah's program, the famed talk-show host became extremely nervous and started to cry!

Many different kinds of people also appreciate Madonna for many different reasons. Madonna has zealous fans who are young and old, straight and gay, educated and unschooled, First and Third World, black, white, brown, and yellow, and of every sexual preference, demographic category, and lifestyle imaginable. People who differ from one another in every way can all still find something relevant in Madonna's multidimensional, multimediated public imagery. From the feminist who identifies with Madonna's in-your-face "I take the world on my own terms" attitude to the voyeuristic young male charmed by the explicitly sexy side of her public persona, Madonna resonates widely with multiple, often contradictory, cultural values and lifestyles, personal identities and fantasies. Madonna's significance is discovered, reinforced, and transcended in the various ways her fans enthusiastically put her to work culturally (Schwichtenberg 1993; see also the discussion of symbolic power in chapter 7).

Mary Tyler Moore and Madonna both appeal to a multiple fan base, and that is the key to mega stardom. During the peak of his career, Michael Jackson had the same kind of appeal. It was not only Jackson's talent but his unfixed, even oppositional image system (black/white, child/adult, male/female) that propelled him to the top of international pop culture. These media stars are richly polysemic, and the more polysemic (open ended) the image, the greater the popular potential. The more diverse the range of people who recognize, relate to, or identify with a media "product" for a diversity of reasons, the greater the potential for popular success. People interpret media stars to fit their needs, interests, and fantasies.

Preferred interpretations

We must be careful here not to fall into any trap that would pretend that people have total freedom to interpret their worlds any way they please. Such is definitely not the case. Media and all communication sources exercise tremendous influence over the creation and transmission of messages. They always arrange agendas and styles in front of their intended receivers with specific purposes firmly in mind. Senders frame their messages to encourage interpretations that advance their interests, not necessarily ours. Media genres and formats create certain expectations. This framing of message content is what we mean by *preferred interpretations*, which refers to *the interpretations that message sources would prefer us to make.* No doubt, assimilation of predictable message structure and content into everyday social interaction introduces, reinforces, and extends fundamental themes of the dominant ideology and culture.

Conclusion

In the midst of celebrating human initiative, creativity, and transcendence, therefore, let us not lose perspective. The autonomy and power of individuals and groups in front of dominant ideological and cultural sources are not infinite. For this reason, I do not want to argue completely against the strident and simple line of reasoning that underlies theories of media and cultural imperialism. Clearly there is more than a grain of truth to the idea that society's major ideology-producing institutions, communications technologies, and mainstream messages do serve in many ways to reinforce each other and reaffirm complementary modes of substantial economic, political, and cultural power. And, although people do indeed selectively interpret, invent, and reinvent ideology and culture within the situated realms and moments of their lives, the dominant forms do not go away.

In this chapter, however, we have seen that social institutions, especially the mass media, articulate a wide range of ideas, all of which are open to guided but ultimately unlimited interpretations. Ever-expanding communications technologies cannot be fully controlled. People do in fact connect with symbolic forms and communications technologies in ways they believe promote their interests. As institutions grow and technology becomes more accessible, particularly in the age of the Internet, symbolic forms and their underlying ideologies expand and diversify. User freedom and creativity increase too.

Given all this, any argument that ideology and technology simply smother the senses with some corporate master plan – an idea basic to the media and cultural imperialism argument – does not stand up well to the evidence. Although societies' elite institutions and leaders find ways to use symbolic forms and other resources at their disposal, in the final analysis no totalizing, controlling, hegemonic effect is possible.

In this chapter we have explored institutional diversity in the mass media and culture industries, the undetermined role of technology in social influence, and the polysemic nature of symbolic forms. These are the first three zones of indeterminacy in communication processes. We now turn our attention to the fourth zone, the socio-cultural worlds of "receivers," by exploring how cultural territories and identities shift about in the era of global communication.

9

Globalization and Cultural Territory

Somewhere in the Middle East a half dozen young men could well be dressed in jeans, drinking Coke, listening to rap, and between their bows to Mecca, putting together a bomb to blow up an American airliner.

Huntington 1996: 58

It is true that Coke, tourist T-shirts, and transistors have become universal . . . the things and symbols of Western culture have diffused into the daily lives of many of the world's peoples, even if they are made in Hong Kong.

Friedman 1994: 100

We are witness to an ever-increasing penetration of the mass media, uniformity in our dress, the victory of the fast food outlet; and at the same time we can also see the development of local communication, the rise of individual fashions, local produce and cuisine, so that it would sometimes seem that we are in the process of reappropriating our existence. One is drawn to this conclusion by the fact that, far from erasing the strength of our ties . . . technological advances sometimes even bolster them.

Maffesoli 1996: 41

Mass and micro communications media today easily reach across national and cultural borders, a technological development that directly influences international political relations as it intensifies debates about cultural sovereignty. The impact of global communications has been a major policy focus of the United Nations Educational, Scientific, and Cultural Organization (UNESCO) since the early 1970s. The most common concern is that Western powers, spearheaded by American-owned transnational corporations, have monopolized world communications to such a degree that the economic well-being and cultural identity of less powerful nations have been mightily damaged.

This contemporary transnational, transcultural drama – the globalization of material and cultural resources – is, according to Anthony Giddens, an inherent consequence of high modernity (1990: 63). But the point that some critics keep coming back to is that modernity and globalization should not be regarded simply as stages in world history, but as destructive, irreversible developments driven by First World economic interests. Globalization is not just a *flow,* according to these critics, but a *world system* of exploitation. One of the harshest commentators, Swedish social anthropologist Jonathan Friedman, argues that the world system is based on "multinational economic organizations, global investment and speculation machines" and:

> there has also emerged a global class structure, an international elite made up of top diplomats, heads of state, aid officials and representatives of international organizations such as the United Nations, who play golf and take cocktails with one another, forming a kind of cultural cohort. This grouping overlaps with an international elite of art dealers, publishing and media representatives, and culture industry VIPs who are directly involved in media representations and events, producing images of the world and images for the world. (Friedman 1994: 205–6)

Friedman makes the important point that elite forces in the world system cooperate to advance their mutual interests. Echoing other critics like Herbert Schiller, Friedman argues that multinational corporations use modern communications media to assert and reinforce global economic and cultural domination. According to this view, the world has become one big market driven by the dominating forces of global capitalism. Competition pervades everything from warfare, religion, international trade, and scientific breakthroughs to the production of popular music and mail-order brides.

No doubt such tendencies exist. Students from the more developed countries compete with each other to win advanced business degrees from reputable universities with specializations such as "Global Management." Favorable trade balances and economic productivity favor nations and corporations that use aggressive global marketing strategies. Powerful nations wield tremendous influence over decisions made by the International Monetary Fund, World Bank, and World Trade Organization. Newly emerging economies must integrate into the Global Information Infrastructure, which is also manipulated to advantage by the world's political-economic superpowers. Third World countries – seen by big corporations as cheap labor sources and future markets, and desperate to attract capital so as not to get left behind in the global dollar chase – compromise cultural values in their international joint ventures and trade policies. Western rationalism, individualism, and competitiveness are celebrated worldwide as key to economic success. The world adopts a "northern" sense of time and property. Everything from food to sex to religion becomes more and more commercialized on a global scale.

Box 9.1 Warning: The Global Environment is in Danger!

(The following paragraphs were written by a world authority on environmental issues, Dr Michael Marx, executive director of the Coastal Rainforest Coalition based in San Francisco, California. He argues that the environmental consequences of globalization spell disaster for all of us . . .)

As an environmentalist who deals with the steady decline in the Earth's ability to support its human, animal, insect, and plant environment, I find globalization to be a very disturbing reality. It has accelerated the rate at which eco-systems are being destroyed in order to feed the voracious appetites of major corporations and their shareholders.

I would be less disturbed about globalization if we could simply exchange culture and art without transmitting cultural values, or if the cultures being exchanged were based on a deep respect for the sanctity of all beings, like many original indigenous cultures were. Unfortunately, the global transmission of culture inherently entails the transmission of values. And Western culture, which is the dominant culture being sold worldwide, considers all of nature to be little more than a storehouse of natural resources to be mined, processed, sold, and discarded. By selling American culture, we also sell American business, which in turn sells products that hasten environmental destruction.

Those who are not bothered by the effects of globalization on their environment, and on their democracies, should consider just what big money can buy in the global political economy. Let me provide a representative example. Chile is a member of the World Trade Organization (WTO), the international agency that regulates world trade and represents more than 130 member nations.

Because Chile is integrated into the privileged world economic system administered by the WTO, it can invite Boise Cascade, a US company, to build the world's largest wood chip mill in southern Chile's Ilque Bay. There, Boise Cascade is logging five million acres of native, old-growth forests, turning these trees into paper and building materials for US and Japanese consumers. Chile's ruling elite is enriched. Boise Cascade is enriched. Unfortunately, however, a splendid part of one of the world's most endangered eco-systems – temperate rainforests – is permanently impoverished.

The WTO has the power to overrule city, state, and national jurisdictions that seek to protect their environments by restricting certain destructive business practices. So, countries using turtle-deadly shrimping practices appealed to the WTO to overturn US regulations that restricted their ability to sell their shrimp in America. The WTO, in closed-door session, and without input from citizens or scientists, wiped out the US law with the stroke of a pen. The WTO exercised the same power to negate the Dolphin Protection Act that embargoed tuna caught with nets that destroy dolphins. The WTO has also taken the position that the state of Massachusetts cannot pass a law prohibiting the investment of state dollars in the environmentally destructive, brutal military dictatorship in Burma. Just the threat of a WTO challenge can force countries to back down. For instance, when Canada refused to allow an American company to sell a carcinogenic additive to a Canadian company, the American company threatened a WTO challenge to the decision. As a consequence, Canada was forced to compensate the company for millions of dollars in lost profits.

So here's where I depart from the optimistic view expressed by this book's author, my friend James Lull. Those who celebrate the globalization of popular culture unfortunately overlook how such cultural materials contribute to corporate dominance, and to the subsequent role of corporations in the destruction of the very life systems we all require. In effect, popular culture serves the same function for large corporate interests today as early (and present-day) missionaries served (and serve) for their religious institutions and governments. While the missionaries were selling religion, they also sold their cultures and their values. Pop cultures' idolized icons are the new global missionaries. They not only sell their own products (CDs, TV shows, computer games, teeshirts, and so on), they also (intentionally or not) sell Western economies' values of materialism, overconsumption, and waste. For instance, MTV videos – with their fabulous scenes of huge houses, lavish furnishings, expensive cars, and chic clothing – send a message to students in Indonesia and Malaysia, home of some of the world's most important natural resources, that if they imitate American culture, they too can have these luxuries.

Michael Rothschild (1995) has described corporations as living organisms that evolve rapidly as they grow larger and increase their ability to adapt. This is partly the basis of the often-heard phrase in business, "Grow or die." Popular culture, when spread to other countries, is like an invasive species that modifies the environment and makes it receptive to even more destructive invasive species – transnational corporations. As corporations invade foreign cultures, their ability to attract, control, and focus immense amounts of resources squeezes out competitors. Some of their *real* competitors, in fact, are non-profit organizations like Greenpeace, Rainforest Action Network, and the Sierra Club – groups that defend the environment, human rights, religious freedom, and true democracy.

The WTO was created to increase global corporate profitability. Business is ultimately about reducing costs, increasing profits, and concentrating wealth in the hands of executives and shareholders who wrongly think they live comfortably removed from the consequences of their actions. The global spread of popular culture sets the table for just such economic and environmental exploitation. Imagine how the diversity of cultures throughout the world will change as large corporations amass more power and global presence. Just as the religious state was replaced by the nation-state, the nation-state is now being replaced by the corporate state. The global spread of American values and business, regulated by the WTO, is the primary vehicle which propels this disastrous historical transition. Globalization, it must be said, does not bode well for the planet, or for its inhabitants.

Michael Marx makes a strong and credible argument. The global ecosystem clearly suffers from the frantic consumption of natural resources by countries in the more developed parts of the world, especially northern nations like Britain and the United States. Capitalist cultural values no doubt underlie and help stimulate such overamplified consumer activity. We very well may be planting the seeds of global environmental deterioration, even destruction.

And it's certainly not just the rainforests and the ozone layer that suffer. The famed Polish sociologist Zygmunt Bauman – whose work we considered in chapter 1 – is among those who fear "the human consequences" of globalization. Bauman's sobering view reminds us that progress never moves forward in any egalitarian way, and that contemporary communication modalities tend to serve business interests over humanitarian objectives, reinforcing social divisiveness instead of creating social unity and harmony (Bauman 1998).

We therefore face an uncomfortable paradox with no happy solution in sight. The fact is that modernity and globalization exist. These trends will not go away or be reversed, despite the best efforts of well-meaning environmentalists and academics. Other social tendencies overpower the still too abstract notion of "responsibility to the global environment," or any development of a global welfare state. Nearly everyone prefers not to contemplate seriously the apocalyptic consequences that environmentalists predict.

Without downplaying the importance of the environmental and human issues, it must be said, however, that *globalization's influences are not all predictable and not all bad*. Nations, cultures, economies, corporations, social movements, and the rest must either integrate into the global scene, ignore, or disconnect from it. To integrate means compromise, no doubt. But to ignore or disconnect from the global stage is to self-destroy in other ways. Economic self-sufficiency and cultural isolation simply are not viable options any more for any society that aspires to improve its standard of living. And calls for environmental responsibility almost always emanate from experts in countries that consume the greatest share of the earth's natural resources. Environmentalists' pleas for consumer restraint, therefore, don't always appeal much to people who live in less materially developed societies, because such messages can easily be interpreted as sincere but elitist condemnations to eternal premodernity and marginalization.

Communication receivers: the making of global cultures

Beginning with the very first paragraph of chapter 1, we have emphasized the intentionality, creativity, and productivity of human "agents." In the last chapter, we described three "zones of indeterminacy" in contemporary human communication as a way of arguing against the pessimism of media and cultural imperialism theories. We analyzed communication sources, technologies, and messages. The fourth component of any communication system, "receivers," has already been discussed at length in chapter 5. In that chapter, we illustrated how media audiences cleverly navigate their structured, symbolic worlds in ways that are not determined by ideological structures. We continue now with the critique of imperialism by focusing on how "people on the move" construct their cultural worlds in the era of globalization.

Although popular culture forms such as TV shows, movies, and pop music clearly express particular cultural values, these popular forms and values are never simply received, digested, and acted upon in any uniform way by their global audiences. *Symbolic representation of any type is not the same as interpretation and use.* As we have seen repeatedly in these pages, symbolic forms sometimes produce effects unintended by message senders, even opposite from what is desired by those senders. Some cultural products become very popular in certain parts of the world, but are simply rejected in other parts. Cultural forms tend to circulate better regionally than globally because cultural and linguistic similarities promote greater understanding and appreciation than less resonating forms can inspire (e.g. Tomlinson 1997, 1999). This is especially true in today's hyper-connected world.

In any case, cultural groups never simply imitate other cultural groups. The flow of popular culture from one part of the world to another produces some similarities, but deep differences remain. The typical result of global cultural interaction is the creation of hybrid forms. Although symbolic representations of culture arrive from distant locations powered by mass and micro media technologies, they are mediated critically and appropriated socially and culturally in the contexts they enter.

Moreover, many consequences of modernization and globalization are positive. This tendency is by no means limited to the current era. As Thomas Sowell observes, for example:

> Some may lament that colorful local fabrics in non-Western societies have been superseded by mass-produced cloth from the factories of Europe or the United States. They may regret seeing traditional drinks replaced by carbonated sodas, or indigenous musical instruments put aside while people listen to American popular songs on Japanese made portable radios. Those who deplore such things are also deploring the very process of cultural diffusion by which the human race has advanced for thousands of years. (Sowell 1994: 226)

Sowell's comments pertain just as well to the domestic "Buy American" campaigns waged by United States industrial producers over the years. Americans have been encouraged to buy American cars, for example, simply because they are made in America, even though Japanese models have been far better investments. Must we all consume only what our individual nations produce? And what about the flow of ideas? Is the transnational flow of information about democracy and the rule of law a bad thing for the world? Does raised awareness about women's rights or about the struggles of indigenous peoples do a disservice to women, men, and children who live in repressive conditions? Indeed, all national and global social movements – including the environmental and human rights movements – require an intervention that only the symbolic weight of mediated communications can provide.

Such processes presume global sociality. Mediated visibility and interaction give us more "contemporaries," according to Ulf Hannerz (1992). By contemporary, he means "people whom we are aware of as living at the same time, about whom we make assumptions and whom we may influence in some ways, although we never meet in person" (Hannerz 1992: 30). Combining the potential of communications technology with popular culture provides a new "spirit of the times" (Maffesoli 1996: 73).

Globalization promotes shared emotion too. Globalized media often broaden emotional connections and inspire "electronic empathy . . . a view of the other which has more to do with notions of a shared human nature than with cultivated differences" (Hannerz 1996: 121). The outpouring of sadness and sympathy following Princess Diana's death is one remarkable example of how common emotion can surface and be made visible in ways that foreground a good side of human nature. Global aid agencies too, though they can rightly be criticized for certain financial abuses, inspire global awareness and response to the social tragedies unfolding in Africa, Latin America, and elsewhere. The international Red Cross, for example, is a trusted, globalized disaster relief organization whose logo circulates just as effectively as the Nike swoosh or the American flag. Indeed, in many cases the "global" actually improves conditions at the "local" level.

We are left therefore to conclude that the monolithic world system thesis, while properly critical in orientation and tone, overstates what is actually happening. The conspiratorial power of the repressive global "cultural cohort" Jonathan Friedman imagines, or the threat of Anglo-American popular culture creeping around the planet as an "invasive species" as Michael Marx describes, are insightful and important perspectives, but they simplify very complex cultural processes.

Indeed, some recent theorizing concludes that something quite different is happening. In a book that attracted much attention, not all of it favorable, the American political scientist Samuel P. Huntington (1996) uses considerable historical evidence to argue that the political, economic, ideological, and cultural power of the West, especially the United States, is fading. According to Huntington, "We are witnessing 'the end of the progressive era' dominated by Western ideologies and are moving into an era in which multiple and diverse civilizations will interact, compete, coexist, and accommodate each other" (Huntington 1996: 95). He argues that Christianity, pluralism, individualism, and the rule of law made it possible for the West to invent modernity, expand throughout the world, and become the envy of other societies" (pp. 56–78). But the dominance may be coming to an end. While the West and Japan still dominate advanced technology industries, the international market encourages sale of that very same technology worldwide. This means that eventually the West and Japan will lose whatever competitive advantages such technological superiority provides (Huntington 1996: 87–8).

Is the world becoming more or less homogeneous? What many contemporary observers conclude is that the global circulation of images, ideologies, and cultural styles – facilitated by the multinational culture and communications industries – actually fuels symbolic creativity, lessens homogeneity, and increases cultural diversity. One inevitable, profound, and incontrovertible consequence of globalization is the diversification of symbolic power, its cultural uses and contexts. By the same token, it certainly isn't very wise or forward-thinking to hold onto the idea that traditional cultures ought to be preserved like tombs in a museum. History shows that culture – like multinational corporations perhaps, but like biological body and mind as well – must also grow or die.

The global cultural mix

- A Peruvian band playing traditional Andes folk music at a tourist restaurant in Playa del Carmen, Mexico, suddenly breaks into the English band Queen's "We Will Rock You" to the delight of German and Canadian girls in the audience.
- Many New Yorkers born in the Dominican Republic regularly return to the Caribbean island nation to vote in national elections and say they consider themselves as much Dominican as American.

- Jamaican reggae music by Bob Marley, Peter Tosh, and Black Uhuru pulsates at high volume in clothing boutiques located in the people's markets of Fez, Morocco.
- The Milano collection of lamps sold in the United States are made in Taiwan and distributed by a French wholesaler.
- More than 400 million people worldwide, in countries including Russia, Tunisia, Zimbabwe, and Switzerland, regularly watch TV soap operas that originate in Spanish-language nations.
- German pop music bands travel to the United States where they perform solely for Vietnamese-American immigrants who use the music to unite their community.
- The two top-rated radio stations in Los Angeles broadcast only in Spanish. One of them features *banda* music – regional Mexican folk music blended with traditional Bavarian rhythms and instruments including the tuba.
- The police department in Santa Barbara, California, patrols the Latino section of town in a police car customized with airbrushed door-panel murals, metallic sparkle, and magnesium wheels to resemble the "low-rider" vehicles young Latino men drive.
- The Argentine veejay on MTV Latin America explains to Mexicans, Colombians, Venezuelans, and other Latinos why Black Sabbath was such an important influence on Korn.

Globalization does not mean that some universal, technology-based super-society covers the globe and destroys local social systems and cultures. Despite technology's awesome reach, we have not, and will not, become one people. It is true that potent homogenizing forces such as English, Chinese, Arabic, and other dominant languages, military weaponry, advertising techniques, Internet protocol, media formats, international airports, and fashion trends undeniably affect consciousness and culture in every corner of the world. Such spheres of influence unquestionably introduce and reinforce certain standardizing values and practices. But these political-economic-cultural influences do not enter cultural contexts uniformly. They always interact with local conditions to produce diverse and dynamic consequences. Languages are great examples of linguistic hybridity and cultural borrowing. And just as TV programs, films, and popular music don't turn individual consumers into passive dupes in any single society, the power to transmit information worldwide likewise does not stimulate automatic imitation or conformity. To the contrary. By delivering culturally-rich symbolic resources, television, the Internet, and all other mass and micro media open up and extend the possibilities of cultural work in every direction – invention, creolization, and retrenchment.

Forces of modernity and globalization no doubt have changed the face of world cultures and influenced political-economic relationships. But the overall effect is "more an organization of diversity than a replication of uniformity" (Hannerz 1990). Local and regional ways of thinking and living do not disappear in the face of imported cultural influences. While globalization is irreversible, the global has not destroyed or replaced the local. The very concept of culture presumes difference. As British sociologist Anthony D. Smith points out:

> If by "culture" is meant a collective mode of life, or a repertoire of beliefs, styles, values, and symbols, then we can only speak of cultures, never just culture; for a collective mode of life, or a repertoire of beliefs, etc., presupposes different modes and repertoires in a universe of modes and repertoires. Hence, the idea of a "global culture" is a practical impossibility. (1990: 171)

Image nations

What can your nation do for you that a good credit card cannot do?
Hannerz 1996: 88

Despite the provocative question he asks, Ulf Hannerz, like most observers, believes that while the nation-state is challenged and changing, it is not about to go away. The nation-state still demarcates important ideological, social, and cultural differences. One need look no further than the attempt to harmonize the European Union to see how difficult it is to unify and politicize different nations and national cultures. And if the nation-state is truly in decline in some ways as a legitimate locus for social organization, what will take its place? The American anthropologist Arjun Appadurai wonders, "if the nation state disappears, what mechanism will assure protection of minorities, the minimal distribution of democratic rights, and the reasonable possibility of the growth of civil society?" (Appadurai 1996: 19).

But exactly what is "a nation?" Does the concept refer only to existing political states that occupy particular pieces of ground? Or is nation more a political-cultural state of mind? Where do people's ultimate loyalties lie?

In a world where communications technology, diverse symbolic forms, and the vastness of cyberspace challenge traditional understandings of space and place, geographic territory still counts for a lot. Ethnic struggles over land rage in Yugoslavia, Ethiopia, Tibet, Palestine, Spain, Rwanda, India, Sri Lanka, and elsewhere. Indigenous peoples in New Zealand, Mexico, Australia, Guatemala, Hawaii, and other places focus on land rights and distribution. Colonialization, slavery, wars, and immigration have left in their wake a wide range of "cleft societies" (Huntington 1996), where human communities originating in different civilizations live with varying degrees of discomfort in shared geographical space. Familiar examples include the spread of Muslim peoples throughout Western Europe, and the increase of Hispanic and Asian populations in North America.

The separatist movement in Canada provides a good example of how physical geography, political legitimacy, and communications media sometimes resonate with and reinforce each other in nationalist struggles.[1] Separatists from the French-speaking Canadian province of Quebec for many years have wanted to establish an independent nation. The separatists' national imagination was galvanized and greatly accelerated when the first French-language television channel appeared on the federal, state-supported Canadian television system (CBC) in 1952. The French-speaking channel with its culturally attractive media content over the years has reinforced and further inspired separatist leanings by many French-speaking Canadians. Today, the explosion of more and more culturally specialized media channels on cable and satellite TV, French-speaking radio and print media, video, and popular music together with the Internet and other information technologies make it even easier for French-speaking Canadians to imagine themselves as members of an alternative interpretative community – a symbolic nation they hope will eventually become politically viable too. Modern nations *depend* on mass communication for just such symbolic presence and continuity (Anderson 1991; Chaney 1994).

The media also played a major role in the Islamic nationalist revolution in Iran in 1979, and continue to be a crucial factor. The fundamentalist uprising was stimulated partly by reaction to the spread of Western culture. Together with urbanization, social mobilization, and higher levels of literacy and education, intensified communication and media consumption "expanded interaction with Western and other cultures, undermining traditional village and clan ties to create alienation and an identity crisis" (Huntington 1996: 116). The Islamic state forged by the revolution, like all totalitarian governments, has nonetheless had difficulty managing Iranian culture after taking control of the state media system. Satellite television beams into Iran from the outside, and even though satellite dishes are illegal, many middle-class viewers find ways to import the distant signals. Consequently, Iran's government-controlled TV stations have had to diversify and improve programming in order to attract viewers. And in cyberspace, the government has struggled to find an Internet policy that will allow it to use information technology to spread religious dogma and integrate effectively into the world economic system. But the very same developments mean that Iranians can also access websites that promote a "free Iran," as well as pornography, Western-based news reports, and other politically and culturally unacceptable materials.

This problematic balance between openness and protectionism in a globalized communications environment is a major issue for national governments everywhere, but especially in countries like Iran where regulation is tight and the economy is comparatively poor. These same problems crop up in Vietnam, for example, where it has been impossible to stop anti-communist propaganda, human rights material, and pornography on the Internet. Nations such as Iran and Vietnam cannot ignore or outlaw information technology because economic development depends on rapid data transfer. But as countries open up technological avenues for economic purposes, they simultaneously unleash an incredibly expanded and volatile public space. These micro-media, Internet-related forces then interact socially and culturally with more conventional media.

In Vietnam, much like China, commercial TV programs from America, Japan, and other countries appear on the government television system. The Vietnamese agree to air such programs because the foreign advertising that accompanies them brings in much-needed hard currency, and the programs provide the people with cheap and attractive entertainment fare. Reruns of the American serial *Baywatch*, for instance, are very popular now in Vietnam. The famous Japanese soap opera *Oshin* has also become a favorite there. The lead character's likeness has been used to sell products on television, and tapes of early episodes are played in video cafés and video stores. A restaurant named Oshin opened in Hanoi. The ideological and cultural consequences of simply showing glamorous images of life outside the borders are profound in an impoverished country like Vietnam.

With two-thirds of the world's population, Asia is the home of many fast-growing economies. With its strong cultural traditions, Asia is also a global hot-spot for these complex, modern-day struggles over nation.

The dynamics of global culture

Arjun Appadurai deals precisely with the diverse global economic and cultural activity going on today that threatens the nation-state (1990). At the base of his argument is the idea that culture is heterogeneous; it always takes many forms. Appadurai specifies five factors he thinks shape the dynamics of contemporary global cultural diversity. He calls these dimensions "scapes." Appadurai argues that the five scapes insure that cultural homogeneity and domination are not possible. The dimensions (scapes) of global culture are ethnoscapes, technoscapes, finanscapes, mediascapes, and ideoscapes. Each concept refers to a type of movement. Ethnoscape, for example, denotes the flow of people from one part of the world to another. This includes tourists, immigrants, refugees, exiles, guest-workers, and so on. Technoscape describes the transporting of industrial technology across national borders. India, China, Russia, and Japan, for instance, have all exported technology to Libya in order to construct a huge steel complex there. Finanscape refers to patterns of global money transfer. Foreign investments channeled through the World Bank for energy and transportation development projects in Brazil are examples of this. Rather than advance only the interests of the world's political-economic-cultural super-powers, Appadurai argues that relationships between and among ethnoscapes, technoscapes, and finanscapes are "deeply disjunctive and profoundly unpredictable, since each of these landscapes is subject to its own constraints and incentives . . . [and] each acts as a constraint and a parameter for movements of the other" (Appadurai 1990: 298).

Added to these disjunctive factors are two more interrelated concepts – mediascapes and ideoscapes. Mediascape refers to mechanical and electronic mass media hardware and the images it produces. Viewers use these images to construct cultural "narratives of the other." For example, by portraying African culture on European television, the medium supplies symbolic resources which invite people to imagine life on the southern continent. The last factor, ideoscape, also refers to images, but specifically to the political aspects – the ideological contours of culture. Ideoscapes represent partisan positions in struggles over power and the allocation of resources in a political state. The articulation and dissemination of ideologies are always modified by context. Thus, ideological domains such as rights, freedom, responsibility, equality, discipline, democracy, and so on make up ideoscapes of differing significance in Cuba, the United States, Scotland, South Africa, Peru, Norway, and Thailand, for example.

The five scapes influence culture not by their hegemonic interaction, global diffusion, and uniform effect, but by their differences, contradictions, and counter-tendencies – their "disjunctures." Communications technology is fundamental to the argument. The mass media do much more to expand cultural diversity than to standardize it. And contrary to theories of media and cultural imperialism or doomsday arguments about globalization, the global economic market is not simply there for the taking by multinational corporations either. Volatile currencies, corruption, vague and shifting laws, the risk of big capital investments, local competition, and market saturation all work against economic and cultural domination. As Appadurai concludes, "people, machines, money, images, and ideas follow increasingly non-isomorphic paths" in the construction of contemporary global cultures (Appadurai 1990: 301).

Globalization therefore is best considered as a complex set of interacting and often countervailing human, material, and symbolic flows that lead to diverse, heterogeneous cultural positionings and practices which persistently and variously modify established vectors of social, political, and cultural power. Or as Jesús Martín-Barbero puts it, "the steady, predictable tempo of homogenizing development is upset by the countertempo of profound differences and cultural discontinuities" (1993: 149).

Culture thus oscillates dialectically between permanence and change, between tradition and innovation. How people organize these cultural stresses is key to understanding modern personal and social stability.

Cultural territory is a very important issue for Third World scholars. Along with Jesús Martín-Barbero, none of them has argued more convincingly and elegantly in recent years than Néstor García Canclini (1989). From the outset García Canclini joins with the chorus of contemporary thinkers who no longer accept the argument that political-economic-cultural realities are dominated and manipulated by large metropolitan consortia. Consistent with our earlier discussions, García Canclini points out that theories of cultural imperialism do not account for the ways ideological and cultural images are created and distributed by the centers of production. The subjectivity and creative unruliness of the arts, mass media, and cultural production generally prevent cultural homogenization and manipulation: "The aspirations of artists, journalists, and all types of cultural workers to function as a mediator between symbolic camps and in relations between and among diverse groups contradicts the motion of the market toward concentration and monopolization" (p. 344).

With this understanding of the basic tendencies of global cultural activity, we shift focus now to specific types and examples of human and symbolic movement in our quest to understand what cultural territory means in the era of globalization.

Deterritorialization and migration

The first step in the formation of new cultural territories is *deterritorialization*. This refers to "the loss of the 'natural' relation between culture with geographic and social territory" (García Canclini 1989: 288), or "the release of cultural signs from fixed locations in space and time" (Rowe and Schelling 1991: 231). In Anthony Giddens's terms, deterritorialization means the "disembedding" (lifting out) of people and symbolic forms from the places we expect them to be. Deterritorialization is the partial tearing apart of cultural structures, relationships, settings, and representations.[2]

The migration of Third World peoples into more developed countries – a social uprooting that provokes major cultural disruptions and adaptations – is one primary and often troubling form of deterritorialization. Economic incentives usually are at the heart of such human movements. The African and Asian slave trade in colonial North America, Brazil, and the Caribbean region centuries ago, for example, was inspired by a search for cheap labor. Today the market for menial labor attracts poor immigrants to wealthy societies. For instance, California money tempts Mexican farm workers and domestic workers to leave home. About one-third of the Mexican workers arrive illegally, sometimes after dangerous clandestine border crossings. After landing in the United States they find themselves living in sprawling ghettos which spawn gang violence, drug abuse, and eventual unemployment, among many other social problems. Los Angeles in particular has become a powerful magnet for low-paid immigrants from everywhere.

The United Nations Population Fund calls contemporary immigration the "human crisis of our age" because poverty, wars, and overcrowding force people to push into territory that is already occupied by others. Ethnic Albanian refugees huddling in the rain, cold, and mud under flimsy pieces of plastic in Macedonia during the Yugoslavian War were among only the most recent, globally circulated images of such tragedies. Political refugees from armed conflicts in Vietnam, Chile, Somalia, China, Cambodia, and elsewhere have migrated all over the world.

Cultural deterritorialization is a profoundly human matter. Deterritorialization can be totalizing and horrible. Taking away a group's language, social customs, religion, and music – as was done to African slaves in the American colonies, for instance – is tantamount to cultural assassination. But culture never dies, even in conditions of orchestrated repression. It adapts and survives in modified forms. Furthermore, the effects of cultural dislocation are never limited only to those who are forced to move. For example, Turkish guest-workers in Germany have an ethnic/cultural relation with the Germans, with each other in Germany, and with the Turkish homeland. All three cultural zones are negotiated simultaneously. Modern communications technology plays a key role in all the negotiations: how Turks learn about Germans (and, to a lesser degree, how Germans learn about Turks); how Turks maintain and nurture their identities as Turks in Germany; and how Turks maintain contact with their culture and people in Turkey. This situation, of course, is not peculiar to Turkish people in Germany. Similar circumstances develop wherever migrant populations congregate.

One common by-product of widespread cultural dislocation is political extremism involving the homeland. Many immigrants live physically in one place, but emotionally in another. Vietnamese in California, for example, have mounted a tenacious clandestine effort to overthrow the communist government in Vietnam. This ideological/political struggle became violent when fierce anti-communist protests were waged against a bookstore in southern California in 1999. The Vietnamese owner of the store had displayed a color portrait of the legendary communist leader Ho Chi Minh and the communist Vietnamese flag, a symbolic act that inflamed reterritorialized Vietnamese who detest communism. California Vietnamese also regularly stage protests against Vietnamese-language newspapers that support normalization of political and economic relations with communist Vietnam. Such reactionary activity is not unusual for peoples who are forced to flee their homelands: "Deterritorialization . . . sometimes creates exaggerated and intensified senses of criticism or attachment to politics in the home-state. Deterritorialization, whether of Hindus, Sikhs, Palestinians, Ukrainians, or Albanians, is now at the core of a variety of global fundamentalisms, including Islamic and Hindu fundamentalism" (Appadurai 1990: 301; 1996). The African-American repatriation movement of the early twentieth century and today's black Muslim political activity also exemplify this tendency.

Conflicting immigrant groups often maintain and even increase their hostilities in their new lands. Chinese students from China,

Taiwan, and Hong Kong, for example, form their own student organizations on California college campuses, and Chinatown neighborhoods and social groups often divide up by origin. Young Mexican immigrants to the United States form gangs according to their geographical origins in Mexico ("northerners" v. "southerners"), and export these contrived hostilities back to Mexico, a development that is reinforced by media images, especially movies, which depict and glorify the gang wars.

Not all human migrations are unwanted or forced by political or economic necessity. The brain drain of highly educated and technically skilled specialists from places like India, China, Taiwan, Iran, and Brazil to the United States and Europe reflects how the global economic market encourages even relatively comfortable people to voluntarily leave their lands of origin too. The consequences can be dramatic. As Thomas Sowell points out, "much of the commerce and industry of whole regions of the planet was created by large-scale migrations – whether of Chinese into Southeast Asia, Indians into East Africa, or Germans and Italians into Brazil and Argentina" (Sowell 1994: 69). Professor and student temporary exchanges and relocations are common. International tourism, among the most profitable of all global industries, and employment reassignments for multinational corporations and federal governments also account for a tremendous number of people living outside their native lands. Modern forms of transportation and communication have made all types of human migration faster and easier.

Cultural melding and mediation

> Immigrants cross the city in many directions and install, precisely in the crossings, their baroque places of regional sweets and contraband radios, their curative herbs and videocassettes.
>
> *García Canclini 1989: 16*

When Angolans relocate in Brazil, Indians in Zimbabwe, Koreans in Japan, Vietnamese in the United States, and Jamaicans in England, for example, they certainly don't keep strictly to themselves – especially not the young adults and children. In one way or another deterritorialized peoples mix in with their new surroundings. What results is a kind of cultural give-and-take. These cultural interactions are variously termed transculturation, hybridization, and indigenization. Each concept emphasizes a different aspect of cultural melding and mediation.

Transculturation and hybridization

Transculturation refers to a process whereby cultural forms literally move through time and space where they interact with other cultural forms and settings, influence each other, produce new forms, and change the cultural settings. As we have seen, such syntheses often result from the physical movement of peoples from one geographic location to another. But we must not think of transculturation simply as the consequence of shifting populations. Many cultural crossings are also made possible by the mass media and culture industries. Some of the most significant and vast cultural territories and movements are mediated, symbolic lands and migrations.

Media imagery routinely brings together people who don't know each other. "Interpretative communities" are relatively anonymous groups of people who interpret particular mediated materials with shared enthusiasm or a common viewpoint. Female readers of romance novels, regular donors to Pat Robertson's TV evangelism crusade, fans of the Grateful Dead ("Deadheads") who followed the rock group around the world, daily Rush Limbaugh listeners, and *Star Trek* fanatics ("Trekkies") are all interpretative communities. They are audiences defined more by shared identities and discourses than by demographic similarities or differences.

Modern technology reconstructs the essential axes of cultural distance – space and time. This is the case most obviously in terms of physical space. We have already discussed at length how transmission and reception of information and entertainment from one part of the world to another inspire new cultural syntheses. But communications technology also permits new perceptions and uses of cultural time. Film, still photography, kinescope, audiotape, videotape, and today's sophisticated digital audio and video information storage and retrieval systems provide access to the symbols which make up cultural histories. Electronic and digital media preserve culture in ways print media can never do, and make it available for creative reinterpretation. People today can experience, edit, and use cultural symbolism in new temporal and spatial contiguities, greatly expanding the range of personal meanings and social uses. Mixing the traditional with the modern is fully reasonable and practical. Cultural archives of symbolic forms can be creatively accessed and reconstructed using consumer communication technology.

Transculturation processes synthesize new cultural genres while they break down traditional cultural categories. Modern communications technology and the culture industries facilitate the creative process. As García Canclini observes with reference to South American culture:

> technologies of reproduction allow everyone to equip their home with a repertoire of discs and cassettes that combine high culture with the popular, including those who have already synthesized many sources in the production of their works: Piazzola who mixes the tango with jazz and classical music; Caetano Veloso and Chico Buarque who have appropriated the poetry of Afro-Brazilian traditions with . . . experimental music. (1989: 283)

The information superhighway travels through contexts of both cultural production and reception as it simultaneously moves in many directions in space and time. Certain genres, images, and stories appeal quite universally and move rapidly from one cultural space to another. Not all categories of information or entertainment travel at the same fast speed, however. For example, most national and local news, even juicy scandals, is far more provincial, and therefore more likely to occupy a dusty county road than a superhighway (Tomlinson 1997).

Transculturation produces cultural *hybrids* – the fusing of cultural forms. Hybrid forms and genres are popular almost by definition. Consider, for example, the global flow of rap music. Originating in America's inner-city ghettos, rap music and hip-hop culture travel all over the world where they encounter and influence many kinds of local pop music. Some of the biggest-selling Latin American pop music artists, for example, fuse rap with pop, salsa, tropical, and reggae. Mainland Chinese pop singers have rap songs in their repertoires. Christian rap is here. The hybrid is not a simple "impregnating of one culture with the contents of another" but "involves an ambivalence about both of the original cultures" creating a sense of "freedom, nomadism . . . even opportunism" (Naficy 1993: 127).

Indigenization

> Claims of creeping global homogenization invariably subspeciate into either an argument about Americanization, or an argument about commoditization, and very often these two arguments are very closely linked. What these arguments fail to consider is that at least as rapidly as forces from the various metropolises are brought into new societies, they tend to become indigenized in one way or another: this is true of music and housing styles as much as it is true of science and terrorism, spectacles and constitutions.
>
> *Appadurai 1990: 295*

Photo 9.1 Hybridization. Japanese cuisine meets soul food in San Francisco (photo by James Lull)

The concept *indigenization* helps explain how transculturation and hybridization occur. Indigenization means that imported cultural elements take on local features as the cultural hybrids develop. The exotic, unfamiliar, and foreign is domesticated. Continuing with our example of transcultural hip-hop culture, for example, consider what happens when rap music is exported to a place like Indonesia, Hong Kong, or Spain. The unfamiliar, imported cadence and attitude of rap are appropriated by local musicians. The sounds become indigenized at the same time. Indonesian, Hong Kong, and Spanish rap is sung in local languages, with lyrics that refer to local personalities, conditions, and situations. The resulting musical hybrid is an amalgam of American black culture and Indonesian, Hong Kong, or Spanish culture.

Photo 9.2 Indigenization. Malcolm X as a commercial product and cultural resource in Brazil (photo by Vicente de Paulo)

Of course hybrids such as these never develop from "pure" cultural forms in the first place. American black culture has already been strongly influenced by African cultures and by European-American cultures, while Indonesia, Hong Kong, and Spain reflect long and complex histories of cultural mixing too. They were hybrids themselves long before they met each other.

Box 9.2 The Maori Hip-Hop Hybrid

(The following analysis draws from a visit I made to New Zealand in the late 1990s, and also from the work of New Zealand-born, Australian performance studies theorist Tony Mitchell (1996). Readers should consult Mitchell's work for an expanded account of the Maori hip-hop scene.)

> With our links to the land broken, our alienation from the mode of production complete, our culture objectified, we have become marginalized and lost. This is not to say beaten. And this is what we have in common with black America.
>
> *Kerry Buchanan, cited in Mitchell 1996: 246*

> Fuck the status quo!
>
> *Song from the hit album,* Movement in Demand, *by the Maori rap group Urban Hutt Posse*

> *Haka!* There is going to be a fight between us. May it mean death for you and victory for me!
>
> *Maori war chant adopted by British lawn bowling teams in New Zealand*

Photo 9.3 Maoris from *Once Were Warriors* (reprinted with permission of New Zealand Film Commission)

British explorer Captain James Cook sailed around the two big islands in the South Pacific known today as New Zealand in 1769. He was not the first European to touch ground there. A Dutch navigator arrived on the northern shores more than one hundred years before, but was met by hostile inhabitants, the Maoris, who killed and cannibalized most of his crew.

Cook claimed New Zealand for England, opening the area for maritime industry, agriculture, mining, international trade, and Christian missionaries. The Maori population, meanwhile, suffered greatly from the British settlers' arrival. Deadly diseases were introduced, prostitution and other social maladies developed, land was taken over by the Europeans, and inter-tribal warfare escalated. In order to restore order to the islands, and to create a fair balance of interests between the British and the Maoris, a legal agreement, the Treaty of Waitangi, was signed between representatives of the British crown and Maori tribal chiefs in 1840. Land disputes between settlers and Maoris continued nonetheless, and rights that had been promised to the Maoris by the treaty gradually eroded.

Over the years New Zealand has prospered as a nation and as an economy. New Zealand has a positive international image. It was ranked fourth "least corrupt" country in the world recently by a respected international organization,[3] and prides itself on civil rights and racial harmony. But compared to New Zealand's citizens who descend from England and other European countries, the Maori inhabitants continue to suffer. The educational level and standard of living of the Maoris, who make up between 10 and 15 percent of New Zealand's population, average well below that of the Pakeha (European settlers). During the economic boom which followed World War II, many Maoris left their rural homes and communities and moved to New Zealand's cities, especially South Auckland, in search of jobs. Many of these urban and suburban areas have become blighted by poverty, violence, unemployment, and drug trafficking. As they attempted to assimilate into mainstream "kiwi" society, many Maoris disconnected from their cultural traditions, histories, and languages.

The Sixties brought radical changes to New Zealand, just as it did to much of the rest of the world. The civil rights movement and anti-war protests in the United States and elsewhere provoked activity on the streets of Auckland and other cities. Legal actions were mounted by Maoris against the federal government. Land claims and cultural rights were at the heart of the unrest. A Maori separatist movement gained momentum. In the midst of all the political and legal challenges, many young Maoris started to take greater interest and pride in their cultural heritage, including language, art, and music.

As discussed in chapter 7, communications media and popular culture proliferated on a global scale beginning in the Sixties. New Zealand was no exception. Young Maoris became especially avid consumers of imported cultural materials, in part because they had been largely excluded from New Zealand's mainstream media over the years. Like people everywhere, the Maoris became particularly fascinated by African-American cultural forms. Rhythm and blues, disco, jazz music, and breakdancing were quickly adopted by Maori youth. But the African-American cultural form that has really struck a responsive chord is rap music and all the accoutrements of hip-hop culture.

New Zealand's political and cultural tensions were brought to global attention in the mid-1990s by the international award-winning film *Once Were Warriors*, directed by Maori Lee Tamahori. The soundtrack features the most famous and uncompromising Maori rap group, Urban Hutt Posse. Director Tamahori explains how African-American rap music and hip-hop cultural style inspired his work:

> I look around the streets. Young Maori look absolutely fantastic. Pride, well being. A sense of costume. An awareness of how they look. I dare say most of it comes from MTV and other television, but the key is that they take all that and change it, make it their own. You'll see bits of black liberation from Africa, a touch of reggae, a touch of East LA, all filtered through their own culture. (Mitchell 1996: 252)

The adoption of an international black identity by New Zealand's Maori youth works in several ways. It compensates in part for a lack of knowledge of Maori culture, avoids the conservative, hierarchical demands of Maori elders, is easily accessible through media and the international culture industries, is relatively easy to adapt, and harmonizes well with Maori culture overall, including its tropical roots and oral communication tradition. Many young Maoris believe (even subconsciously) that their situation in New Zealand resembles the well-publicized political and ethnic struggles of American blacks. The Urban Hutt Posse even traveled to the United States to meet with black political and cultural leaders. Among their main influences were the rap group Public Enemy, and black Muslim leader Louis Farrakhan, from whom they borrowed the title of their strongest LP, *Movement in Demand*.

The international culture industries and the globalized market make audio and visual images of African-American popular culture available to even the poorest Maori living in another hemisphere 10,000 miles from the United States. Such resources have been indigenized in specific ways that reinforce and advance the political and cultural causes of the minority Maori population. But that is not the end of the cultural cycle. In much the same way as African-American popular culture is consumed and used by white Americans and every other ethnic group in the United States, Maori hip-hop culture, and more traditional cultural elements such as Maori language, clothing, and especially the distinctive, colorful body tattoos, have also become very popular among white youth in New Zealand and around the world.[4]

"Glocalization"

Although transculturation, hybridization, and indigenization may indeed bring about "the mutual transformation of cultures" (Rowe and Schelling 1991: 18), and involve considerable cultural creativity from both sides, the transformations often entail unequal economic power relations between the interacting cultures. One extremely visible and often criticized symbol of global popular culture is the McDonald's restaurant chain. One scholar even uses McDonald's as the paradigmatic instance of how he believes a Western concept, fast food, and an ensemble of specific food products can combine to do significant damage to local cultures. The author refers to this alleged cultural subversion as *The McDonaldization of Society* (Ritzer 1993).

A more careful analysis, however, reveals that no hamburger hegemony exists. No doubt eating at McDonald's originally was an American-style cultural experience, but that does not make it exploitative, culturally corrupting, or unhealthy. Why wouldn't McDonald's be successful all over the world? Are the world's peoples bound to eat the same food, and consume it the same way, as their parents and grandparents? Should we expect world cultures to be so static?

Photo 9.4 Hamburger hegemony? The familiar McDonald's golden arches, now in Moscow too (photo by James Lull)

The American anthropologist James Watson has studied the impact of McDonald's in Asia (1997). He points out that, of course, McDonald's did clash at first with established culinary and cultural territory in Asia. But over time the hamburger franchise has become just as familiar in the Asian cultural landscape as noodle houses, lumpia stands, and bento box lunch bars. For more than twenty years now in Japan and Hong Kong, "an entire generation of children has grown up with McDonald's; to these people the Big Mac, fries, and Coke do not represent something foreign. McDonald's is, quite simply, 'local' cuisine" (Watson 1997: 2). And while McDonald's introduced certain nuances of public dining to Asia – like encouraging Japanese customers to eat with their fingers – overall the Asian accommodation of McDonald's has taken place as much on Eastern terms as Western. The McDonald's menu, for instance, is localized (mutton-based Maharaja Mac and vegetable nuggets in India; teriyaki burgers in Japan, Taiwan, and Hong Kong; McSpaghetti in the Philippines, and so on). In the face of McDonald's worldwide policy to move customers in and out of its restaurants as fast as possible, young people in Hong Kong have instead turned McDonald's into after-school hangouts. They spend hours there "studying, gossiping, picking over snacks; for them, the restaurants are the

Photo 9.5 No building? No problem. The Burger King franchise went into the former East Germany so quickly after the fall of communism they didn't wait for building space to become available. A mobile storefront opens at the train station in Dresden c.1991 (photo by James Lull)

equivalent of youth clubs" (Watson 1997: 7). Sometimes McDonald's even performs as a socially liberating cultural force. Watson cites the case of Taiwan where McDonald's serves as a rare public space that is not dominated by men. McDonald's functions this way in Taiwan precisely because it does not derive from traditional Chinese cultural structures, traditions, or histories.

Of course one of the keys to McDonald's success is a fundamental standardization of the menu, fast and friendly service, reliable standards of product quality, and cleanliness. Because McDonald's has been a global phenomenon for many years now, it has also become familiar for non-Americans traveling in foreign countries. A Danish person who arrives in Jakarta, for example, might very well find it quite comfortable to stop in at the "Golden Arches" as an occasional alternative to the less familiar and predictable local food and restaurants.

But let's be careful not to give McDonald's too much credit. True, Norwegian customers can order a grilled salmon sandwich at McDonalds, Turks can get their chilled yogurt drinks there, Italians get pasta with their burgers, Germans can drink beer while munching McSausages, and Israelis can choose from a kosher menu. The McDonald's in Rio de Janeiro promotes meal specials such as "McCarnaval" and "Lanche Carioca" (the Rio resident's lunch). In all these cases McDonald's, the external cultural form, has been indigenized. But to whose advantage? From McDonald's point of view, the idea is to sell more hamburgers by tapping into local culture. This blending of local features into global products has been called *glocalization* (Robertson 1995). The Rio McDonald's may have a slightly Brazilian edge to its personality, for instance, but the Brazilian McDonald's employees still scurry about for minimum wage and most of the profits end up at the home office in San Diego, California. By the turn of the century, considerably more than half of McDonald's profits were coming from outside the United States (Watson 1997: 3).

Global advertising companies have become very alert to the opportunities and the limitations of transculturation, hybridization, and indigenization. They employ three basic strategies to maximize profits. They can "adopt" (by taking an idea from one market and using it in another without changing it), "adapt" (by taking an idea from one market, tailoring it for another market while maintaining the core values and executional elements of the original idea), or "invent" (by introducing new ideas into markets when research shows adopt and adapt won't work). In a globalized world of sophisticated marketing and advertising strategies, we must always ask: on whose terms, for what purposes, and to whose benefit do cultural hybrids develop?

Cultural indigenization and "glocalization" also take place within national boundaries. For example, as we discussed in chapter 4, the spectacular Brazilian cultural tradition, Carnival, is telecast throughout the country on the national TV system, Globo. But rather than imitate the famous Rio version of Carnival, people throughout Brazil modify the "TV stimulus" (not only of Carnival, but of national TV fare generally) by diffusing it in ways that integrate local preferences and traditions (Kottak 1990: 174). Furthermore, the Brazilian audience, especially lower middle-class, working-class, and lower-class viewers, definitely prefer Brazilian programs over imported television shows. This is the case in other Latin American countries too (Straubhaar 1989; Sinclair 1999). Imported television programs that succeed anywhere in the world usually resonate harmoniously with local cultural orientations or represent universal genres such as melodrama and action. Doing so, of course, they make money for their distant sponsors.

Reterritorialization and diasporas

Deterritorialized by modernity and globalization, people attempt to re-establish a new cultural "home" wherever they go (Tomlinson 1999: 148). These cultural ambitions and activities compose the processes of *reterritorialization*.

Fusing imported traditions with resources in the new territory, immigrant groups all over the world create local versions of distant cultures. For those groups who work together to maintain their traditional ethnic or cultural identities and lifestyles, these hybrid cultures are sometimes known as *diasporas*. Disaporic cultures can be formed and maintained much more easily today than ever before. Cultural goods such as food, clothing, and domestic items of all kinds flow much more rapidly around the world now, thanks mainly to transportation advances and market incentives for global import/export businesses.

Communications media, information technology, and culturally relevant symbolic forms such as popular music, videos, newspapers, magazines, books, and computer software are extremely important in reterritorialization processes generally, and in the establishment of diasporas in particular. Culture, communication, and connectivity are essential ingredients in the formation of *diasporic public spheres* (Appadurai 1996: 21). The "ethnic media" are especially useful to diasporas in America for sharing information about immigrants' legal rights and opportunities, for example. Meeting the informational, entertainment, and cultural needs of diasporic communities has become a modern growth industry. Deterritorialization and reterritorialization create new markets for entrepreneurs of all types, but especially for those in the media and culture industries who "thrive on the deterritorialized population for contact with its homeland" (Appadurai 1990: 302). In the slow and painful process of cultural assimilation to a new geographic space, particularly in the alienating, huge metropolises where immigrants and exiles tend to congregate, popular culture products from "back home," as well as local materials produced in the native language and reflecting core cultural values from the homeland, are crucial for creating peace of mind and ethnic solidarity for reterritorialized peoples. These cultural materials are rented or sold not in department store chains or at Blockbuster Video, but in "ethnic" grocery stores and video rental shops. There is also a growing market for videos, pop music, and software produced in exile and sent to the home countries. Vietnamese cultural materials produced in California sell well in Vietnam, for instance, as do Persian products exported from Los Angeles to Iran (Naficy 1993).

Connecting to traditional values, religion, popular arts, and language, communications media help to maintain, enliven, and transform cultural life for cultural diasporas. Older members of deterritorialized peoples often use traditional cultural materials to reinforce their preferred modes of living and social statuses within their new communities. Younger members may find comfort in tradition too, though they are just as likely to form their reterritorialized identities at least partly in opposition to imported values, ways of life, and cultural products, which they often find outdated, uncool, or otherwise uninteresting. Many children of London's deterritorialized Indian Sikh diaspora, for example, find their parents' heavy political commitments to fundamentalism irrelevant – something for the older generation, maybe, but not for them. While some young Indian males appropriate Sikh style to construct machismo displays, "the great majority aspire not to reterritorialize their ethnic group, but rather to transcend it" (Gillespie 1995: 21).

Photo 9.6 Diasporic cultures. Vietnamese Americans in California attend a semi-annual celebration of their traditional culture. The shirts say, "I love the language of my country . . ." (photo by James Lull)

Photo 9.7 Mobile media. Left out of the mainstream, Vietnamese immigrants to the United States create alternative media to communicate publicly. Billboards made of scraps of wood propped up against Vietnamese storefronts announce music concerts and other cultural events (photo by James Lull)

Widespread, affordable, point-to-point consumer communication technologies facilitate mediated interpersonal communication that is used to construct hybrid satellite cultures in new locations and maintain ties to cultural homelands. Immigrants who live thousands of miles away from their places of geographic origin regularly use email and telephones to nurture relationships with family and friends back home, and to expand their cultural territory in new geographical locations. Communications technology sustains and enlarges the very nature of a given cultural field by facilitating social interaction that is not bound by physical space. Put another way, culture can be actively reterritorialized by the ability of communications technology to facilitate social interaction that transcends physical distance.

A tremendous advantage of reterritorialized immigrant culture is that the perceived good things about the "old country" can be preserved in the new locations, without having to directly confront the typical repressive political and economic realities that were left back home. Heavy nostalgia – a highly selective, fond remembering of the distant culture – is common for reterritorialized peoples as they seek emotional comfort in their new lands. Dominant cultural values and familiar behaviors back home are reduced to memory traces and figments of the imagination. Immigrants usually face co-cultural or subcultural status in their new territories, a reduced role that is frequently difficult to accept.

Adaptation is key. Ethnic Chinese immigrants from China, Taiwan, Hong Kong, and elsewhere coming to San Francisco, Los Angeles, London, New York, Sydney, and other world cities over the past two centuries, for instance, staked out their physical territory as Chinatowns, each with its own political and cultural structure and hierarchy. They did so in part because of discrimination they encountered. Chinatowns became hubs of economic and cultural activity. Links to the homelands were maintained through family and business activities. Indeed, whatever prosperity was to be enjoyed by "overseas Chinese" depended on the ability of members of the deterritorialized group to nurture an international "bamboo network of family and personal relationships and a common culture" (Huntington 1996: 170).

More recent Asian immigrants, however, have had to look outside the Chinatowns, Koreatowns, Japantowns, and other Asian towns for space to live and work. In California, a cultural nuance was waiting for them to use – the shopping mall.[5] Ethnic shopping malls have become the new meeting grounds for California's immigrants, providing culturally familiar merchandise and food, negotiations in their own languages, and most important, a place to meet friends. The ethnic mall has become a social support system and center for self-sufficiency – much like the original urban enclaves – that helps immigrants make the transition to life in America. But of course this changes with time too. One immigrant to the Silicon Valley, for instance, told a *San José Mercury News* reporter that first-generation immigrants spend 85 percent of their leisure time at the ethnic malls, the second generation 50 percent, and the third generation 25 percent with the remaining time spent at McDonald's and Pizza Hut!

Circular migration

Immigration need not be a one-way, permanent state of affairs where mediated cultural forms become the only contacts with the original culture. Some people move back and forth frequently between national cultures, functioning well, often in quite different ways, in both. This is known as *circular migration*.

Photos 9.8–9.9 Ethnic malls in California. Helping immigrants make the transition in new cultural space. Above, a Spanish-language radio station promotes the grand opening of *Mi Pueblo* food center. Below, Vietnamese Americans spend a Saturday afternoon socializing at Lion Plaza in San José (photos by James Lull)

Learning how to live in multiple places and spaces is a kind of cultural competency in globalization. Even conservative governments are getting used to the idea that their people are irretrievably on the move. India, for example, introduced a "Persons of Indian Origin" card in 1999 to encourage their diasporas in England, the United States, and elsewhere to travel, work, and invest in India with minimal legal or bureaucratic difficulty.

Some Puerto Ricans, Jamaicans, Dominicans, and Mexicans travel from South to North and return South, or vice versa, several times every year. The Latinos often share common neighborhoods in New York, Miami, and Los Angeles, where they interact and influence each other. Spanish-language television, radio, cinema, and dancehalls in the United States bring Latinos together physically and symbolically. Mexican kids whose parents work in the United States legally can attend school half the year in Mexico, the other half in the United States, and receive a legitimate joint diploma. The positive syntheses forged among the reterritorialized cultures, as well as the conflicts that emerge in contested social and cultural space in America, are then exported back to the Caribbean, Mexico, Central and South America as cultural products (popular music especially), and as perceptions of the Latino "other." Circular migrations greatly influence regional identities in the countries of origin too (Gendreau and Ibarra 1999).

Box 9.3 Singing to the Heart of Mexico

Our bilingual, bicultural, binational experience is a form of schizophrenia, rich and poor, sun and shadow, between realism and surrealism. To live on the border is to live in the center, to be at the entrance and the exit; to inhabit two worlds, two cultures, and to accept both.

Burciaga 1993: 66

If you want us to come back, hire a Mexican player.

*Banner held by Mexican immigrants to northern California at
a San José Quake professional soccer match*

Divorced in time and space from the familiar terrain of everyday life back home, Mexican immigrants to the United States depend greatly on symbolic links to their imagined native ways of life. Mexico is by no means just a geographical place. More than anything it is a cultural space, and nostalgic journeys to that space are taken by people as they establish their new cultural territories.

Those types of symbolic connections to romanticized Mexico are very strongly felt when Juan Gabriel – Mexico's greatest composer and singer of popular music – performs concerts in California. The state's huge Latino community, composed mainly of Mexican immigrants, connects intimately to cultural feelings inspired by Juan Gabriel.

Photo 9.10 Juan Gabriel (printed courtesy BMG Latin)

Gabriel performs songs such as "The Mexico that Has Left Us" (*El Mexico que se nos fue*), a particularly emotional portrait of political and cultural tensions between Mexico and the United States. The song laments the transformation of Mexican towns and villages in the wake of immigration, the devastation of the Mexican economy since the recent peso devaluation and recession, the industrialization and contamination of the countryside that have been accelerated by hemispheric trade agreements, and the modernization and commercialization of life in general. Juan Gabriel sadly describes the replacement of adobe homes with cement structures in Mexico, the breaking up of nuclear families, even the preference of television over local music groups for entertainment in Mexican villages.

Juan Gabriel presents a poignant Mexican interpretation of the downside of modernization and globalization. He creates a vivid, nostalgic view of old Mexico which may not promote Mexican economic development, but touches the hearts and souls of Mexican immigrants – those with and without legal papers – who reside and toil in California. His concerts are attended almost exclusively by Mexican Americans and Mexicans in America. He draws huge crowds without advertising in English-language media. Like the Vietnamese and other cultural groups in California, Mexican Americans learn about their cultural events mainly through alternative media and informal social networks. They really don't expect much more.

What Juan Gabriel offers his compatriots in the United States is access to their own sense of cultural well-being, hopes for the future, and potential to enjoy popular pleasures. Performers like him are unifying resources of enormous importance. For thousands of immigrants to countries all over the world, symbolic representations of culture such as music are much more accessible and democratic than traditional political, economic, or coercive power because they help individuals from all walks of life exercise real influence over their experiences and feelings.

Because culture is constructed and mobile, it is also synthetic and multiple. The abundance, power, and convenience of modern communications technology give reterritorialized peoples opportunities to keep their ethnic identities alive. This is true for Mexican immigrants in northern California who watch three Spanish-language cable TV stations in the Bay Area, listen to many Spanish-language radio stations, rent the same video classics their friends and families view in Mexico, and buy the latest Juan Gabriel, Julieta Venegas, Café Tacuba, or Alejandro Fernández album. Because of the robust and efficient American market, many Mexican cultural materials are actually easier to find and less expensive in California than they are in Mexico.

Mexican towns and neighborhoods have grown up all over California. These settlements often have profound attachments to particular parts of Mexico. Their inhabitants make frequent journeys back and forth between their homes in the United States and their homes in Mexico. Aguililla, Michoacan (Mexico), and Redwood City, California, are one such pair of communities. Aguililla is known as "Little Redwood City" in Mexico, and Redwood City is "Little Aguililla" in California. The Mexican national economy depends on dollars coming in from laborers working in the United States. Because Mexicans living abroad have the right to vote in Mexican elections, Mexican politicians come to California and Texas to campaign for votes.

The transnational flow of communications technology and cultural materials helps make Mexicans feel more Mexican in Mexico too. For instance, when famous popular music groups like Los Tigres del Norte, Bronco, or Los Tucanes de Tijuana play their hits in outdoor stadiums in Mexico, they depend on Japanese, German, and American audio technology to amplify the music with minimal distortion. The effect is loud, pure, sound that drives Mexican emotions, feelings, language – Mexican culture – deep into the bones of concert goers. Far from destroying Mexican culture, the imported equipment enhances the *puro Mexicano* cultural experience.

The sites and styles of cultural territories have changed in the late modern and postmodern world, but people still organize themselves culturally in order to carve out their personal identities and feel secure. No doubt, the "disembedding [lifting out] . . . of social relations from local contexts of interaction and their restructuring across indefinite spans of time and space" can be very disorienting and intimidating (Giddens 1990: 21). But by developing new cultural territories and "re-embedding" (inserting) social relations in new contexts, people can overcome the depersonalizing tendencies of fractured postmodern life to find emotional relief and security (pp. 141–2). New ways of conceptualizing time, space, and culture thus provide one basis for refashioning stable social relations (Giddens 1991: 17). Cultural reterritorialization is not something done to people over which they have no control.

Ramp-up to postmodernity

Reterritorialization is a process of active cultural selection and synthesis drawing from the familiar and the new. Cultural environments today are made up of mediated and unmediated elements, of the highbrow and the popular, of the personal and the mass, of the public and the private, of the here and the there, of the familiar and the strange, of yesterday, today, and tomorrow. People draw ambitiously from all available material and symbolic domains to socially construct their cultural worlds.

Culture has never been motionless; it is invariably reinvented by subsequent generations. But cultural forms and environments today are changing in unprecedented ways and in greater measure than ever before. Modernity demands such disruptions and alterations. Anthony Giddens describes modernity as a "juggernaut... like a runaway engine of enormous power which, collectively as human beings, we can drive to some extent but which also threatens to rush out of our control" (Giddens 1990: 139).

But what happens to a society after its members' quest for modernity's material comforts and conveniences has been largely satisfied? One popular academic theory has it that people living in those societies suffer an overly stimulated, confusing, and ultimately unfulfilling existence. The chaotic conditions of such a society have been described as *postmodernity*. In a postmodern society, the traditional pillars of social stability disappear. Simplicity gives way to complexity. Certainty is provisional. Memory is short. Reality is simulated. Shame disappears. Immediate gratification replaces long-term goals. Style triumphs over substance. Commercialism explodes. Sensations rule.

The social consequences of such a change are real. More marriages end up in divorce. Many more children are born out of wedlock. Job longevity shortens. Corporations shred documents. High-school students shoot each other. Viruses infect computers. Wars are fought on television. Rainforests are destroyed. Music has no melody. Tattoos and tongue studs scream for attention. Any collective purpose in life becomes unclear. Cultural categories, contexts, assumptions, allegiances, and relevancies shift madly about. From social relationships to music and architecture, nothing makes sense any more. The consequences are felt globally. A new world disorder takes shape.

We must not lose sight of the fact, however, that much of the world is not yet modern, and certainly not postmodern. Academic discussions about postmodernity and modernity frequently agonize over the plight of societies, or social groups within societies, that can afford to luxuriate in the "problems" that modernity and its aftermath bring. While it is true that modern and postmodern developments affect people everywhere, at least indirectly, many people do not benefit from current conditions. Furthermore, much of the world's most serious and perplexing confusions, like the ethnic and religious wars raging in Yugoslavia, India, Indonesia, and Africa, have much more to do with ideologies and cultural traditions deeply rooted in the past than with any collective neurosis brought on by an inability to deal with the directionlessness and despair of life after modernity.

Still, for all of us, the world *is* changing rapidly. How do people interpret their changing worlds, make them meaningful, and advance their personal, social, and cultural interests? To systematically rethink these issues in a way that matches the worlds we live in, we will continue to wrestle with the slippery concept of culture in the next, and final, chapter.

10

Culture, Superculture, Sensation

To speak of culture as ordinary life doesn't make much sense in such an extraordinary world. Although traditional cultural understandings and practices have not outlived their usefulness – not for people constructing shared ways of life, and not for theorists who try to figure out what in the world is going on – culture nonetheless needs serious reconsideration appropriate for the times. Culture's contemporary significance and diverse manifestations make up the focus of this final chapter.

Surviving the culture crash

People struggle over culture, especially when it is associated explicitly with politics of race, ethnicity, or social class, or when it is subject to geographical dispute. And while globalization has altered culture in many respects, traditional forms of culture remain vital for collectively envisioning and organizing social life, for accomplishing serious political objectives, and for fashioning personal and social identities.

Recent historical developments, however, do indeed mark a new era in culture and cultural analysis. The technological advances in transportation and communication that led to postmodernity and globalization have radically expanded the range of perceptions and uses of time and space, while greatly influencing global political and economic activities and relations. The uncertainties and confusions of the times sometimes are said to even evaporate meaning and identity. But in truth, postmodernity and globalization mainly extend, amplify, and accelerate cultural tendencies that have long been in place. It is the rate of change today that has really gotten everyone's attention.

How can culture – which implies significant coordination, coherence, and community – survive in a world where shared values, languages, religions, social institutions, and ways of life are disrupted, even placed in opposition to each other, and where members of cultural groups "invade" the space of others and feel themselves invaded? How do people make sense and make friends in a world that is everyday more fragmented, fast, symbolic, synthetic, contradictory, and conflictive? Sounds like a frantic, isolating, desperate situation.

Precisely because contemporary symbolic forms circulate so widely and easily, and because they invite such diverse interpretations and uses, the ability of human beings to create and organize their worlds in ways that stimulate, comfort, and please them actually increases in the era of postmodernity and globalization. The consequences of contemporary communication develop according to how people use the new technologies and symbolic materials. The locus for this cultural work lies exactly in the essence of the phenomenon itself – symbolic abundance. Today's diverse technological and symbolic environments generate a rich stock of resources for creative cultural engagements.

Moreover, a serious degree of cultural anarchy is at work. As David Chaney puts it, "what seems to distinguish postmodern cultural practice is that the universe of cultural imagery can be pillaged indiscriminately" (Chaney 1994: 183). Symbolic forms of all types are connotational. They stimulate ultimately unbounded interpretations, permutations, and involvements as they enter, resonate with, and change established cultural environments.

Concluding this volume on media, communication, and culture, I will continue to emphasize the positive cultural potential that abounds on the outset of the new millennium. Symbolic resources today are put to work by people for all the same reasons, and in many of the same ways, that cultural activity has always been constructed. At the same time novel cultural alignments are being formed. Although a mastering of new cultural competencies and literacies is required of people today, the generative qualities of contemporary symbolic resources simultaneously expand the range of thought and behavior while actually reducing some of the confusions brought on by postmodernity and globalization.

New communication skills and
the personalization of culture

Middle-class adolescents in countries all over the world unproblematically surf the web while they watch TV, listen to loud music, and do their homework. Their parents conduct business on cellular phones while they oversee their families, listen to the radio, and drive to work.

Communications multi-tasking has become a natural state of affairs for many people in the world's middle class. The ability to simultaneously manage multiple technologies, multiple mediated torrents of information and emotion, and the local jumble of unmediated persons and things makes up the overall complex of communication skills that life today requires. Today's expanded communication environments thus necessitate innovative and more complex skills of cultural assembly and code switching. People navigate endless archipelagos of cultural representation, integrating fresh symbolic forms into familiar, local cultural routines and materials to create new cultural formations, understandings, and activities. Developing such skills is not only a matter of acquiring new communication tools and literacies. It also requires cultivating a mentality and lifestyle that can accommodate the incessant, multi-tributary flows.

Influenced greatly by the Internet and by the miniaturization and privatization of media technology, cultural journeys into the brave new world are becoming eclectic, solo ventures. Consumer-friendly communications and information technology – together with the robust, culturally loaded symbolic representations they transmit – interact exponentially to create new platforms and portals of meaning and experience on an individual "user/consumer" basis.

The rapid development and spread of industrial and consumer communications technology, the robust circulation of symbolic forms, and the reach, frequency, and diversity of communications interactivity transform certain key aspects of basic human experience. Constructing contemporary meaning and experience requires people to monitor their interests, biases, wants, and needs and match them up with the symbolic panoramas opening up dynamically in front of them. Sorting, synthesizing, editing, and bundling cultural options into customized matrices and activities helps people make sense of and enjoy their new surroundings. The ability to create and live simultaneously in dynamic grids of intersecting experience – local and distant, material and symbolic – has become fundamental cultural practice.[1]

Learning how to participate competently in this era of globalized hypercommunication by combining fragments, repositioning cultural impulses into new contexts, linking symbolic elements with material surroundings, negotiating encounters with virtual strangers, and so on is less tied now to geographical localities and "real" time than before. That which is far away can instantly be made close. That which is close at hand can often be ignored. The fluidity and flexibility of the tumultuous symbolic universe encourage and facilitate extremely creative and personalized involvements. The frenzy stimulates new kinds of human contact whose consequences alter and broaden the experiences and expectations of the individual participants while changing the cultural environments at the same time.

We should speak today therefore not just of the "social construction of culture," but of the "creative and highly personalized invention of cultural multiplexes." We have entered a global amphitheater of symbolic cultural "rich points" (Agar 1994: 230–1), which people use to expand their worlds, construct their social and cultural identities, and draw pleasure from their everyday experiences.

The superculture

Culture is a process of multinational assembling, a flexible articulation of parts, a montage of features that any citizen in any country, religion, or ideology can read and use.

García Canclini 1995: 16

Presented with a choice, many people may under some circumstances not opt for what may have seemed to be "their" culture. They were perhaps never wholeheartedly for it in the first place.

Hannerz 1996: 58

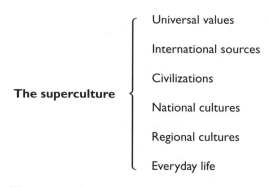

The superculture
- Universal values
- International sources
- Civilizations
- National cultures
- Regional cultures
- Everyday life

Figure 10.1 The superculture

Now I will introduce briefly a new conception of culture that grows out of the complex historical period in which we live. The *superculture* transcends traditional categories to reflect two principal current cultural trends: globalization and personalization. The superculture is the particular matrix of symbolic resources, unmediated everyday scenes, and all other available cultural representations and activities that people sample, evaluate, appropriate, and piece together in order to expand their horizons, share sentiments, create social networks, fashion lifestyles, and organize life in meaningful and pleasing ways.

The superculture necessarily is a janus-faced, transient space between here and there, between society and self, and between the material and the symbolic because *culture today floats tentatively between the local and the global, between the collective and the individual, and between unmediated and mediated forms of experience.*

The trick today is to be culturally light on our feet. We live not in worlds composed of distinct sociocultural influences which we experience in serial fashion, but in shifting universes of cultural impulses that constantly require us to sort, synthesize, and create. We engage complex texts in complex social and cultural contexts. As media and information technologies become more accessible and robust, the cultural possibilities likewise expand. Classic oppositions between real and unreal, authentic and simulated, substance and style have lost their original meanings in contemporary cultural activity.

People today have access to six fundamental spheres of cultural activity and representation (see figure 10.1). As persons expand their range of cultural operation, their cultural experiences become less local and less strictly communal. They construct their supercultures when they assemble cultural syntheses by drawing from resources emanating from the various cultural spheres. Supercultures are fusions of cultural fragments that become intelligible to the self and others in the constitutive construction of cognitive patterns, communicative interactions, and social practices that make up the impermanent cultural profiles of individual persons. To the degree that such personal hybrids contribute to formation of cultural identities, such identities and allegiances are not necessarily the enduring types we have traditionally associated with language, blood, and ethnicity, for example.

The cultural spheres

The spheres are predigested repositories of cultural resources which are interpreted and synthesized into clusters of relevant elements by cultural programmers – everyday human beings. The specific configurations this cultural work produces are the supercultures.

The six cultural spheres range from the most distant and global locales to the closest and most traditional venues. What specifically are these spheres of cultural utility?

First, people widely draw from *universal* values – those principles of life and social behaviors which, though they are by no means uniformly interpreted, nonetheless appear and signify quite commonly across diverse cultural groups. These include fundamental moral principles embedded in the worlds' major religions, and utopian notions of universal human rights embodied by global organizations such as the United Nations, the International Red Cross, and the International Red Crescent. Other domains of universal awareness and appeal include the widespread desire humans have for material objects represented in codes and acts of consumption, standards of aesthetics and physical beauty, sexual and survival needs, and varieties of emotional experience and expression.

Second are the abundant *international* symbolic cultural resources available to users of mass media and information technologies around the world. As we have seen throughout this book, satellite television, cable, the music industry, computer hardware and software, and the Internet circulate symbolic content of incredible quantity and variety. The hybrids people can create from these sources are limitless. Also at play here are the logos, styles, and transactions international trade and commerce, the cross-cultural influence of tourism, educational and cultural exchange programs, political treaties and agreements, and so on.

Third is the most encompassing of the traditional cultural categories – *civilizations*. Samuel P. Huntington (1996) among others argues that the world is divided into eight or nine basic cultural groups – civilizations – which demarcate fundamentally stable and contrasting ways of life. Civilizational differences are so central and important that people even make war over them. The bloody stand-off of the late 1990s between Serbians and Albanians – cultural groups from different civilizations occupying the same geographical territory – is but one example. Border stresses between Mexico and the United States also reflect the kinds of tensions that grow between different civilizations living side by side. The struggle between Israelis and Palestinians in the Holy Land is legendary civilizational discord.

The world's great civilizations have evolved along three different historical trajectories: some civilizations are based on a common world view based in religion (Islamic, Buddhist, Hindu, Orthodox, Sinic); others were created by colonial expansionism (Western civilization, Latin America); a third category traces its origins to geography (Japan, Africa). Of course not all people who live in the various civilizations have the same cultural orientations and biases, and civilization theory has been harshly criticized by some scholars who believe it crudely and misleadingly essentializes people. Furthermore, civilizational theory as an overarching theoretical framework can oversimplify culture in the era of postmodernity and globalization. Nonetheless, as people assemble their cultural matrices they do indeed draw in part from the familiar languages, religions, food, rituals, and customs that make up their civilization. The ability to do so is facilitated in large measure today by strong economic and cultural ties – including especially the exchange of telecommunications hardware and content – which develop and endure between nations of the same civilization.

Fourth, dominant *national* ideologies and cultures continue to be pervasive and potent resources. The national sphere carries with it all manner of codification, legitimization, and authority. Collective consciousness and daily life are organized in large measure by the discourses, demands, and routines required and suggested by dominant national ideologies and cultures. Laws, rules, customs, languages, religions, systems of commerce, education, and so on, all backed up by unifying material and symbolic forms such as constitutions, flags, national anthems, school curricula, military forces, media, and advertising, make the nation an unsurpassed cultural resource for most people, whether they like the idea or not (Price 1995: 40–59).

Fifth, *regions* within nations play a crucial role as they offer accents and alternatives – riding on, but sometimes contrasting with, national ideology and culture – that people use to fashion their cultural preferences, habits, and identities. To imagine oneself as part of a region – a northern Californian, for example, or a midwesterner, southerner, or New Englander – is a regional badge of cultural identity in the United States. The differentiating effect of regionalism applies to all nations, sometimes in ways that have important political implications. In Spain, for example, Catalonian separatists struggle for political independence in the north, while in the south newly formed culture industries promote regional traditions and styles – flamenco music and dance in Andalucia, for example – which generate lively varieties of collective cultural capital for this long-neglected part of the country.

Finally, we come to *daily life* as a cultural resource. Daily life, of course, is influenced by universal values, international symbolic forms, civilizations, national ideology and culture, and regional orientations. It draws greatly from all these sources, but is not the same as any one them. Because everyday life is not just the sum of given values, rules, and practices, the most micro environments and activities also contribute to the culture of groups and individuals. The superculture thus accommodates the important ethnographic notion of culture as everyday life, but everyday life today exists in complex relation to very attractive and powerful external cultural forces. We cannot think of the routine local practices of everyday life in and of themselves, therefore, as a satisfactory explanation for what constitutes culture in the current era.

Cultural actualization

> In the play of consumption and style, the practical actors of everyday life formulate their own versions of cultural diversity.
>
> *Chaney 1994: 82*

Culture actualizes in this robust material and symbolic environment when people select and combine ingredients from the spheres of available resources. Basic cultural work is a process and product of synthesis – a blending of available signs into combinations that give meaning, comfort, or pleasure. The multidimensional superculture – a constellation of cultural elements from near and far – is fundamental to personal well-being. As García Canclini argues:

> It is indispensable to have international information, not only to be technologically and aesthetically up to date, but also to nourish symbolic elaboration in the multiculturality of migrations, exchanges, and crossings. But beyond this there are moments when we need to re-enfold ourselves into that which is our own, whether this is national or ethnic peculiarities, interpersonal interactions in domestic spaces, or the modest searches of the individual person. (García Canclini 1995: 189)

Elements of the superculture do not stand independent from each other. We don't simply pick and choose from autonomous material and symbolic fields to construct our cultural profiles. Although the superculture implies a profound multiculturality, it also reflects transculturality, interculturality, and hybridization, as García Canclini himself argues so well (García Canclini 1989; 1995). The superculture is therefore a dynamic, transtextual, transdiscursive polylogue of available materials, signs, and stories evaluated and put into practice by social actors in the dreams and dramas of their everyday lives. It is composed of an expansive intersection of resources ranging from deep within the collective consciousness of the civilization, nation, and region to the alluring contours of less familiar cultural elsewheres. The superculture is manifest in functional circuits of self-understanding, well-being, and exploration that are brought to fruition when people combine resources from the extraordinarily wide range available. As one striking example from Latin America, some rural dwellers rely on traditional healing methods and old techniques of artisanal and agricultural production, while "at the same time they use international credit cards and computers" (García Canclini 1995: 153). In England, the rest of Europe, the United States, and nearly everywhere else, people combine distant digital and virtual realities brought to awareness by information technology, with close, body-oriented cultural elements – sports, dance, food, and fashion, for example – to forge creative supercultural synergies.

Flexibility is fundamental. Symbolic cultural forms – especially those from far away – can often be much more easily manipulated than relatively fixed and enduring local cultural elements. This is because distant resources can provide attractive opportunities for creative cultural work that eludes supervision by local cultural authorities. Familiar, institutionalized sources of cultural authority – schools, national media systems, churches, mainstream mass media, and so on – have lost some of their power in this transformation of the locus and manner of cultural construction. As more cultural power is assumed by individuals and small groups, authority changes from societal mandates, rules, and regulations to modern and postmodern styles related more to personal and small-group politics, lifestyles, and pleasures. The superculture phenomenon thus is nothing less than a cultural revolution where the basic terms of institutionalized social power are contested by individuals and groups as they appropriate newly attainable resources from the cultural spheres.

Sensations

No overly coherent, globalized world will ever emerge – not for individuals, nor for groups, and not just because of the sometimes contradictory and conflictive pull of the cultural spheres. Symbolic forms circulated by mass media and information technologies stimulate much more than cultural hybrids and unities. Human beings may be organizing animals, but they are also drawn to physical and emotional pleasures that have little or nothing to do with the stabilizing influence of culture. The tendency to disengage from cultural work can be just as strong as the tendency to make or intensify social and cultural connections. People sometimes use communications media and popular culture to stimulate their senses just for the fun of it.

Take American horror movies. While the storyline matters in horror films, what the audience really wants is a guaranteed, post-industrial-strength emotional roller-coaster ride. Or consider the striking rise in popularity of television shows such as *The World's Most Amazing Videos* or *When Wild Animals Attack* where one disaster after another amuses audiences for hours. Countries have their own versions of this genre. In Spain, for example, *Impact TV* strings together video fragments of the worst bullfight gorings and falls from horses that can be found every week. The glut of American TV talk shows – especially those of the Jerry Springer variety – are all based on shock and sensation. The appeal of much television news – particularly media scandals – rests on sensory provocations. Extreme sporting games, professional wrestling, and extreme martial arts shock the senses. Sports channels keep viewers interested by replaying the emotional highlights – slam dunks, home runs, touchdowns, and gooooooooooooals! Erotic media content – magazine, film, video, and Internet pornography – depends on the capacity of symbolic forms to stimulate culturally decontextualized physical reactions. Even email, which ostensibly facilitates the exchange of information, has been appropriated to a large extent to serve emotional purposes and promote erotic fantasies. We have indeed moved into "a world of dreams (or nightmares) driven by the sensuality of representation" (Chaney 1996: 53).

But representation does not cover all the ground. Media sensations are driven just as much by form as by content, if not more so. Media technologies themselves stimulate physical and emotional involvements and reactions. Techniques of media production have become so sophisticated that much media content is based primarily on technical manipulation of image and sound. Many fans of the latest *Star Wars* films, for instance, say the reason they like the movies so much is because they enjoy the technical effects – they like submitting to the feelings the technical effects provoke. The story basically just strings the sensations together. When *Matrix* was released in 1999, all the talk was about the film's amazing, unprecedented visual effects which were themselves enough to draw huge audiences to movie theaters worldwide. Science fiction, disaster, horror, and action films depend on technical effects to carry the story and conquer audiences through sensory stimulation.

The sensory attractiveness of contemporary media experience is not based solely on manipulation of fictional or technical content, however. Sophisticated communications technologies in and of themselves arouse the senses. The sheer capacity of audio systems to produce extremely high levels of volume at concerts, in movie theaters, and at home, for instance, can greatly excite the senses. Many young people demand high volume when they listen to popular music. Volume delivers the sensation – creating, changing, or elevating the mood of listeners (Christenson and Roberts 1998; Lull 1992a). People even become physically addicted to the volume itself.

Digitalization of media technologies has dramatically increased the emotional effects of audio and visual-based genres. Digital technologies produce extremely high-resolution images and sounds which elevate the intimacy and emotional impact of mediated experience to unprecedented levels. By dramatically increasing the signal-to-noise ratio (wanted-to-unwanted video and audio "information"), ambient distractions are reduced, allowing users of digital media to experience stories and songs with stunning levels of personal involvement. By turning up the volume of a digital video movie, for example, the viewer can hear and feel the sounds of emotion – cries, laughter, shouts of joy, fear, or ecstasy – with a closeness not available in the "real" world.

By obliterating the constraints of traditional perceptions of time and space, digital technologies also turn symbolic archives into widely accessible resources and create virtual neighborhoods composed of strangers.

But we ought not think of media content and form as independent sensory streams. Combinations of content and form take sensations to their greatest heights. Audiences gripped their seats tightly while they watched *Titanic*, for example, because they were caught up in the passionate story and frantic action on the big screen as it interacted with and was enhanced by loud, clear, digital "surround sound" that filled the theater. Such mediated mega-experiences can nearly overwhelm the senses, and please audiences in the process. Such experiences stimulate strong emotional and physical reactions – laughing, crying, screaming, yelling, moving the body, initiating contact with other people. The significance of some symbolic experiences therefore stems from the ability of media to penetrate our hearts, souls, and bodies to scare us, energize us, thrill us, stoke our emotions, make us lose control. This is not something media do to us. We seek out, pay for, enjoy, and willingly repeat these experiences. Some people further heighten the effect of sensational media experiences by ingesting alcohol and drugs as part of the pleasure search and ritual of consumption.

Experience without culture

Media sensations do not require much interpretation to be effective. One need not concentrate too hard at a movie theater, for instance, to sense that the blood-dripping, three-headed monster charging the screen to the sound of deafening music and shrieks of terror is dangerous. Sensations driven to ever greater extremes by digital media represent a kind of human experience that does not necessarily combine in any rational way with the structures and assumptions of culture or superculture. Sensations in fact can override the rationality that much cultural work presumes. Sensory stimulation itself is an attractive, but not necessarily culturally evident or meaningful, experience. Furthermore, the global reach of popular media today guarantees that sensory experiences are shared, but shared not does necessarily mean culturally located or significant.

Some media sensations thus promote experience that is lifted out of culture, and create sociality that lacks intimacy and accountability. Mediated signs need not be connected to referents, and the referents themselves don't have to matter either. For example, for many people Rio de Janeiro is not a Brazilian city. It's a sexy, sun-drenched archetype of sensory pleasure. It's just Rio. Fun. A space, not a place.

Sensation is bodily and emotional stimulation and pleasure in and of itself – an autism of delights.

The human consequences of contemporary sensory experience are not well understood, and may never be. Because the senses are open, infinite, and fantastic, anything is possible. Sensations can bring about a rupture between culture and consciousness, producing cognitive structures that are not well integrated. Psychologists who worry about such phenomena refer to a "human disconnect" that has even been blamed for violent outbursts like the mass murders at a Colorado (USA) high school in 1999, and other tragedies since then.

Conclusion

Civil societies appear increasingly less like national communities, understood as unified territories, languages, and political systems. Rather, they manifest themselves as interpretative communities of consumers – that is to say, groups of people who share pleasures ... that give them shared identities.

García Canclini 1995: 196

The duty of the postmodern citizen is to lead an enjoyable life.

Bauman 1996: 34

The most important developments of the past century revolve around the same dynamics that will propel life in the next hundred years – the compression of time and space through advances in transportation and communication, the remaking of social communities provoked by human migrations and technological interfaces, and the diversification and intensification of experience stimulated by media and the symbolic forms they circulate.

The consequences of such developments were not predictable last century, and will be even less certain in the next. Nation, class, religion, and ethnicity will be further relativized. Cultures will continue to fracture into personalized supercultures. Human experience will increasingly become an expansive grid of temporary relevances and sensations. And through it all, more for some than others, opportunities will abound and creature comforts will soothe.

We do indeed live in a "global pillage" of symbolic cultural activity, but – as we stressed from the beginning of this book – not all the world's people face the challenges and opportunities of the current era with the same resources, competencies, interests, or motivations. The consequences of technological and symbolic complexity, modernity, postmodernity, and globalization do not by any stretch of the imagination apply in a standard way to the world's six billion inhabitants, although as we have observed throughout this journey into contemporary media, communication, and culture, all the consequences of the current era by no means militate against the poor or disenfranchised. Still, while the transnational middle class has embarked on an unimaginable adventure in the twenty-first century, many of the world's people will watch what's happening on an old TV set or hear about it from friends. Despite awesome advances in all forms of scientific knowledge and technology, it appears that the gaps among people unfortunately will widen to the point where in many ways it will seem that we aren't even living on the same planet.

The potential dangers of the current era are not limited to gaps and differences between and among people. What kind of a world are we creating? Are we all just selfishly pursuing personal interests, rampant consumption, and the fleeting pleasures of instant gratification? Does the world benefit in some relatively democratic way from the "*anarchy* of the market," as Paul Willis (1990) believes, or does it suffer systemic global discrimination from the "*tyranny* of the market," as Pierre Bourdieu (1998) argues? As always, upon careful reflection, answers to such profound and complex questions are not easily found. In the end, it must be said, not Bourdieu nor anyone else has been able to finesse a viable alternative to the idea that cultural activity today is based on a dynamic, sometimes volatile, always differentiating play of image and consumption driven by the logic and energy of global market forces. That's not a world toward which we're headed; it's the place where we've already arrived.

Notes

Chapter 1   Introduction

1   Nokia is Finnish, not Japanese.
2   It must also be said, however, that Finland has maintained a very restrictive immigration policy over the years, a fact that minimizes socioeconomic differences within the nation.
3   The statistics and trends discussed here are supplied by the Organization for Economic Cooperation and Development, Paris.

Chapter 4   Social Rules and Power

1   The depths to which the affair went include the nicknames they had for each other. Clinton called Lewinsky "Kiddo," which she said made her think he often didn't remember her name. Lewinsky, in turn, referred to the former president as "Butthead" in her taped telephone conversations with Linda Tripp.
2   I must point out that this social inversion directly involves mainly people from the lower socioeconomic classes. The vast majority of middle-class and upper-class Brazilians take no part in the ritual, and many of them detest the entire thing. Many families in Rio de Janeiro escape the city during Carnival. Those who stay home are likely to watch parts of the celebration, especially the parade of the schools of samba, on television. For many Brazilians today, Carnival has become a TV ritual.

Chapter 5   Media Audiences

1   Some educators and researchers in the United States experimented with "TV education" in the classroom, but so far this has not sparked much

interest and is fraught with legal, technical, and bureaucratic problems. England and the Nordic countries have done more in this area, and Latin American researchers are also active in such work (for example, see Orozco Gómez 1990, 1991, 1996 concerning Mexico, and Fuenzalida 1997 about Chile).

2 Marcuse's provocative concept of "false needs" is likewise subject to criticism, especially for its elitism. Is Marcuse any more qualified than anyone else to tell us what we need? John Tomlinson (1991) has written extensively and sharply about Marcuse's argument in this debate.

3 Within the uses and gratifications framework, *methods* (cognitive plans and associated activities) that involve mass media are routinely termed "uses." The term "use" conflates cognition with action, thereby short-circuiting the explanatory potential of uses and gratifications research and theory.

4 See Chaney (1996) for an extended analysis of "lifestyle."

5 Still, big stars and big production budgets continue to characterize the major commercial TV networks in the United States and elsewhere: "It is apparent from currently available data that traditional, mass appeal network television still dominates media consumption in the United States" (Webster and Phalen 1997: 114).

Chapter 6   Culture

1 Anthropologists also suffer from their disciplinary history with culture. Ethnographic research on "exotic, Third World cultures" was linked to the imperialist, colonizing exploits of England, northern European countries, and the United States.

2 Nation as a political state continues to function in certain key respects, however. It is one way to organize social life, and provides a vital symbolic homeland even for people who emigrate from their former lands. This crucial theme will be taken up in much greater detail in chapters 9 and 10.

3 English will change to become more multi-dialectical, a World Standard Spoken English (Crystal 1997). The rising economic and cultural power of China signals a distinct challenge to the domination of English in the long term.

4 The *Wall Street Journal* article reports that the United States government has tried to cover up the controversy as politically too hot in the current era of multiculturalism.

5 In order to accommodate the skyrocketing increase of multiracial people in the United States, the American government allowed respondents to the 2000 census to check more than one racial category, but not one "multiracial" box. This caused tremendous problems for the Census Bureau to properly count individual persons. Furthermore, African-American and Latino-American political organizations opposed any change that recognizes multiracial people because such a move reduces

the numbers of blacks and Latinos these groups claim to represent, sub-sequently weakening the organizations' political bargaining power.

Chapter 7   Symbolic Power and Popular Culture

1   "Audience" is an industry expression that should not be taken for granted. For a lengthy critical discussion of how commercial and public service broadcasters conceptualize "audience" to their advantage, see Ang (1991).
2   One high-school teacher in Chicago found an especially effective means for punishing troublemakers at school. He formed the "Frank Sinatra Detention Club." Students who were required to stay after school could do nothing during those hours but sit in their chairs and listen to old Frank Sinatra records. Disobedience soon declined sharply. The musical culture gap has also been effectively manipulated by the manager of a convenience store in Sacramento, California, who couldn't find a way to stop young people from loitering in the parking lot outside the store. The manager piped classical music into the lot, scaring off the urban youth who previously could not even be intimidated by armed security guards. The manager joked that the only potential problem with this approach is that "next thing you know, we'll be getting senior citizens loitering out there!"
3   Indonesian workers make about $2.20 US per day assembling the shoes while Jordan made up to $20 million US as the principal hype artist.
4   Consumer warning! Despite the hype, the award-winning *Lauryn Hill* album is truly one of the most boring records ever made.
5   But see Grindstaff (1997) for a critique of how people are manipulated by the producers of TV talk shows to make pathetic spectacles of themselves.

Chapter 8   Meaning in Motion

1   The comparative analysis I present in the next few paragraphs was inspired by a lecture-discussion given by the American sociologist Stanley Aronowitz at the University of California–Santa Barbara.
2   *Machismo* is a complex cultural trait. It is often used inside and outside Mexico to refer very negatively to an arrogant domination, even mis-treatment, of women by men. The term can also be interpreted more liberally as "masculinity," and in this sense *machismo* has positive connotations, such as the responsibility that men assume for their families.
3   Piracy facilitated by easy access to tape recorders accounts for two-thirds of all pop music sold in Asia, 30 per cent in Africa, 21 per cent in Latin America, and about 11 per cent in Canada and the United States accord-ing to Frith (1992: 72), and other estimates are even higher.

4   The VCD players were developed in California's Silicon Valley, further
    demonstrating how "global hegemonic control" is simply not possible.
    This technology has undermined the profit potential of the American
    motion picture industry by promoting piracy in China and elsewhere.
5   A German television comedy series based on the bigoted Archie Bunker
    character, *Motzki*, was developed soon after the fall of the Berlin Wall.
    The lead character viciously ridiculed East Germans and their national
    culture. The program provoked strong reactions from Germans through-
    out the uncomfortably reunified nation in the early 1990s. Both *All in
    the Family* and *Motzki* were originally based on a British TV series of
    the 1960s and 1970s, *Till Death Us Do Part*.
6   This point must be qualified. As I pointed out earlier, considerable exper-
    imental and survey research has been conducted on the question of media
    violence. One of the major findings within the vast body of research is
    that children who are predisposed to violence in some way (aggressive
    personalities in general, victims of abuse, those frustrated as an experi-
    mental precondition) react much more aggressively to violent portrayals
    on TV and film than their calmer peers. This well-documented finding
    supports the point being made here. However, it is also the case in many
    studies that children who are *not* so predisposed react aggressively to
    violent programming, though the effect is less strong. What I want to
    stress here is that at least in the case of violent TV/film and aggressive
    behavior among children (especially boys), the media can stimulate
    responses that do not necessarily reflect a predisposition on the part of
    the viewer.

Chapter 9   Globalization and Cultural Territory

1   Backgrounding for this brief analysis of Quebec was taken from an article
    in *New Republic* written by Robert Wright (1995).
2   See Tomlinson (1999) for an especially comprehensive discussion of the
    complexities of deterritorialization.
3   Rated by Transparency International 1997 Corruption Perception Index.
4   Of course, the usual cultural contradictions abound. While Maori claims
    for land settlements are based on their rights as "indigenous" peoples,
    the Maoris, like the British, are not the original inhabitants of New
    Zealand. An earlier Polynesian population was displaced by the Maoris
    sometime around AD 950, with the largest migration arriving around
    1350, just a few centuries before the Dutch and English got there, accord-
    ing to Maori legends.
5   See Bauman (1996) for a discussion of the role of the American shop-
    ping mall in the construction of cultural identities.

Chapter 10   Culture, Superculture, Sensation

1   See Thompson (1995: 229), Tomlinson (1997: 71–5), and Tomlinson (1999) for good discussions of cultural proximity.

Glossary

accountability: The idea that media and information technology hold powerful people in society accountable for their actions.

active audience: A theoretical perspective claiming that audience members are not passive receivers or victims of their experiences with television and other media, but instead actively interpret and use the media in ways that benefit them.

agency: A concept promoting the idea that people are knowledgeable, capable agents of social action. Refers to the ambition, intelligence, and creativity that people bring to bear on their everyday life experiences.

agenda setting: A social science term meaning that the mass media "set the agenda" (i.e. determine the topics) for social discourse by presenting certain information (news stories, entertainment, and cultural themes) while avoiding other topics.

appropriation: Making use of something for your own purposes, sometimes in direct contradiction of its original intention.

articulation: When an ideological or cultural idea or theme connects to and influences other ideas or themes.

capitalism: An economic/ideological system that relies on market forces (the relatively unfettered buying and selling of goods) rather than state planning, which is characteristic of communism.

circular migration: A process of migratory movement by people from their original homelands to a second location (usually in another country), and back again. Often correlating with vocational opportunities in the adopted homeland, this process typically repeats in regular cycles.

class/social class: Groups of people categorized by their relative economic and social standing (upper class, middle class, working class, lower class).

code: A system of signs understood culturally. Language is one example.

cognition/cognitive: Emphasizes the rational, thinking dimensions of mental activity (rather than the emotional aspects). Acquiring knowledge.

commodity: Anything that is produced or offered for sale. These goods and services always have ideological origins and consequences.

communication(s):   Can be understood many ways. The two most common basic definitions are (1) the transmission of information through time and space, and (2) the construction of meaning through symbolic exchange.

consciousness: The essence or totality of attitudes, opinions, and sensitivities held by individuals or groups. It is what the articulation and spread of particular ideas produce in society.

constructivism: Social theory based on the idea that people invent their worlds through social practice and communication. This perspective differs from approaches that imply that consciousness and culture are received rather than created.

convention: A rule-governed pattern of social behavior. Conventions embody and reflect cultural orientations. They prescribe social activity as "norms."

critical theory: Various streams of social theory that call attention to the problems inherent in the economic and political structures and processes of capitalism. This intellectual tradition is typically associated with Marxist critical theory, especially as developed by the "Frankfurt School" in pre-World War II Germany, and its philosophical and political derivatives.

cultural capital: Cultural knowledge and style as resources in the formation of personal identities and the exercise of social influence.

cultural identity: The cultural values, lifestyles, practices, images, and other characteristics of a group or groups with which persons associate or affiliate themselves. People are then often recognized by others as members of that cultural group(s).

cultural imperialism: The critical notion that the diffusion of modern cultural artifacts, images, and styles (from dominant languages and popular music to TV sets and computer hardware) around the world is a contemporary form of cultural oppression or "imperialism" These processes favor the economic, political, and cultural interests of international superpowers such as the United States, the United Kingdom, Germany, and Japan.

cultural media: Communications technology whose message content inherently carries cultural information and biases.

cultural territory: The geographical and symbolic spaces where culture is created through human communication.

culture: An extremely complex concept defined for our purposes as shared values, assumptions, rules, and social practices that make up and contribute to personal and collective identity and security, *see also* **superculture.**

determinism: A cause-to-effect theoretical relationship. Examples are economic determinism (social class positions develop according to a hierarchy of material relations), ideological determinism (dominant ideas necessarily overrule competing thoughts), and technological determinism (the social effects of a medium such as television are linear and predictable). For an opposing view, *see* **negotiation.**

deterritorialization: The tearing apart of cultural structures, relationships, settings, and representations.

diaspora: A community of ethnically or culturally-related people living outside their places of geographical origin.

direct effects: Early theory of electronic media's influence on society where the impact of media was thought to be powerful, immediate, negative, and unaffected by other factors.

discourse: Most generally, the way objects or ideas are talked about publicly that gives rise to particular widespread understandings. *See also* **agenda setting.**

disjuncture: The differences, contradictions, and counter-tendencies in culture that tend to neutralize the concentration and potency of dominant forms of political-economic power.

dominant ideology: A system of ideas that asserts, reinforces, and advances the interests of a society's elite socioeconomic group.

elites: Refers generally to the highest socioeconomic class in capitalist societies.

empower: To engage in an activity that brings out a sense of worth, confidence, or ability in an individual or group. To enable.

ethnography: A qualitative empirical research method, grounded in anthropology, that depends on participant observation, depth interviewing, and the use of informants as primary evidence in cultural analysis.

ethnomethodology: Routine, often taken-for-granted strategies of sense making and social behavior that people employ to construct their everyday lives.

framing: The way an object, image, or idea is represented thereby influencing the way the object, image, or idea will be interpreted. *See also* **preferred interpretation.**

functionalism: A controversial theory which fundamentally claims that society "functions" well as a system because various institutions (e.g. schools, political parties, mass media) help maintain social stability.

genre: A category of media fare such as "soap opera," "Tejano music," "slasher films," etc.

globalization: The flow of people, images, commodities, money, ideas, and information on a global scale, which some theorists argue is creating a homogeneous world culture.

glocalization: The fusion of "global" cultural influences with "local" cultural contexts, usually with serious economic consequences. *See also* **indigenization.**

gratification: The experience of deep personal satisfaction/pleasure or the reduction of biological or psychological deficiencies.

habitus: A system of socially learned cultural predispositions and activities that differentiates people by their tastes and lifestyles.

hardware: Technological forms, media, or communications equipment such as television stations and sets, telephones, computers, compact disc players, newspaper presses, etc.

hegemony: A process through which dominant ideology is transmitted, consciousness is formed, and social power is exercised. The power or dominance that one social group holds over others. Rather than direct manipulation of people against their interests, hegemony depends on social actors accepting their subordinate status as normal. Ideology-dispensing institutions such as schools, government, business, and mass media reinforce each other by perpetuating the status quo as common sense.

hybridization: The fusing of cultural forms often facilitated by the flow of mass-mediated imagery.

ideational image systems: Systemic forms of ideological expression that combine particular images, message structure, and preferred meanings into an integrated whole.

identity: Emphasizing the cultural aspect, this term refers to the sense of belonging, security, recognition, and importance someone can feel by being a member of a group that is bound together by common values and lifestyles.

ideology: A system of ideas expressed in communication.

image: A symbolic, often visual, display or representation of an object or idea.

image system: An ideological formation whose influence is facilitated by how the ideas are represented and framed and how they are circulated via technology and interpersonal communication.

imperialism: Originally, political-economic-cultural hegemony exercised by one nation over others. In contemporary critical theory it usually refers to "cultural imperialism" or "media imperialism," reflecting concern about how communications hardware and software are used by world superpowers to impose their political-economic-cultural values and agendas on less powerful nations and cultures.

indigenization: The process by which imported cultural materials ranging from food to architecture and popular music are adapted to local cultural conditions.

information technology: Data-transmitting, storage, and retrieval systems ranging from personal computers to the Internet.

institution: Societal organizations such as public schools, political parties, prisons, and mass media industries that help regulate human behavior and, in doing so, reinforce dominant ideologies and cultures.

interpretation: The construction of meaning from symbolic representation.

interpretative communities: Groups of people who may be very different from one another demographically, and may never actually meet each other, but share cultural experiences, preferences, identities, and discourses. Their sense of community is usually facilitated by mass media and information technology.

limited effects: An important theoretical development in media studies and mass communication that claims people are not simple victims of their experiences with media. According to this view, the effects of media are limited by a variety of intervening psychological, social, and cultural factors.

macrosocial: Large-scale social institutions, structures, systems, contexts, collective actions, and cultural tendencies.

mainstream: Conventional, dominant sociocultural patterns.

margin/marginal: Individuals, groups, nations, and cultures that hold relatively little political-economic-cultural power.

Marxism: A socialist theory of economics and politics based on the mid-nineteenth-century writing of Karl Marx and Friedrich Engels. Marxist theory criticizes capitalism as an inherently unfair system wherein the economic elite ruthlessly exploit workers. Marx focused on economic power as the locus of social control, but later versions of Marxism emphasize the influence of ideology and culture.

mass audience: When readers, listeners, or viewers of mass media are considered as an anonymous group, rather than individuals.

mass communication: The transmission and reception of information and entertainment through media technology such as newspapers, magazines, radio, television, and film. A communication process featuring few sources, many receivers, and limited opportunity for feedback.

mass media: Communication industries and technologies that include newspapers, magazines, radio, television, and film. The term "mass" refers to the ability of the communication technologies to send messages over broad expanses of space and time in order to reach many people.

mass society: Isolated, powerless, alienated persons who labor under oppressive work conditions and end up depending on the mass media for information, entertainment, and companionship. The concept was important in critical theory in the first half of the twentieth century.

meaning: What something signifies or represents to a person. Meaning is not inherent in symbolic forms, but is constructed by people who interpret the structured symbolic environment in accord with their own orientations, interests, and competencies.

media imperialism: *See* imperialism.

mediational image systems: How ideology is expressed and elaborated by technological intervention and interpersonal communication.

message: The content of communication. Symbolic forms that are generally created to represent particular intentions on the part of the sender, but are open to many possible interpretations.

message system: A way of conceptualizing the totality of a medium's content as an integrated ideological whole.

method: A term that is used two ways in this book. From the sociological tradition of ethnomethodology, method refers to the particular ways people construct, make meaningful, and rationalize even the most basic actions in their everyday lives. From the perspective on audience "uses and gratifications" discussed in chapter 5, method refers to media-related strategies people use to gratify their human needs.

methodology: The strategies and procedures that social scientists use to conduct their research.

microsocial: In contrast to the overarching, structural nature of the macrosocial, this term refers to small-scale, local, intimate, technologically-unmediated social settings and relationships.

modernity: A status of economic, technological, political, and cultural development usually discussed in terms of nations. Modernity typically refers to a combination of post-industrial, consumer-oriented economic practices, a high level of technological development, some form of democratic politics, and the overall ascendancy of secular influence. The term "modernity," like "postmodernity," also frequently refers to a stage in world history. This use of the term is problematic, however, because many parts of the world are not yet modern. *See* **postmodernity**.

motive: An impulse or drive that incites human action.

multisemy: The idea that all symbolic forms have not only various possible meanings for many different people, but multiple meanings for single individuals too.

needs: According to many psychologists, needs are biological, cognitive, and emotional requirements that give direction to human behavior. By gratifying needs, people maintain their physiological and mental stability.

negotiation: The idea that the meanings of symbolic representations and cultural patterns are not determined or self-evident, but subject to many possible interpretations and uses. In semiotics and cultural studies, negotiation often refers to the ways audience members interpret and use media texts like TV shows, films, or popular music. The negotiation is between the apparent intended significance of a text (representing the political-economic-cultural interests of media sources) and the construction of meaning fashioned by receivers/interpreters who act as agents for their own interests. For an opposing view, *see* **determinism**.

norm: A structured, patterned, rule-governed way of thinking and doing things that conveys an expectation of social conformity.

patriarchy: Social dominance of women, and society in general, by men.

political economy: A critical theory deriving from Marxism that claims socioeconomic elites control global communication and culture through massive political and economic influence.

polysemy: A concept from semiotics which asserts that signs (symbols, images) have many possible meanings or interpretations.

popular cultural capital: Means that popular symbolic resources can be used as a kind of valuable currency in social interaction.

popular culture: Typically refers to commercially successful, mainstream, mass-mediated cultural artifacts and personalities. Popular culture is often contrasted negatively with "high culture." For our purposes, however, the term refers to cultural experiences produced by ordinary people as originators, interpreters, and users of symbolic resources.

postmodernity: A chaotic, fragmented, confused, groundless state of affairs in society that manifests itself in everything from interpersonal relations to art and architecture. The directionlessness and ennui of postmodernity are said to develop after a society has become fully modern. *See* **modernity**.

preferred interpretation: Refers to the way a society's dominant ideological, social, and cultural forces want audiences to interpret symbolic communications emanating from major social institutions, especially the mass media, in order for the elites to maintain their power.

reception theory/research: Focuses on how people create meaning and experience in their interaction with media texts and technologies.

representation: The encoding and display of symbolic forms that reflect ideological positions.

reterritorialization: The dynamic recasting of cultural territory – often influenced by mass media – that alters traditional cultural boundaries and characteristics.

rules: The explicit codes and implicit understandings that constitute and regulate social behavior. Rules assert what is normal, acceptable, or preferred and how social interaction is to be carried out.

selectivity: Psychological processes underlying how people choose, avoid, perceive, interpret, remember, and forget symbolic imagery.

semantics/semiotics: The study of how symbolic forms (signs) are interpreted. The scientific study of meaning construction.

sensation: Basic physical and emotional reactions to media.

site: The location (physical or theoretical) where some struggle over meaning and power takes place.

social mediation: The way mass-mediated ideology is spread, reinforced, and altered through interpersonal communication.

social practice: Routine, unmediated social interaction, including verbal and nonverbal interpersonal communication.

social rules: *See* rules.

social uses of media: How the form and content of mass media are used for specific purposes as resources in the construction of desired microsocial relations.

software: The content of technologically mediated communication (e.g. TV programs, news on the radio, computer programs, etc.).

spatial consciousness: How physical distance and space are perceived, ranging in scope from the influence of telecommunications media on a global scale to the meaning of domestic and other local settings.

structuration: A social theory developed by British sociologist Anthony Giddens that attempts to synthesize the apparently confining forces of "structure" with the empowering forces of "agency."

structure: Can refer to (1) the interrelated complex of institutions in a society or (2) the dominant ideological themes those institutions produce.

subconscious: Below or outside conscious awareness.

subculture: A group of people whose values and lifestyle differ from dominant or mainstream culture, thereby unifying the group and creating an identity for its members. Subcultures can embrace total or partial ways of life, and can oppose mainstream culture or exist alongside it as a complementary, non-resisting alternative.

subjectivity: The uniqueness or individuality that people possess. For our purposes here, how a person's particular life history, orientations, feelings, and preferences come into play when that person interprets media texts or engages in other communicative activity.

subliminal persuasion: Attempts to influence thought and action by using mediated imagery that exists below the threshold of conscious perception. Appeals to subconscious desires.

superculture: A personalized matrix of symbolic forms, unmediated everyday scenes, and all other available cultural representations and activities.

symbol: As used in this book, a general term referring to any image or representation that stands for something else.

symbolic form: The content of human communication mediated by print, photographic, filmic, audio, televisual, or digital technologies of reproduction and transmission.

symbolic power: The use of symbolic forms, especially media imagery, to influence the course of social action and events.

taste culture: A sociological concept, depending in part on social class position, that describes how people can be grouped according to their cultural preferences or "tastes."

technological mediation: The intervention of communications technology in social interaction, particularly the influence of mass media on the diffusion of ideology.

temporal consciousness: How time is perceived. For our purposes here, how the mass media alter conceptions of time.

text: The content of symbolic communication, often used in terms of what the mass media (and not just the print media) present. A text, therefore, can be a TV program, movie, CD-Rom, or rock song, among many other possibilities.

Third World: The less developed parts of the world, especially Africa, Latin America, and parts of Asia.

transculturation: A process by which a cultural form (e.g. language, food, music) moves from one physical location to another where it interacts with and influences the local forms (languages, food, music, etc.) and produces new cultural hybrids.

uses and gratifications: A theoretical development in communication studies associated with the idea that media audiences are "active." According to this perspective, people use the media and other sociocultural resources to gratify basic human needs.

value: A constellation of deeply held, enduring attitudes, beliefs, and predispositions that reflect the ideological and cultural orientations of an individual or group of people.

visibility: The idea that media and information technology reveal (make visible) to the wider public the actions of persons and institutions who wield political, economic, and cultural power.

wants: In contrast to "needs," which are core biological and psychological states said to motivate human behavior, wants are the less weighty desires people have.

References

Adorno, T. (1989). Perennial fashion – jazz. In S.E. Bonner and D.M. Kellner (eds), *Critical Theory and Society: A Reader*. New York: Routledge.

Adorno, T. (1991). *Culture Industry: Selected Essays on Mass Culture*. London: Albert Britnell.

Adorno, T. and Horkheimer, M. (1972). *Dialectic of Entertainment*. New York: Herder and Herder.

Agar, M. (1994). *Language Shock: The Culture of Conversation*. New York: William Morrow and Company.

Anderson, B. (1991). *Imagined Communities*. London: Verso.

Ang, I. (1985). *Watching Dallas: Soap Opera and the Melodramatic Imagination*. London: Routledge.

Ang, I. (1991). *Desperately Seeking the Audience*. London: Routledge.

Appadurai, A. (1990). Disjuncture and difference in the global cultural economy. In M. Featherstone (ed.), *Global Culture: Nationalism, Globalization, and Modernity*. London: Sage.

Appadurai, A. (1996). *Modernity at Large*. Minneapolis: University of Minnesota Press.

Bagdikian, B. (1997). *The Media Monopoly*. Boston: Beacon Press.

Barrios, L. (1988). Television, *telenovelas*, and family life in Venezuela. In J. Lull (ed.), *World Families Watch Television*. Newbury Park, CA: Sage.

Bauman, Z. (1989). *Legislators and Interpreters*. Cambridge, UK: Polity Press.

Bauman, Z. (1996). From pilgrim to tourist – or a short history of identity. In S. Hall and P. duGay (eds), *Questions of Cultural Identity*. London: Sage.

Bauman, Z. (1998). *Globalization: The Human Consequences*. Cambridge, UK: Polity Press; New York: Columbia University Press.

Bausinger, H. (1984). Media, technology, and everyday life. *Media, Culture and Society*, 6, 340–52.

Behl, N. (1988). Equalizing status: television and tradition in an Indian village. In J. Lull (ed.), *World Families Watch Television*. Newbury Park, CA: Sage.

Berelson, B. (1949). What "missing the newspaper" means. In P.F. Lazarsfeld and F.N. Stanton (eds), *Communications Research, 1948–49*. New York: Duell, Sloan, and Pearce.

Bird, S.E. (1997). What a story! Understanding the audience for scandal. In J. Lull and S. Hinerman (eds), *Media Scandals: Morality and Desire in the Popular Culture Marketplace*. Cambridge, UK: Polity Press; New York: Columbia University Press.

Blumler, J.G. and Katz, E. (1974). *The Uses of Mass Communications: Current Perspectives on Gratifications Research*. Beverly Hills, CA: Sage.

Boggs, C. (1976). *Gramsci's Marxism*. London: Pluto Press.

Boorstin, D.J. (1961). *The Image: A Guide to Pseudo Events in America*. New York: Harper.

Bouissac, P. (1976). *Circus and Culture: A Semiotic Approach*. Bloomington, IN: Indiana University Press.

Bourdieu, P. (1984). *Distinction: A Social Critique of the Judgement of Taste*. Cambridge, MA: Harvard University Press.

Bourdieu, P. (1990a). *In Other Words: Essays Toward a Reflexive Sociology*. Cambridge, UK: Polity Press.

Bourdieu, P. (1990b). *The Logic of Practice*. Cambridge, UK: Polity Press.

Bourdieu, P. (1993). *The Field of Cultural Production*. Cambridge, UK: Polity Press.

Bourdieu, P. (1998). *Acts of Resistance: Against the Tyranny of the Market*. Cambridge, UK: Polity Press; New York: New Press.

Burciaga, J.A. (1993). *Drink Cultura: Chicanismo*. Santa Barbara, CA: Joshua Odell Editions.

Cavalli-Sforza, L., Menozzi, P., and Piazza, A. (1996). *The History and Geography of Human Genes*. Princeton, NJ: Princeton University Press.

Chaney, D. (1994). *The Cultural Turn*. London: Routledge.

Chaney, D. (1996). *Lifestyles*. London: Routledge.

Chomsky, N. (1972). *Language and Mind*. New York: Harcourt, Brace, Jovanovich.

Christenson, P. and Roberts, D. (1998). *It's Not Only Rock & Roll: Popular Music in the Lives of Adolescents*. Cresskill, NJ: Hampton Press.

Collett, P. (1977). The rules of conduct. In P. Collett (ed.), *Social Rules and Social Behavior*. Totowa, NJ: Rowman and Littlefield.

Condit, C. (1989). The rhetorical limits of polysemy. *Critical Studies in Mass Communication*, 6, 103–22.

Cooper, E. and Jahoda, M. (1947). The evasion of propaganda: how prejudiced people respond to anti-prejudice propaganda. *Journal of Psychology*, 23, 15–25.

Crystal, D. (1997). *English as a Global Language*. Cambridge, UK: Cambridge University Press.

DaMatta, R. (1991). *Carnivals, Rogues, and Heroes: An Interpretation of the Brazilian Dilemma*. Notre Dame, IN: University of Notre Dame Press.

Degler, C.N. (1971). *Neither Black nor White: Slavery and Race Relations in Brazil and the United States*. Madison: University of Wisconsin Press.

Dorfman, A. and Mattelart, A. (1972). *Para Leer al Pato Donald: Comunicacion de Masa y Colonialismo*. Mexico City: Siglo XXI.

Edgerton, R.B. (1985). *Rules, Exceptions, and Social Order*. Berkeley, CA: University of California Press.

Elliott, P. (1974). Uses and gratifications research: a critique and a sociological alternative. In J.G. Blumler and E. Katz (eds), *The Uses of Mass Communications: Current Perspectives on Gratifications Research*. Beverly Hills, CA: Sage.

Erikson, E. (1982). *The Life Cycle Completed*. New York: Norton.

Fiske, J. (1989). *Understanding Popular Culture*. Boston: Unwin Hyman.

Fiske, J. (1993). *Power Plays, Power Works*. London: Verso.

Fiske, J. (1994). Audiencing: cultural practice and cultural studies. In N. Denzin and Y. Lincoln (eds), *The Handbook of Qualitative Research*. Thousand Oaks, CA: Sage.

Fiske, J. (1996). *Media Matters: Everyday Culture and Political Change*. Minneapolis: University of Minnesota Press.

Foucault, M. (1977). *Discipline and Punish: The Birth of the Prison*. Harmondsworth, UK: Penguin.

Frank, T. (1998). *The Conquest of Cool: Business Culture, Counterculture, and the Rise of Hip Consumerism*. Chicago: University of Chicago Press.

Friedman, J. (1994). *Cultural Identity and Global Process*. London: Sage.

Frith, S. (1992). The industrialization of popular music. In J. Lull (ed.), *Popular Music and Communication*. Newbury Park, CA: Sage.

Fuenzalida, V. (1997). *Television y Cultura Cotidiana*. Santiago, Chile: La Corporación de Promoción Universitaria.

Gandy, O. (1993). *The Panoptic Sort: A Political Economy of Personal Information*. Boulder, CO: Westview Press.

Gans, H. (1962). *The Urban Villagers*. New York: Free Press.

Gans, H. (1974). *Popular Culture and High Culture*. New York: Basic Books.

García Canclini, N. (1989). *Culturas Híbridas: Estrategias para Entrar y Salir de la Modernidad*. Mexico City: Grijalbo.

García Canclini, N. (1995). *Consumidores y Ciudadanos*. Mexico City: Grijalbo.

Garfinkel, H. (1967). *Studies in Ethnomethodology*. Englewood Cliffs, NJ: Prentice-Hall. (1984) Cambridge, UK: Polity Press.

Gendreau, M. and Ibarra, M. (1999). Atlixco: Proceso migratorio e identidad regional. Presented to the Fifth Congress of the Asociación Mexicana de Ciencias para el Desarollo Regional, Hermosillo, Sonora, Mexico.

Gerbner, G. (1973). Cultural indicators: the third voice. In G. Gerbner, L. Gross, and W. Melody (eds), *Communications Technology and Social Policy*. New York: Wiley.

Gerbner, G. and Gross, L. (1976). Living with television: the violence profile. *Journal of Communication*, 26, 173–99.

Gerbner, G., Gross, L., Morgan, M., and Signorelli, N. (1986). Living with television: the dynamics of the cultivation process. In J. Bryant and D. Zillman (eds), *Perspectives on Media Effects*. Hillsdale, NJ: Lawrence Erlbaum.

Giddens, A. (1984). *The Constitution of Society*. Cambridge, UK: Polity Press.

Giddens, A. (1990). *The Consequences of Modernity*. Stanford, CA: Stanford University Press. (1991) Cambridge, UK: Polity Press.

Giddens, A. (1991). *Modernity and Self-Identity: Self and Society in the Late Modern Age*. Cambridge, UK: Polity Press.

Gillespie, M. (1995). *Television, Ethnicity, and Cultural Change*. London: Routledge.

Gitlin, T. (1979). Prime-time ideology: the hegemonic process in television entertainment. *Social Problems*, 26, 251–66.

Goffman, E. (1959). *The Presentation of the Self in Everyday Life*. New York: Doubleday.

Goffman, E. (1963). *Behavior in Public Places*. New York: Free Press.

Goffman, E. (1967). *Interaction Ritual*. New York: Anchor.

Goffman, E. (1969). *Strategic Interaction*. Philadelphia: University of Pennsylvania Press.

Goldman, R. and Papson, S. (1999). *Nike Culture: The Sign of the Swoosh*. Thousand Oaks, CA: Sage.

González, J. (ed.) (1998). *La Cofradía de las Emociones (In)terminables*. Guadalajara: University of Guadalajara Press.

Gramsci, A. (1971). *Selections from the Prison Notebooks*. New York: International Publishers.

Gramsci, A. (1973). *Letters from Prison*. New York: Harper and Row.

Gramsci, A. (1978). *Selections from Cultural Writings*. Cambridge, MA: Harvard University Press.

Grindstaff, L. (1997). Producing trash, class, and the money shot: A behind-the-scenes account of daytime TV talk shows. In J. Lull and S. Hinerman (eds), *Media Scandals: Morality and Desire in the Popular Culture Marketplace*. Cambridge, UK: Polity Press; New York: Columbia University Press.

Gripsrud, J. (1995). *The Dynasty Years: Hollywood Television and Critical Media Studies*. London: Routledge.

Gripsrud, J. (ed.) (1999). *Television and Common Knowledge*. London: Routledge.

Gronbeck, B.E. (1997). Character, celebrity, and sexual innuendo in the mass-mediated presidency. In J. Lull and Stephen Hinerman (eds), *Media Scandals: Morality and Desire in the Popular Culture Marketplace*. Cambridge, UK: Polity Press; New York: Columbia University Press.

Grossberg, L., Wartella, E., and Whitney, D.C. (1998). *Media Making: Mass Media in a Popular Culture*. Thousand Oaks, CA: Sage.

Habermas, J. (1989). *The Structural Transformation of the Public Sphere*. Cambridge, UK: Polity Press.

Hall, S. (1977). Culture, media, and the "ideological effect." In J. Curran,

M. Gurevitch, and J. Woollacott (eds), *Mass Communication and Society*. London: Edward Arnold.

Hall, S. (1985). Master's session. International Communication Association. Honolulu, Hawaii.

Halualani, R. (in press). *By, For, and in the Name of Hawaiians: Identities and Articulation*: Minneapolis: University of Minnesota Press.

Hamm, C. (1983). *Music in the New World*. New York: Norton.

Hannerz, U. (1990). Cosmopolitans and locals in world culture. In M. Featherstone (ed.), *Global Culture: Nationalism, Globalization, and Modernity*. London: Sage.

Hannerz, U. (1992). *Cultural Complexity: Studies in the Social Organization of Meaning*. New York: Columbia University Press.

Hannerz, U. (1996). *Transnational Connections*. London: Routledge.

Harré, R., Clarke, D., and De Carlo, N. (1985). *Motives and Mechanisms: An Introduction to the Psychology of Action*. London: Routledge.

Hastorf, A. and Cantril, H. (1954). They saw a game: a case study. *Journal of Abnormal and Social Psychology*, 49, 129–34.

Hebdige, D. (1979). *Subculture: The Meaning of Style*. London: Methuen.

Herzog, H. (1944). What do we really know about daytime serial listeners? In P.F. Lazarsfeld and F.N. Stanton (eds), *Radio Research, 1942–43*. New York: Duell, Sloan, and Pearce.

Horkheimer, M. (1972). *Critical Theory*. New York: Herder and Herder.

Horton, D. and Wohl, R. (1956). Mass communication and para-social interaction. *Psychiatry*, 19, 215–29.

Huntington, S.P. (1996). *The Clash of Civilizations and the Remaking of World Order*. New York: Simon and Schuster.

Huyler, S.P. (1999). *Meeting God: Elements of Hindu Devotion*. New Haven, CT: Yale University Press.

Innis, H. (1950). *Empire and Communication*. Oxford: Oxford University Press.

Innis, H. (1951). *The Bias of Communication*. Toronto: University of Toronto Press.

Innis, H. (1952). *Changing Concepts of Time*. Toronto: University of Toronto Press.

Jensen, J. (1990). *Redeeming Modernity: Contradictions in Media Criticism*. Newbury Park, CA: Sage.

Johnson, S. (1997). *Interface Culture: How New Technology Transforms the Way We Create and Communicate*. San Francisco: Harper.

Katz, E. (1977). Looking for trouble: social research on broadcasting. Presentation made to British Broadcasting Corporation, London.

Kay, R., Cartmill, M., and Barlow, M. (1998). *Proceedings of the National Academy of Sciences*. Washington, DC: National Academy of Sciences.

Key, W.B. (1973). *Subliminal Seduction*. New York: Signet.

Key, W.B. (1976). *Media Sexploitation*. Englewood Cliffs, NJ: Prentice-Hall.

Key, W.B. (1980). *The Clam Plate Orgy and Other Subliminals the Media Use to Manipulate Your Behavior*. Englewood Cliffs, NJ: Prentice-Hall.

Klapper, J. (1960). *The Effects of Mass Communication.* New York: Free Press.

Kottak, C. (1990). *Prime-Time Society: An Anthropological Analysis of Television and Culture.* Belmont, CA: Wadsworth.

Kratochwil, F. (1989). *Rules, Norms, and Decisions.* Cambridge, UK: Cambridge University Press.

Laswell, H.D. (1948). The structure and function of communication in society. In L. Bryson (ed.), *The Communication of Ideas.* New York: Harper.

Latham, K. (2000). Between markets and mandarins: media production in South China. In B. Moeran and L. Skove (eds), *Asian Media Productions.* London: Curzon.

Lewis, G. (1992). Who do you love? The dimensions of musical taste. In J. Lull (ed.), *Popular Music and Communication.* Newbury Park, CA: Sage.

Lull, J. (1980). Girls' favorite TV females. *Journalism Quarterly,* 57, 146–50.

Lull, J. (ed.) (1988). *World Families Watch Television.* Newbury Park, CA: Sage.

Lull, J. (1990). *Inside Family Viewing: Ethnographic Research on Television's Audiences.* London: Routledge.

Lull, J. (1991). *China Turned On: Television, Reform, and Resistance.* London: Routledge.

Lull, J. (ed.) (1992a). *Popular Music and Communication.* Newbury Park, CA: Sage.

Lull, J. (1992b). La estructuración de las audiencias masivas. *Día Logos,* 32, 50–7.

Lull, J. and Hinerman, S. (eds) (1997). *Media Scandals: Morality and Desire in the Popular Culture Marketplace.* Cambridge, UK: Polity Press; New York: Columbia University Press.

Maffesoli, M. (1996). *The Time of the Tribes.* London: Sage.

Marcuse, H. (1964). *One Dimensional Man.* Boston: Beacon Press.

Martín-Barbero, J. (1993). *Communication, Culture and Hegemony.* Newbury Park, CA: Sage.

Marx, K. (1867, 1885, 1894). *Capital.* London: Lawrence & Wishart 1970.

Marx, K. (1975). *Early Writings,* ed. Q. Hoare. New York: Vintage.

Marx, K. (1977). *Capital, Volume I.* New York: Vintage.

Marx, K. and Engels, F. (1845). *The German Ideology.* London: Lawrence & Wishart 1965.

Marx, K. and Engels, F. (1848). *Manifesto of the Communist Party.* In K. Marx and F. Engels, *Selected Works.* London: Lawrence & Wishart 1968.

Marx, K. and Engels, F. (1970). *The German Ideology.* New York. International Publishers.

Maslow, A.H. (1954). *Motivation and Personality.* New York: Harper.

Maslow, A.H. (1962). *Toward a Psychology of Being.* Princeton, NJ: Van Nostrand.

McCracken, G. (1990). *Culture and Consumption: New Approaches to the Symbolic Character of Consumer Goods and Activities.* Bloomington, IN: Indiana University Press.

McDonagh, E.C. (1950). Television and the family. *Sociology and Social Research*, 35, 113–22.

McLuhan, M. (1962). *The Gutenberg Galaxy: The Making of Typographic Man*. Toronto: Toronto University Press.

McLuhan, M. (1964). *Understanding Media: The Extensions of Man*. New York: McGraw-Hill.

McLuhan, M. and Fiore, Q. (1967). *The Medium is the Massage*. New York: Bantam.

McQuail, D. (1997). *Audience Analysis*. Thousand Oaks, CA: Sage.

Mendelsohn, H. (1964). Listening to radio. In L.A. Dexter and D.M. White (eds), *People, Society, and Mass Communications*. Glencoe, IL: Free Press.

Merton, R. (1957). *Social Theory and Social Structure*. New York: Free Press.

Meyrowitz, J. (1985). *No Sense of Place: The Impact of Electronic Media on Social Behavior*. New York: Oxford University Press.

Mitchell, T. (1996). *Popular Music and Local Identity*. London: Leicester University Press.

Moores, S. (1993). *Interpreting Audiences: The Ethnography of Mass Consumption*. London: Sage.

Morley, D. (1986). *Family Television: Cultural Power and Domestic Leisure*. London: Routledge.

Morley, D. (1988). Domestic relations: the framework of family viewing in Great Britain. In J. Lull (ed.), *World Families Watch Television*. Newbury Park, CA: Sage.

Morley, D. (1992). *Television, Audiences, and Cultural Studies*. London: Routledge.

Murray, J., Rubinstein, E., and Comstock, G. (eds) (1994). *Violence and Youth: Psychology's Response*. Washington, DC: American Psychological Association.

Naficy, H. (1993). *The Making of Exile Cultures*. Minneapolis: University of Minnesota Press.

National Institute of Mental Health (1982). *Television and Behavior: Ten Years of Scientific Progress and Implications for the Eighties*. Washington, DC: US Government Printing Office.

National Television Violence Study: Volume 2. (1997). Newbury Park, CA: Sage.

Neiva, E. (2000). Rethinking the foundations of culture. In J. Lull (ed.), *Culture in the Communication Age*. London: Routledge.

Newcomb, H. and Hirsch, P. (1987). Television as a cultural forum. In H. Newcomb (ed.), *Television: The Critical View*. New York: Oxford University Press.

Orozco Gómez, G. (ed.) (1990). *La Comunicación desde las Prácticas Sociales: Reflexiones en Torno a su Investigación*. Mexico City: Universidad Iberoamericana.

Orozco Gómez, G. (1991). La audiencia en frente de la pantalla. *Día Logos*, 30, 55–63.

Orozco Gómez, G. (ed.) (1996). *Miradas Latinoamericanas a la Television*. Mexico City: Universidad Iberoamericana.

O'Sullivan, T., Hartley, J., Saunders, D., Montgomery, M., and Fiske, J. (1994). *Key Concepts in Communication and Cultural Studies*. London: Routledge.

Pearson, G. (1983). *Hooligan: A History of Respectable Fears*. London: Macmillan.

Press, A. (1991). *Women Watching Television*. Philadelphia: University of Pennsylvania Press.

Price, M. (1994). The market for loyalties: electronic media and the global competition for allegiances. *Yale Law Journal*, 104, 667–705.

Price, M. (1995). *Television, the Public Sphere, and National Identity*. Oxford, UK: Oxford University Press.

Rantanen, T. (1994). Howard interviews Stalin: how the AP, UP and TASS smashed the international news cartel. *Roy W. Howard Monographs in Journalism and Mass Communication Research*. Bloomington, IN: School of Journalism, University of Indiana.

Real, M. (1989). *Super Media: A Cultural Studies Approach*. Newbury Park, CA: Sage.

Reeves, B. and Nass, C. (1996). *The Media Equation: How People Treat Computers, Television, and New Media Like Real People and Places*. Cambridge, UK: University of Cambridge.

Reimer, B. (1994). *The Most Common of Practices: On Mass Media Use in Late Modernity*. Stockholm: Almquist and Wiksell International.

Rickford, J. (2000). www.stanford.edu/~Rickford/ebonics/EbonicsExamples.html.

Riding, A. (1984). *Distant Neighbors: A Portrait of the Mexicans*. New York: Alfred A. Knopf.

Riley, M.W. and Riley, J.W. (1951). A sociological approach to communication research. *Public Opinion Quarterly*, 15, 444–60.

Ritzer, G. (1993). *The McDonaldization of Society*. Thousand Oaks, CA: Pine Forge Press.

Robertson, R. (1995). Glocalization: time–space and homogeneity–heterogeneity. In M. Featherstone and S. Lash (eds), *Global Modernities*. London: Sage.

Rogge, J.-U. and Jensen, K. (1988). Everyday life and television in Germany: an empathic-interpretative perspective on the family as a system. In J. Lull (ed.), *World Families Watch Television*. Newbury Park, CA: Sage.

Rosengren, K.E., Wenner, L.A., and Palmgreen, P. (1985). *Media Gratifications Research*. Thousand Oaks, CA: Sage.

Rothschild, M. (1995). *Bionomics: Economy as Ecosystem*. New York: Henry Holt.

Rowe, W. and Schelling, V. (1991). *Memory and Modernity: Popular Culture in Latin America*. London: Verso.

Samuels, F. (1984). *Human Needs and Behavior*. Cambridge, MA: Schnenkman.

Santiago-Lucerna, J. (1997). Pushin' it to the limit: scandals and pop music.

In J. Lull and S. Hinerman (eds), *Media Scandals: Morality and Desire in the Popular Culture Marketplace*. Cambridge, UK: Polity Press; New York: Columbia University Press.

Sassoon, A.S. (1980). *Gramsci's Politics*. New York: St Martin's Press.

Schiller, H.I. (1969). *Mass Communications and American Empire*. Boston: Beacon Press.

Schiller, H.I. (1973). *The Mind Managers*. Boston: Beacon Press.

Schiller, H.I. (1976). *Communication and Cultural Domination*. White Plains, NY: International Arts and Sciences Press.

Schiller, H.I. (1989). *Culture, Inc.: The Corporate Takeover of Public Expression*. New York: Oxford University Press.

Schiller, H.I. (1991). Not yet the post-imperialist era. *Critical Studies in Mass Communication*, 8, 13–28.

Schiller, H. (1996). *Information Inequality*. New York: Routledge.

Schramm, W., Lyle, J., and Parker, E.B. (1961). *Television in the Lives of Our Children*. Stanford, CA: Stanford University Press.

Schwichtenberg, C. (1993). *The Madonna Connection*. Boulder, CO: Westview Press.

Shimanoff, S. (1980). *Communication Rules*. Beverly Hills, CA: Sage.

Simon, R. (1982). *Gramsci's Political Thought*. London: Lawrence and Wishart.

Sinclair, J. (1999). *Latin American Television: A Global View*. Oxford, UK: Oxford University Press.

Smith, A. (1980). *The Geopolitics of Information*. New York: Oxford University Press.

Smith, A. (1990). Towards a global culture? In M. Featherstone (ed.), *Global Culture: Nationalism, Globalization, and Modernity*. London: Sage.

Sowell, T. (1994). *Race and Culture: A World View*. New York: Basic Books.

Stewart, E.C. (2000). Culture of the mind. In J. Lull (ed.), *Culture in the Communication Age*. London: Routledge.

Stewart, E.C. and Bennett, M.J. (1991). *American Cultural Patterns*. Yarmouth, ME: Intercultural Press.

Straubhaar, J. (1989). Mass communication and the elites. In M.L. Conniff and F.D. McCann (eds), *Modern Brazil: Elites and Masses in Historical Perspective*. Lincoln, NE: University of Nebraska Press.

Suchman, E. (1942). An invitation to music. In P.F. Lazarsfeld and F.N. Stanton (eds), *Radio Research, 1941*. New York: Duell, Sloan, and Pearce.

Szemere, A. (1985). Pop music in Hungary. *Communication Research*, 12, 401–11.

Tester, K. (1994). *Media, Culture, and Morality*. London: Routledge.

Thompson, J.B. (1990). *Ideology and Modern Culture*. Cambridge, UK: Polity Press.

Thompson, J.B. (1994). Social theory and the media. In D. Crowley and D. Mitchell (eds), *Communication Theory Today*. Cambridge, UK: Polity Press.

Thompson, J.B. (1995). *The Media and Modernity*. Cambridge, UK: Polity Press; Stanford, CA: Stanford University Press.

Thompson, J.B. (1997). Scandal and social theory. In J. Lull and S. Hinerman (eds), *Media Scandals: Morality and Desire in the Popular Culture Marketplace*. Cambridge, UK: Polity Press; New York: Columbia University Press.

Tomlinson, J. (1991). *Cultural Imperialism*. Baltimore: Johns Hopkins University Press.

Tomlinson, J. (1997). "And besides, the wench is dead:" media scandals and the globalization of communication. In J. Lull and S. Hinerman (eds), *Media Scandals: Morality and Desire in the Popular Culture Marketplace*. Cambridge, UK: Polity Press; New York: Columbia University Press.

Tomlinson, J. (1999). *Globalization and Culture*. Cambridge, UK: Polity Press.

Tufte, T. (2000). *Living with the Rubbish Queen: Telenovelas, Culture, and Modernity in Brazil*. London: Luton Press.

Turow, J. (1997). *Breaking Up America: Advertisers and the New Media World*. Chicago: University of Chicago Press.

Uribe, A. (1995). Entre a autoridade e as gargalhadas. Uma leitura exploratoria da constução da imagem televisiva de Silvio Santos. Unpublished master's thesis, Methodist University, São Paulo, Brazil.

Vidmar, N. and Rokeach, M. (1974). Archie Bunker's bigotry: a study in selective perception and exposure. *Journal of Communication*, 24, 36–47.

Wallerstein, I. (1974). *The Modern World-System I*. London: Academic Press.

Wallerstein, I. (1980). *The Modern World-System II*. London: Academic Press.

Wallerstein, I. (1990). Culture as the ideological battleground of the modern world-system. *Theory, Culture, and Society*, 7, 31–55.

Watson, J.L. (ed.) (1997). *Golden Arches East: McDonald's in East Asia*. Stanford, CA: Stanford University Press.

Webster, J.G. and Phalen, P. (1997). *The Mass Audience: Rediscovering the Dominant Model*. Mahwah, NJ: Lawrence Erlbaum.

Wicke, P. (1992). The role of rock music in the political disintegration of East Germany. In J. Lull (ed.), *Popular Music and Communication*. Newbury Park, CA: Sage.

Williams, R. (1962). *The Long Revolution*. New York: Columbia University Press.

Williams, R. (1975). *Television: Technology and Cultural Form*. New York: Schocken.

Williams, R. (1976). *Key Words: A Vocabulary of Culture and Society*. New York: Oxford University Press.

Williams, R. (1977). *Marxism and Literature*. Oxford, UK: Oxford University Press.

Willis, P. (1990). *Common Culture: Symbolic Work at Play in the Everyday Cultures of the Young*. Boulder, CO: Westview Press.

Wright, C.R. (1975). *Mass Communication: A Sociological Perspective*. New York: Random House.

Yi, W. (1997). From revolutionary culture to popular culture. Unpublished doctoral dissertation. Murdoch University, Australia.

Zermeño, A. (1998). Ya sé lo que va a pasar! Anticipación y telenovela. In J. González (ed.), *La Cofradía de las Emociones (In)terminables*. Guadalajara: University of Guadalajara Press.

Index